You're in the Wrong Direction!!

Whoops! Guess what? You're starting at the wrong end of the comic!
...It's true! In keeping with the original Japanese format, **Naruto** is meant to be read from right to left, starting in the upper-right corner.

Unlike English, which is read from left to right, Japanese is read from right to left, meaning that action, sound effects and word-balloon order are completely reversed... something which can make readers unfamiliar with Japanese feel pretty backwards themselves. For this reason, manga or Japanese comics published in the U.S. in English have sometimes been published "flopped"—that is, printed in exact reverse order, as though seen from the other side of a mirror.

By flopping pages, U.S. publishers can avoid confusing readers, but the compromise is not without its downside. For one thing, a character in a flopped manga series who once wore in the original Japanese version a T-shirt emblazoned with "M A Y" (as in "the merry month of") now wears one which reads "Y A M"! Additionally, many manga creators in Japan are themselves unhappy with the process, as some feel the mirror-imaging of their art alters their original intentions.

We are proud to bring you Masashi Kishimoto's **Naruto** in the original unflopped format. For now, though, turn to the other side of the book and let the ninjutsu begin...!

—Editor

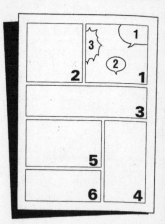

SHONEN JUMP MANGA EDITION

NARUTO

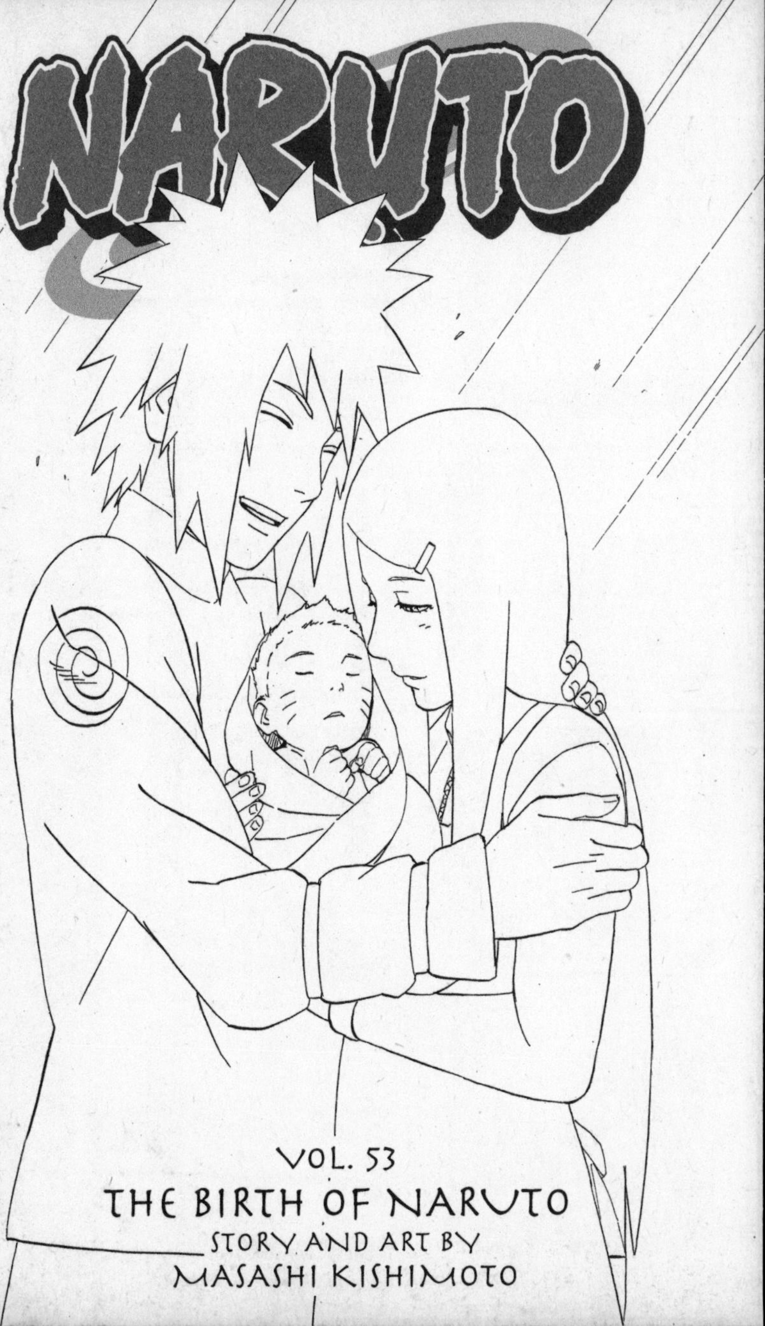

VOL. 53

THE BIRTH OF NARUTO

STORY AND ART BY

MASASHI KISHIMOTO

Naruto ナルト

Sasuke サスケ

Kakashi カカシ

Sakura サクラ

Sai サイ

Yamato ヤマト

Tsunade 綱手

Jiraiya 自来也

CHARACTERS

Jugo 重吾

Karin 香燐

Suigetsu 水月

Kisame 鬼鮫

Itachi イタチ

Madara マダラ

Motoi モトイ

Killer Bee キラービー

Gaara 我愛羅

———— THE STORY SO FAR... ————

Naruto, the biggest troublemaker at the Ninja Academy in the Village of Konohagakure, finally becomes a ninja along with his classmates Sasuke and Sakura. They grow and mature through countless trials and battles. However, Sasuke, unable to give up his quest for vengeance, leaves Konohagakure to seek Orochimaru and his power…

In the years that pass, Naruto engages in fierce battles against the Tailed Beast-targeting Akatsuki. Elsewhere, after winning the heroic battle against Itachi and learning his older brother's true intentions, Sasuke allies with the Akatsuki and sets out to destroy Konoha.

Upon Madara's declaration of war, an Allied Shinobi Force is formed. Naruto, sent away in the name of protecting the jinchûriki, begins training to control Nine Tails. As he struggles, he learns of Bee and Motoi's past, and realizes the importance of trust!!

NARUTO

VOL. 53
THE BIRTH OF NARUTO

CONTENTS

Number 495: Dark Naruto, Defeated!!

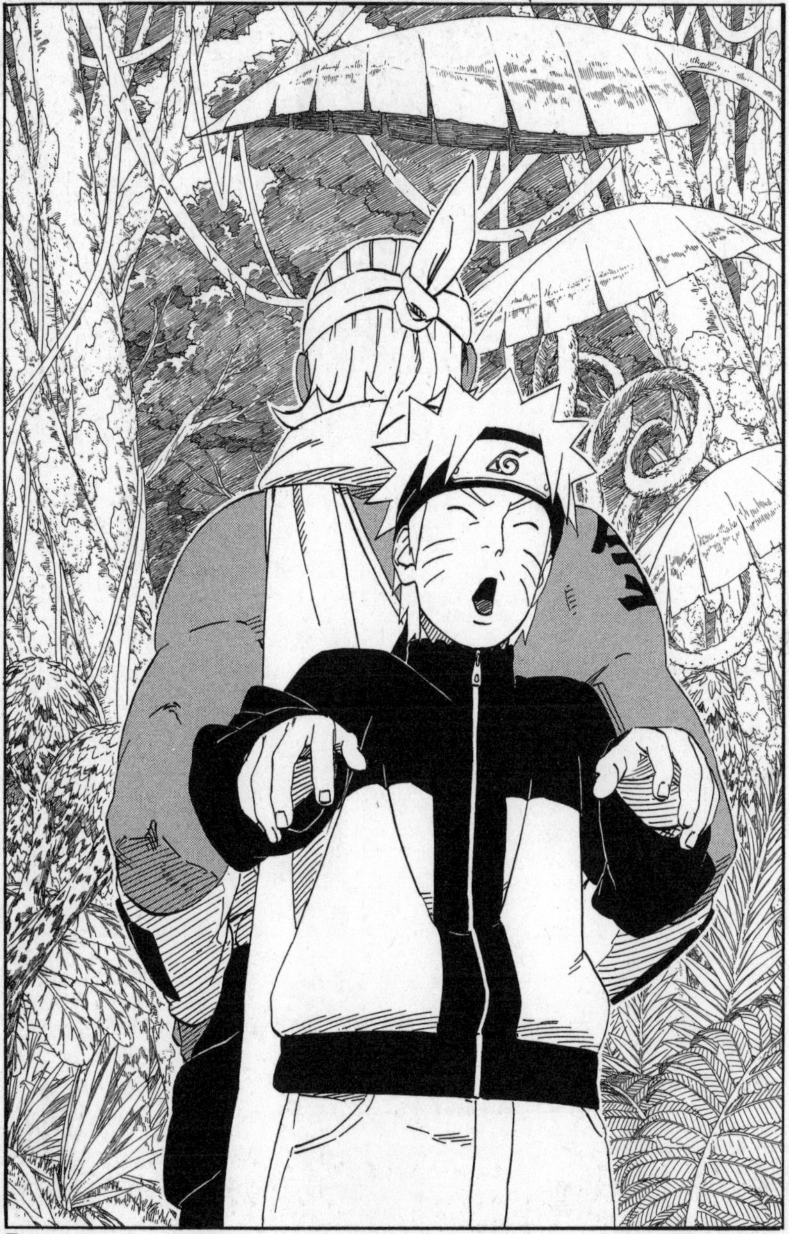

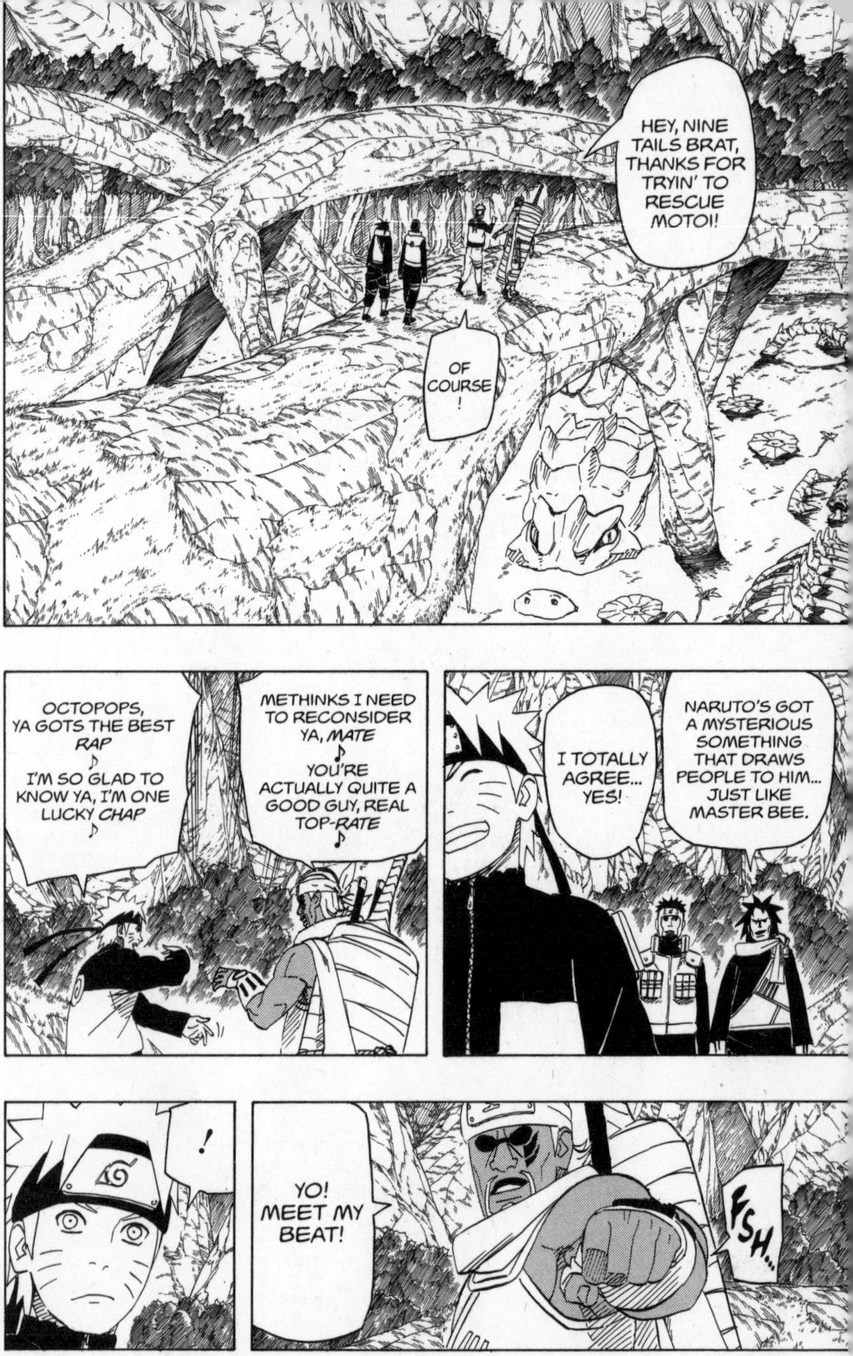
HEY, NINE TAILS BRAT, THANKS FOR TRYIN' TO RESCUE MOTOI!
OF COURSE!
NARUTO'S GOT A MYSTERIOUS SOMETHING THAT DRAWS PEOPLE TO HIM... JUST LIKE MASTER BEE.
I TOTALLY AGREE... YES!
METHINKS I NEED TO RECONSIDER YA, *MATE* ♪ YOU'RE ACTUALLY QUITE A GOOD GUY, REAL TOP-*RATE* ♪
OCTOPOPS, YA GOTS THE BEST *RAP* ♪ I'M SO GLAD TO KNOW YA, I'M ONE LUCKY *CHAP* ♪
FSH...
YO! MEET MY BEAT!
!

READ THIS WAY

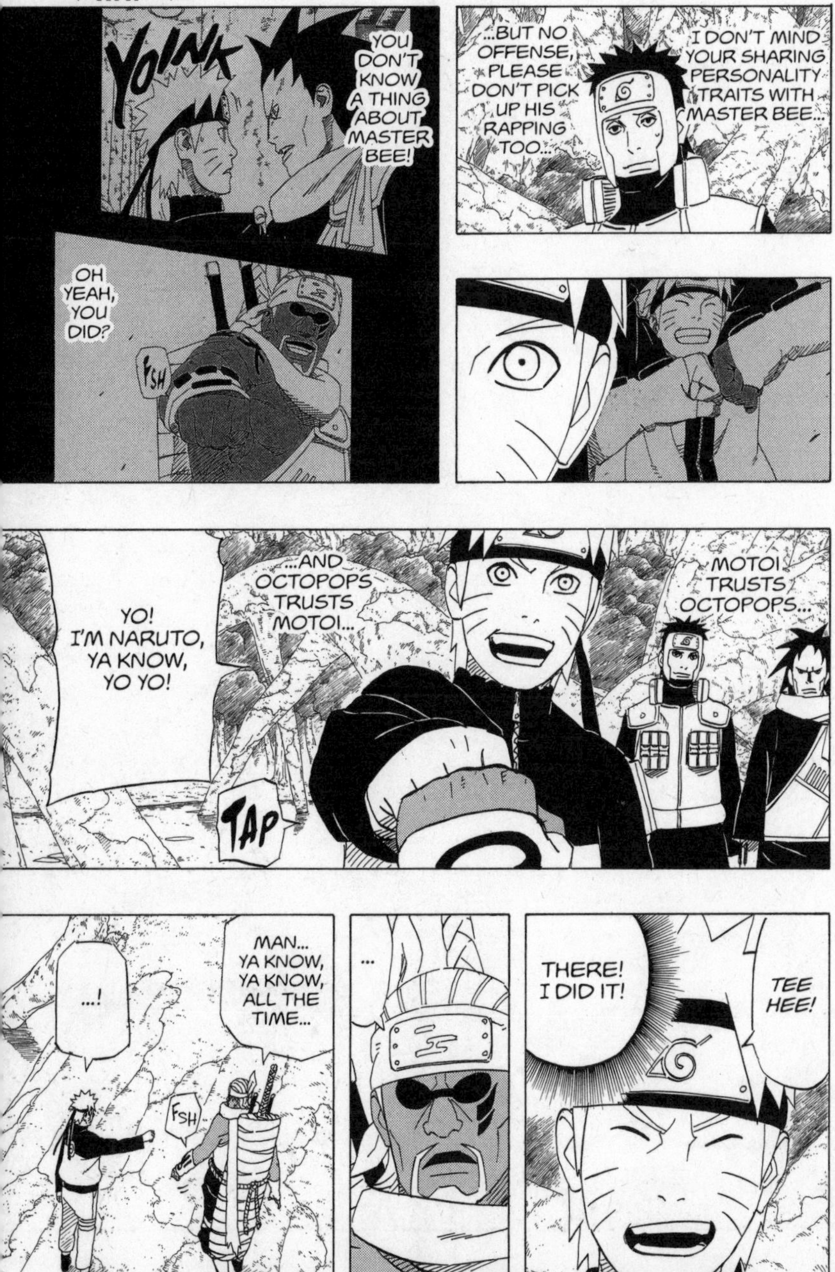
I DON'T MIND YOUR SHARING PERSONALITY TRAITS WITH MASTER BEE...
...BUT NO OFFENSE, PLEASE DON'T PICK UP HIS RAPPING TOO...
YOINK
YOU DON'T KNOW A THING ABOUT MASTER BEE!
OH YEAH, YOU DID?
FSH
MOTOI TRUSTS OCTOPOPS...
...AND OCTOPOPS TRUSTS MOTOI...
YO! I'M NARUTO, YA KNOW, YO YO!
TAP
TEE HEE!
THERE! I DID IT!
...
MAN... YA KNOW, YA KNOW, ALL THE TIME...
FSH
...!

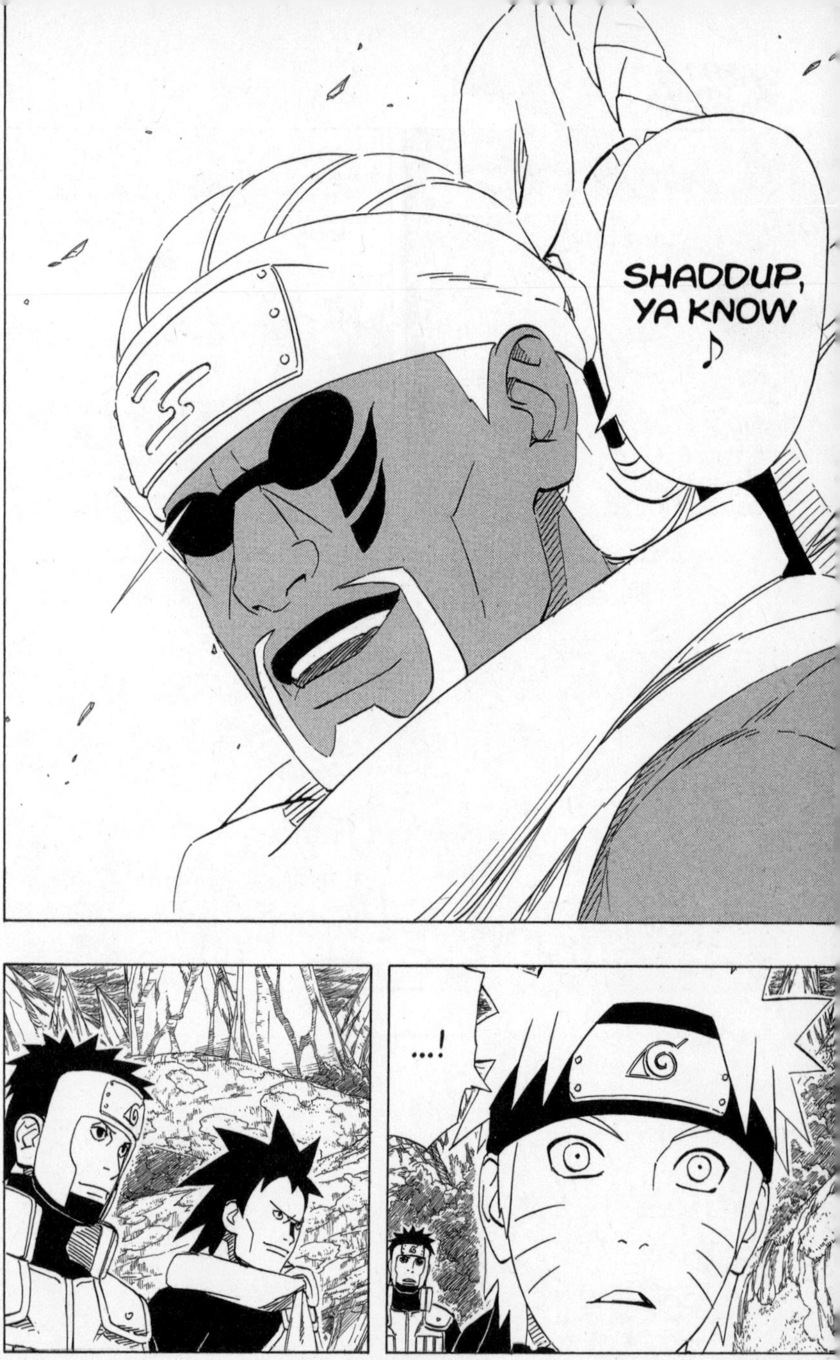
SHADDUP, YA KNOW ♪
...!

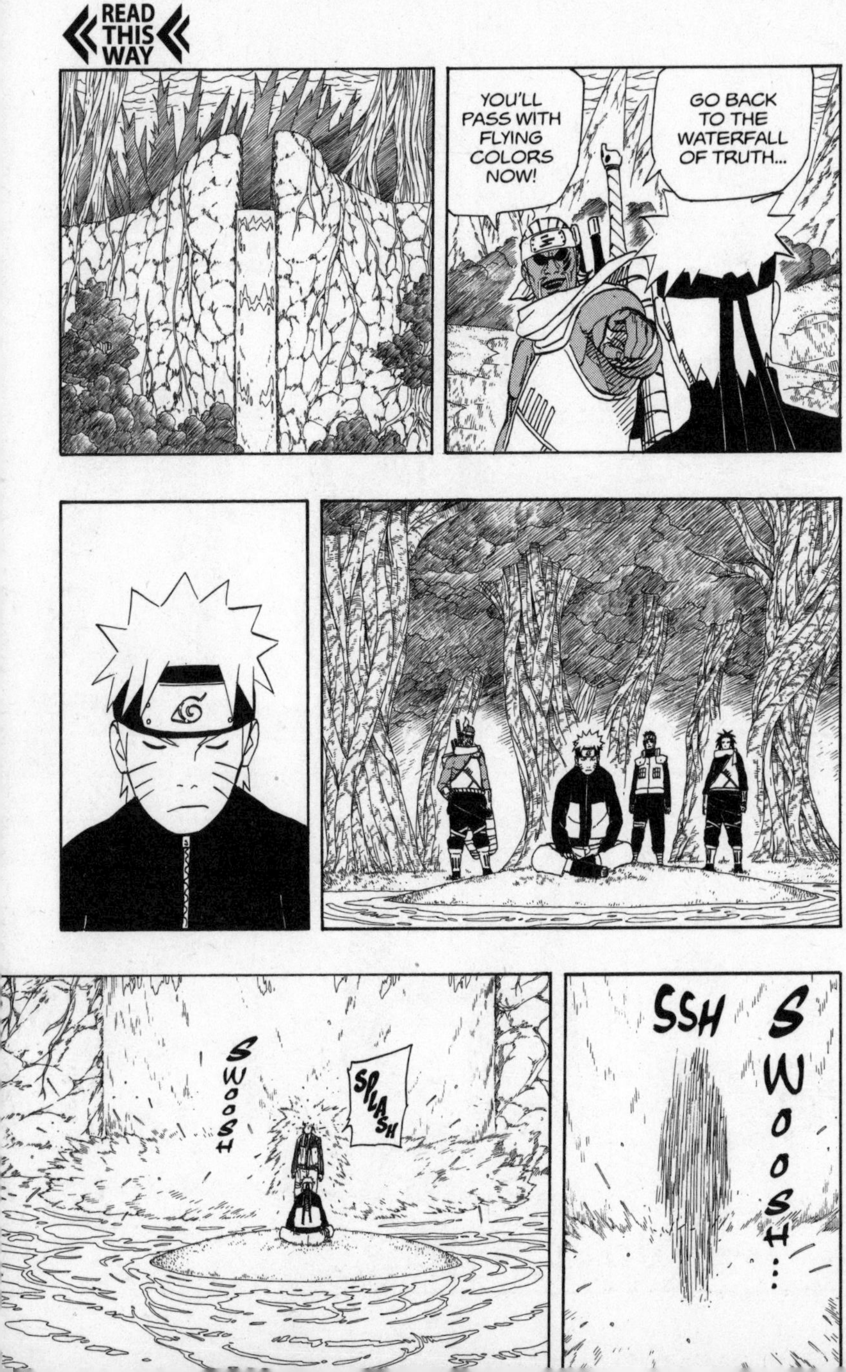
READ THIS WAY
GO BACK TO THE WATERFALL OF TRUTH...
YOU'LL PASS WITH FLYING COLORS NOW!
SSH
SWOOSH...
SPLASH
SWOOSH

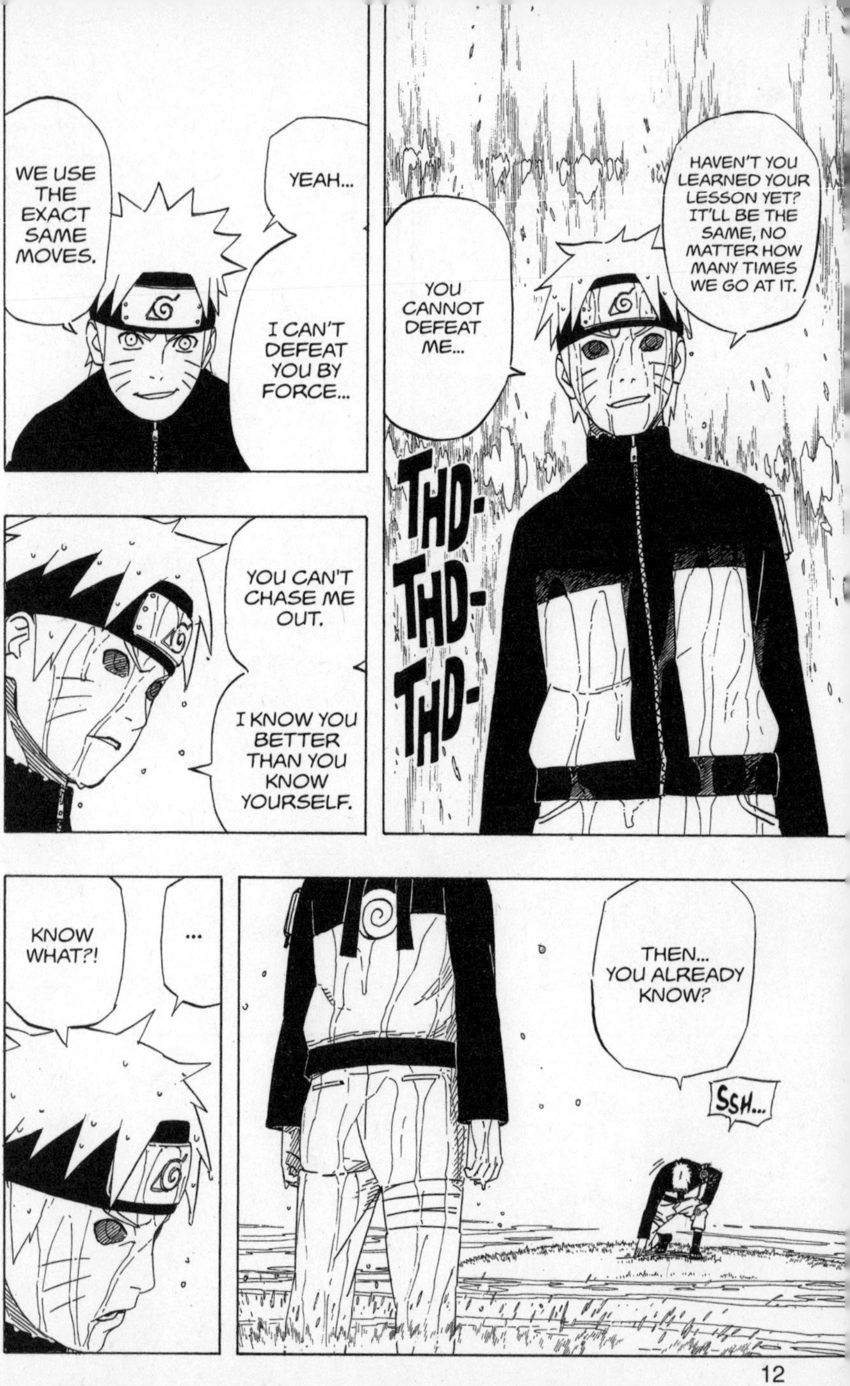
HAVEN'T YOU LEARNED YOUR LESSON YET? IT'LL BE THE SAME, NO MATTER HOW MANY TIMES WE GO AT IT.
YOU CANNOT DEFEAT ME...
THD-THD-THD-
WE USE THE EXACT SAME MOVES.
YEAH... I CAN'T DEFEAT YOU BY FORCE...
YOU CAN'T CHASE ME OUT. I KNOW YOU BETTER THAN YOU KNOW YOURSELF.
THEN... YOU ALREADY KNOW?
SSH...
...
KNOW WHAT?!

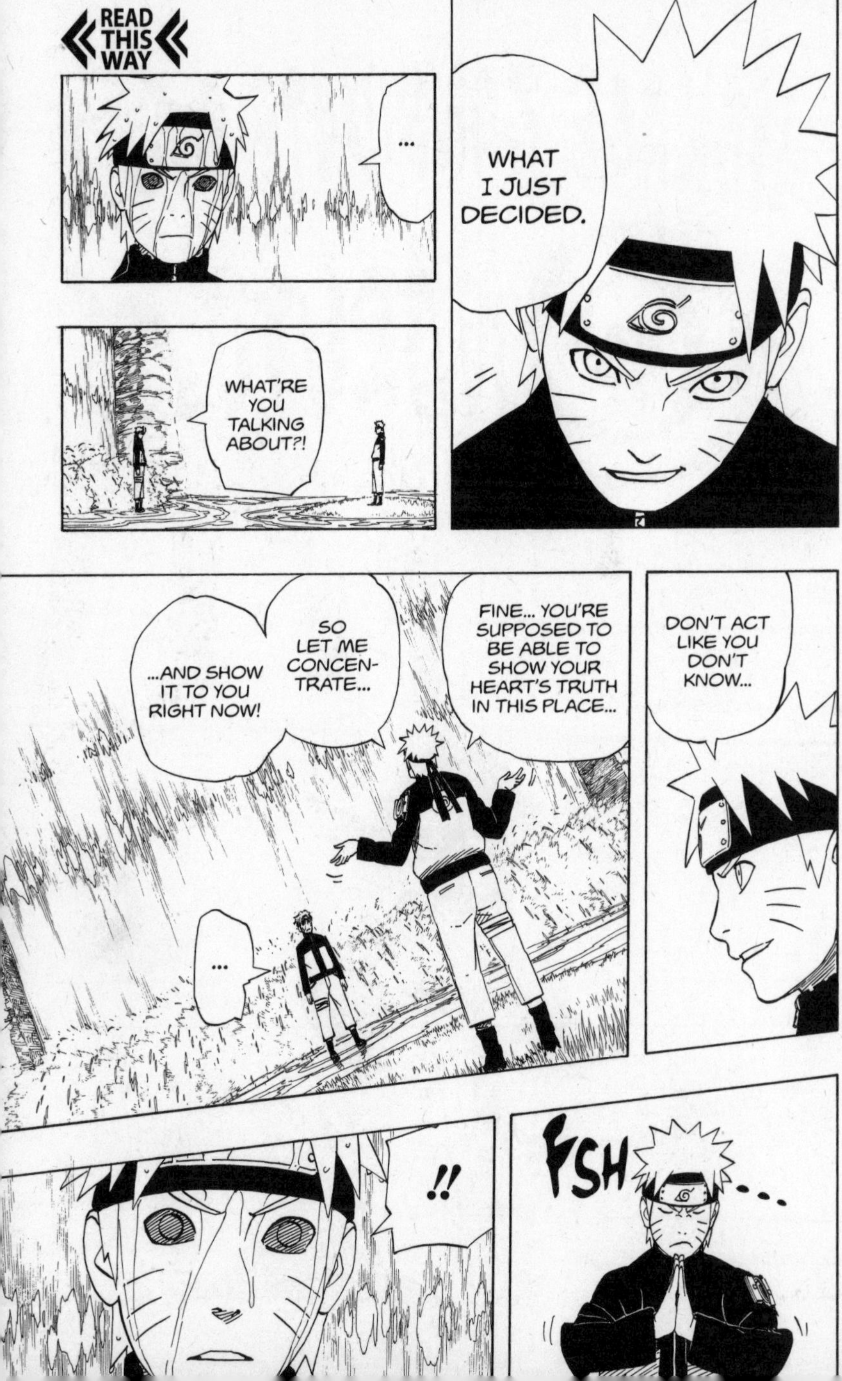
READ THIS WAY
WHAT I JUST DECIDED.
...
WHAT'RE YOU TALKING ABOUT?!
DON'T ACT LIKE YOU DON'T KNOW...
FINE... YOU'RE SUPPOSED TO BE ABLE TO SHOW YOUR HEART'S TRUTH IN THIS PLACE...
SO LET ME CONCENTRATE...
...AND SHOW IT TO YOU RIGHT NOW!
...
FSH...
!!

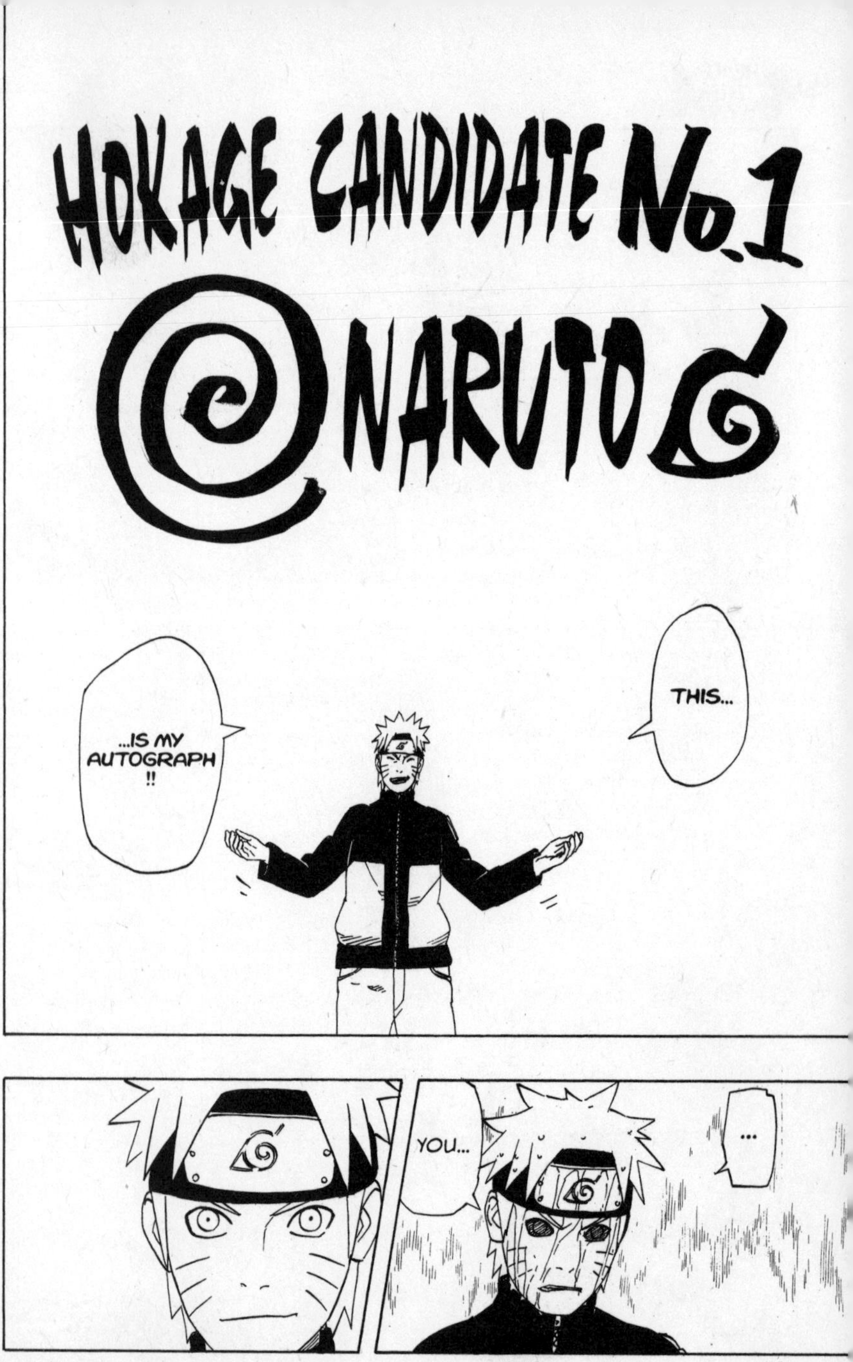
HOKAGE CANDIDATE No.1
NARUTO
THIS...
...IS MY AUTOGRAPH !!
...
YOU...

READ THIS WAY

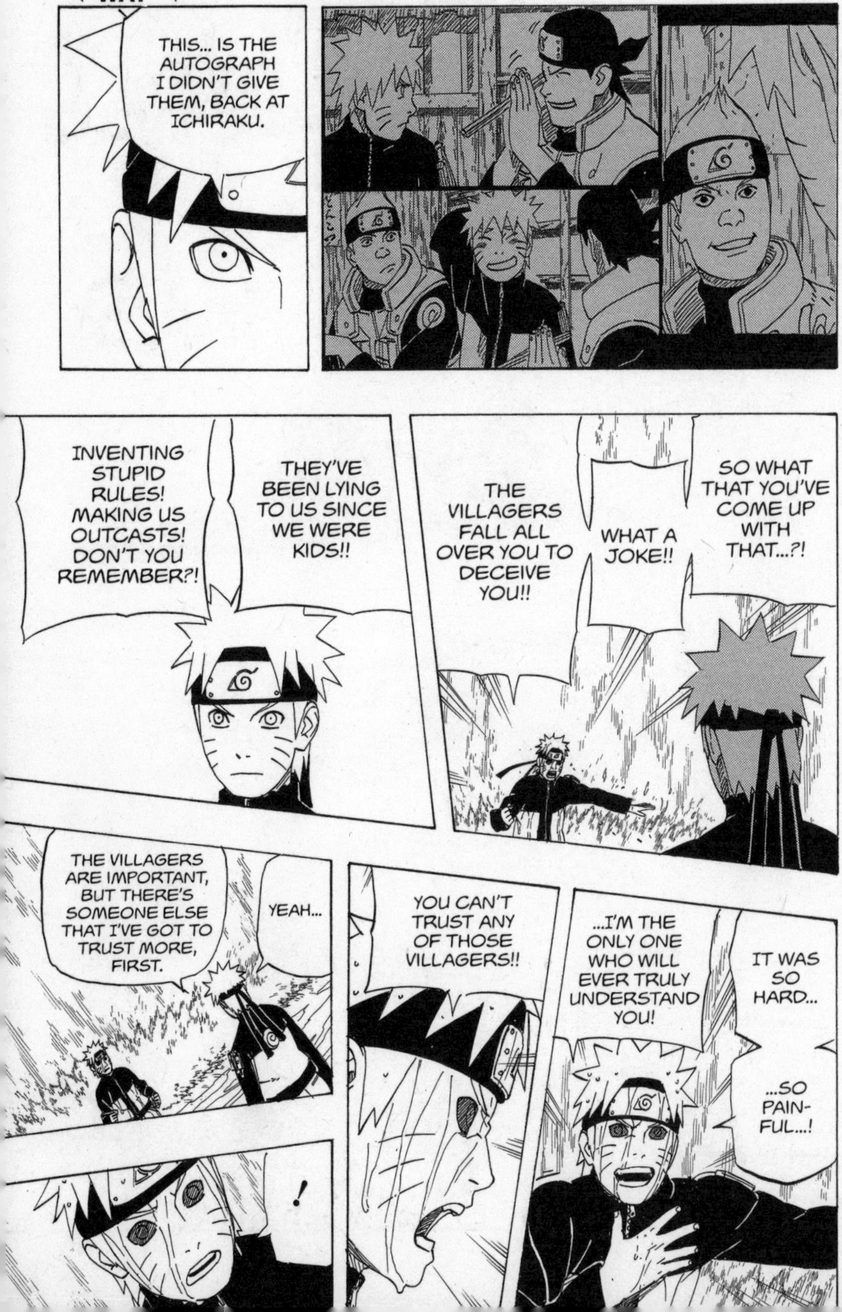
THIS... IS THE AUTOGRAPH I DIDN'T GIVE THEM, BACK AT ICHIRAKU.
SO WHAT THAT YOU'VE COME UP WITH THAT...?!
WHAT A JOKE!!
THE VILLAGERS FALL ALL OVER YOU TO DECEIVE YOU!!
THEY'VE BEEN LYING TO US SINCE WE WERE KIDS!!
INVENTING STUPID RULES! MAKING US OUTCASTS! DON'T YOU REMEMBER?!
IT WAS SO HARD...
...SO PAINFUL...!
...I'M THE ONLY ONE WHO WILL EVER TRULY UNDERSTAND YOU!
YOU CAN'T TRUST ANY OF THOSE VILLAGERS!!
YEAH...
THE VILLAGERS ARE IMPORTANT, BUT THERE'S SOMEONE ELSE THAT I'VE GOT TO TRUST MORE, FIRST.
!

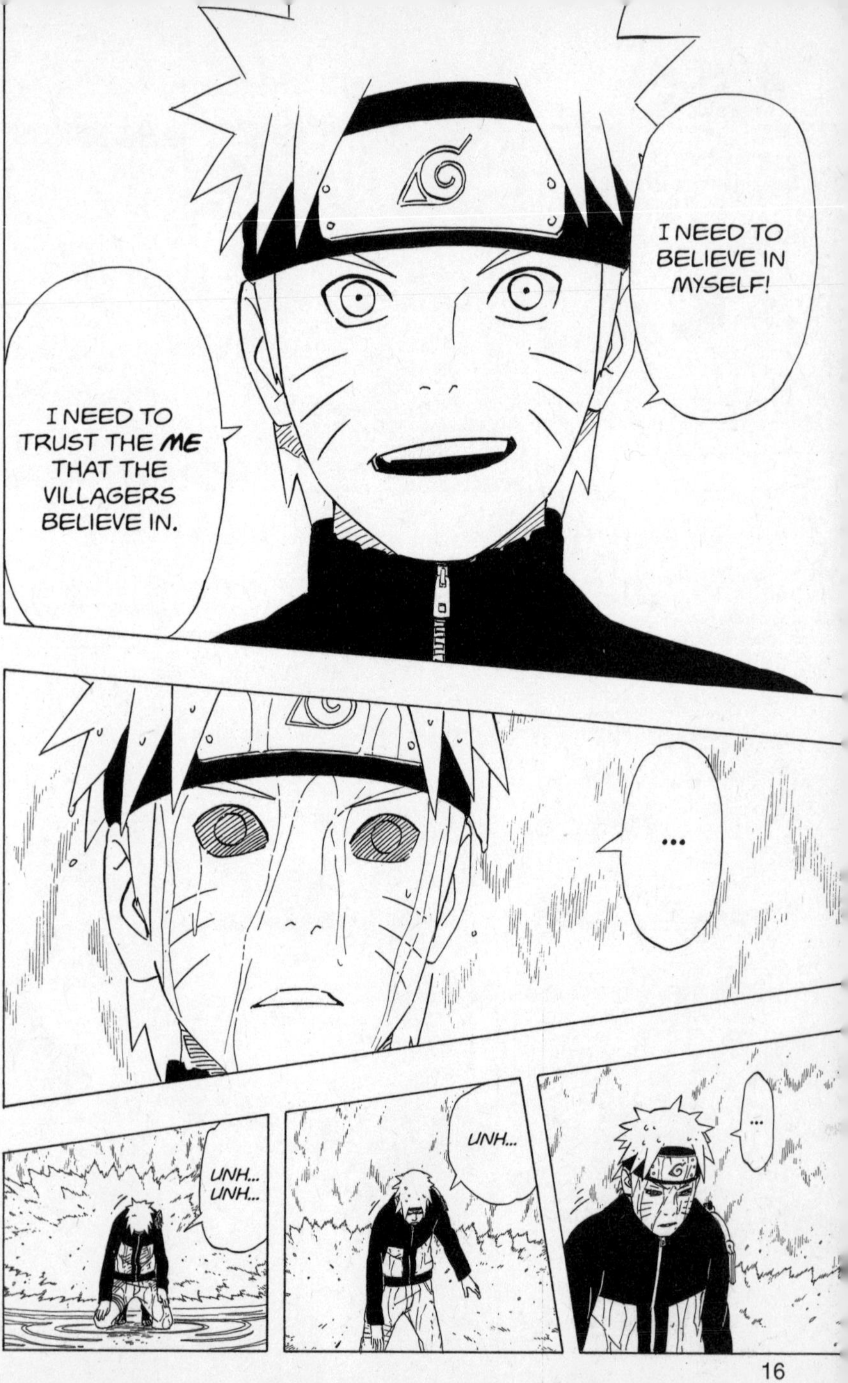
I NEED TO BELIEVE IN MYSELF!
I NEED TO TRUST THE *ME* THAT THE VILLAGERS BELIEVE IN.
...
...
UNH...
UNH... UNH...

READ THIS WAY

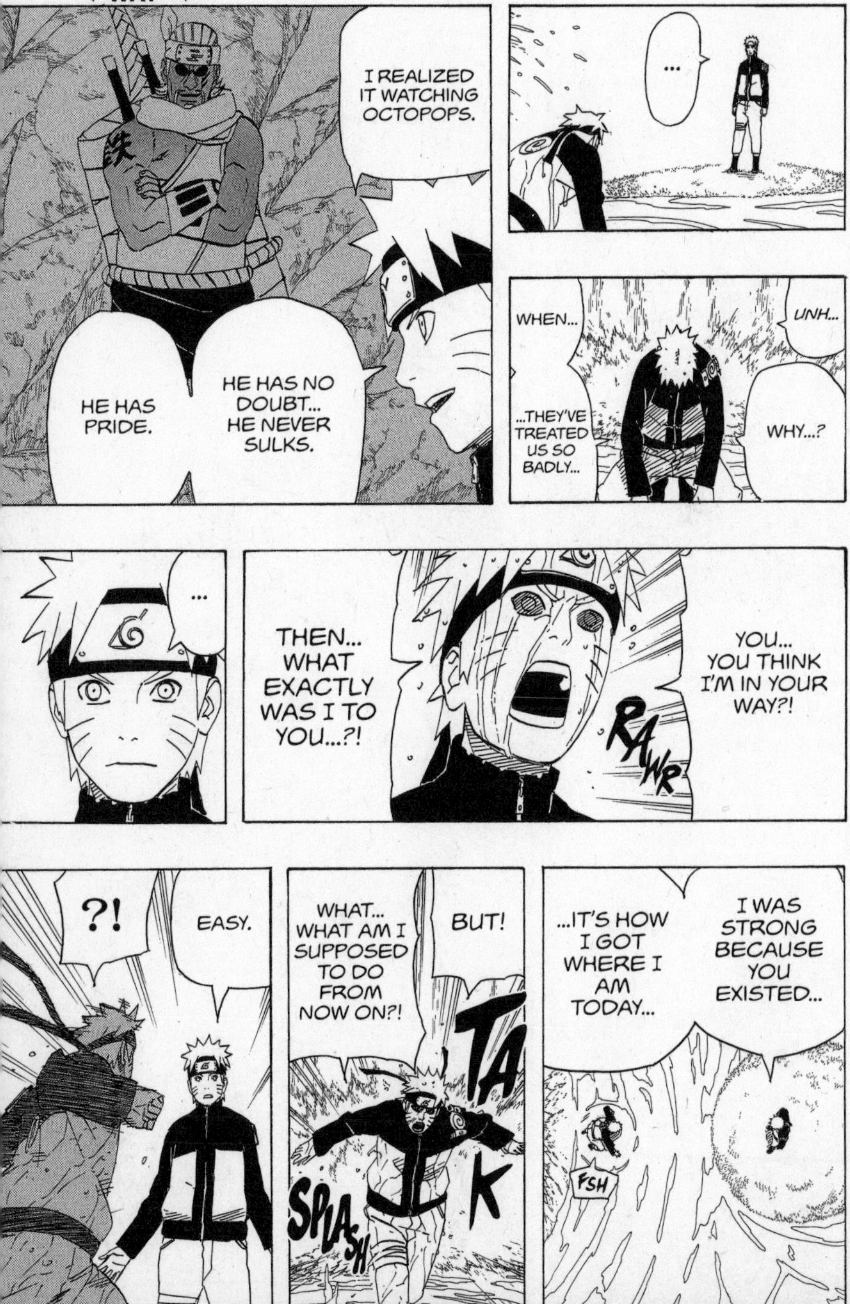
...
UNH...
WHY...?
WHEN...
...THEY'VE TREATED US SO BADLY...
I REALIZED IT WATCHING OCTOPOPS.
HE HAS NO DOUBT... HE NEVER SULKS.
HE HAS PRIDE.
YOU... YOU THINK I'M IN YOUR WAY?!
RAWR
THEN... WHAT EXACTLY WAS I TO YOU...?!
...
I WAS STRONG BECAUSE YOU EXISTED...
...IT'S HOW I GOT WHERE I AM TODAY...
FSH
BUT!
WHAT... WHAT AM I SUPPOSED TO DO FROM NOW ON?!
TAK
SPLASH
EASY.
?!

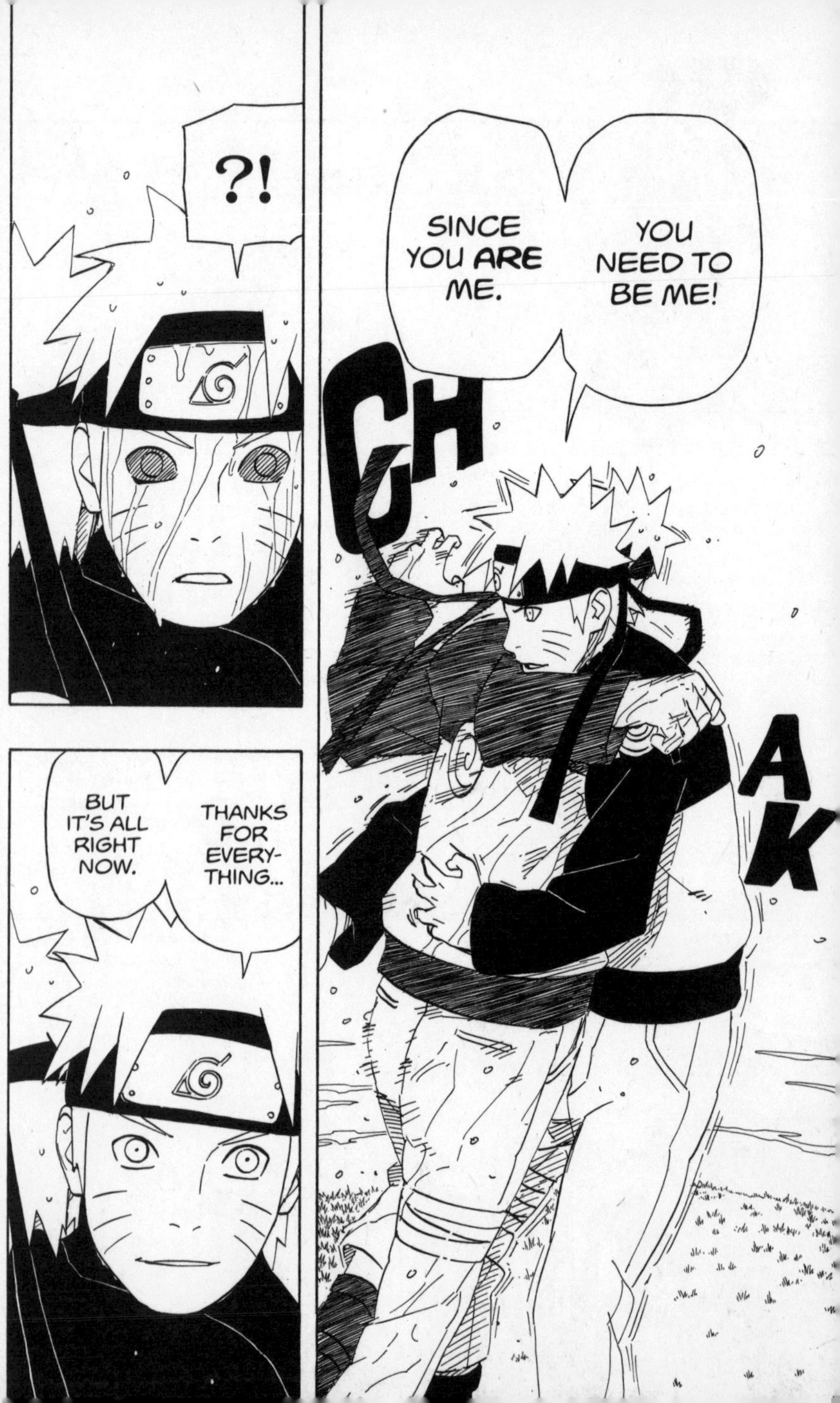
SINCE YOU ARE ME.
YOU NEED TO BE ME!
CH
AK
?!
BUT IT'S ALL RIGHT NOW.
THANKS FOR EVERYTHING...

READ THIS WAY

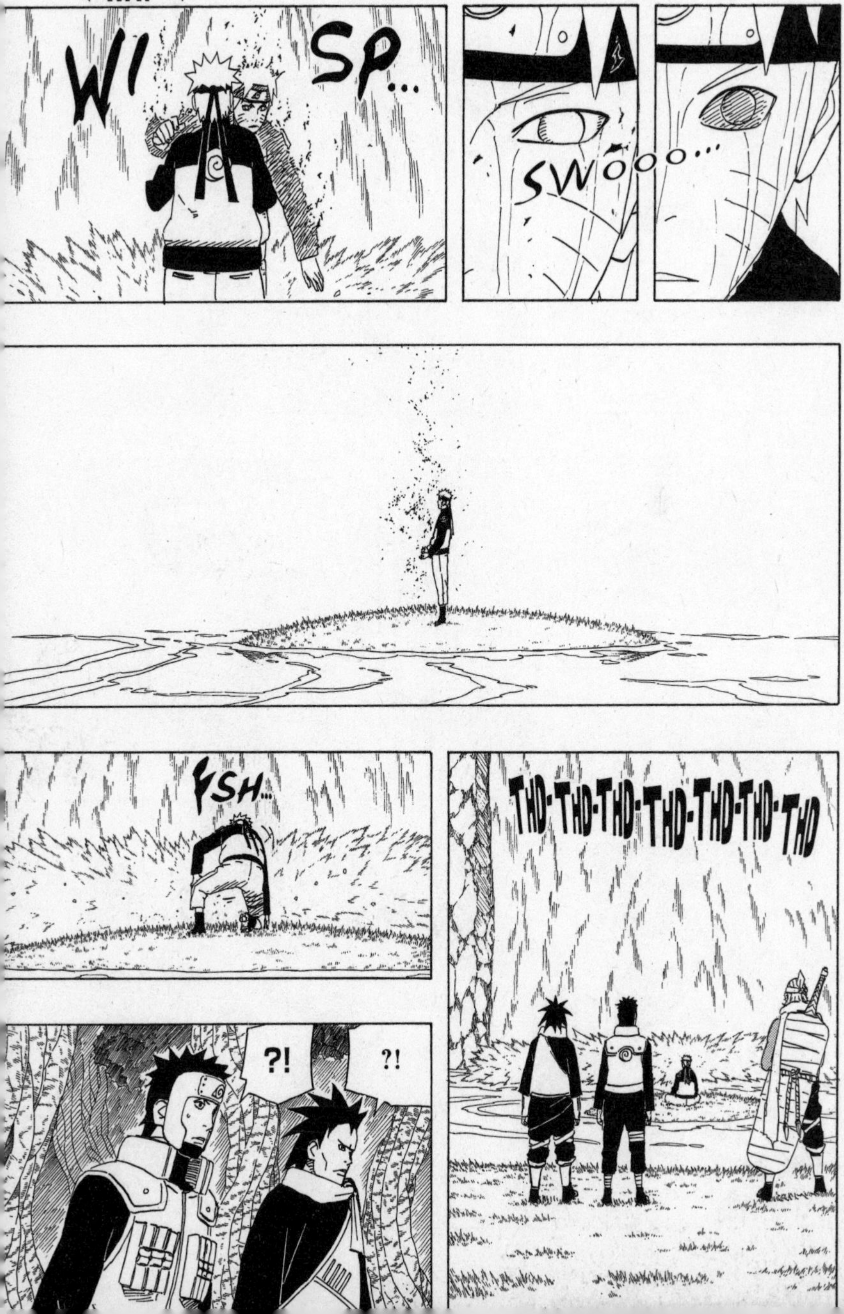
SWOOO...
WI SP...
THD-THD-THD-THD-THD-THD-THD
FSH...
?!
?!

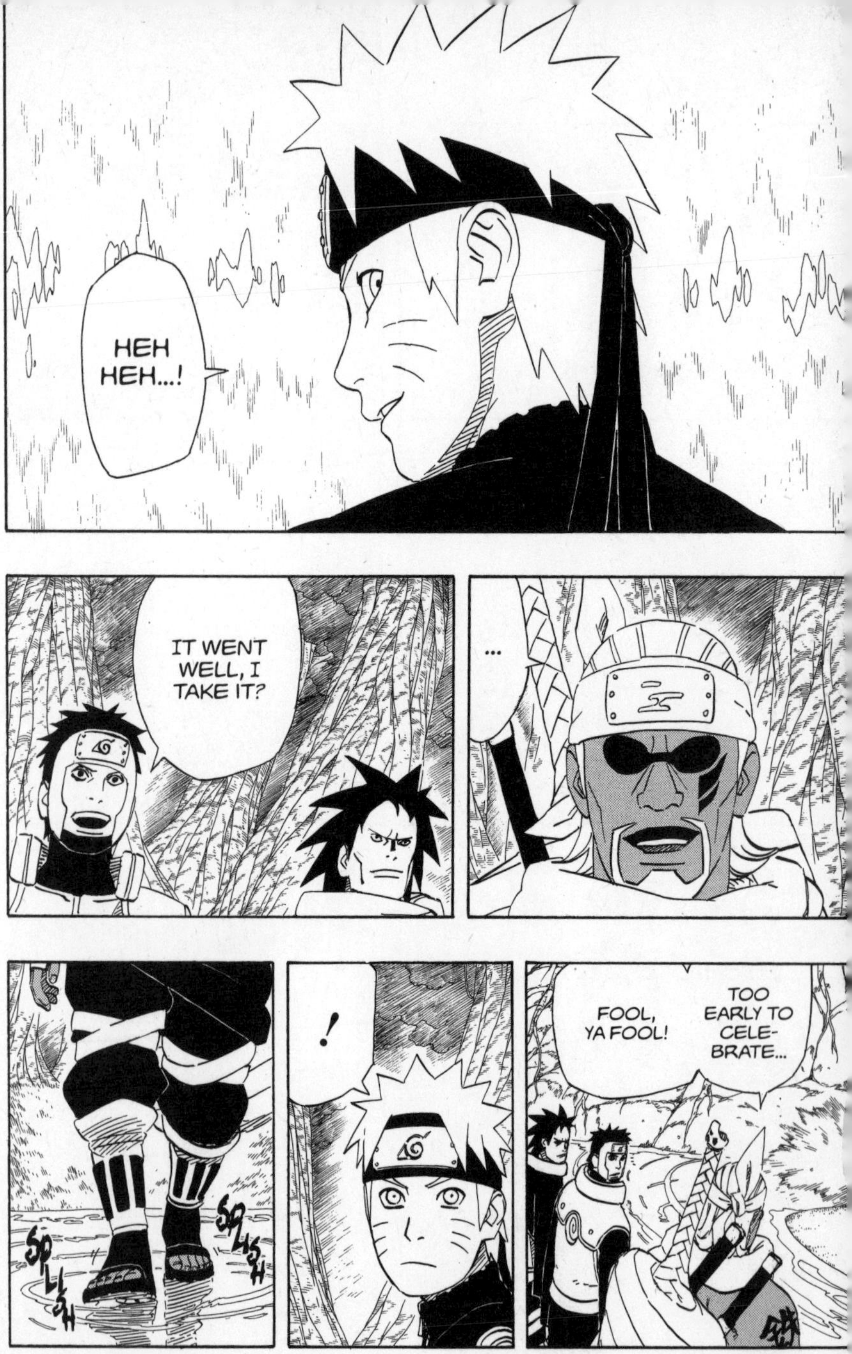
HEH HEH...!
...
IT WENT WELL, I TAKE IT?
TOO EARLY TO CELE-BRATE...
FOOL, YA FOOL!
!
SPLISH
SPLISH

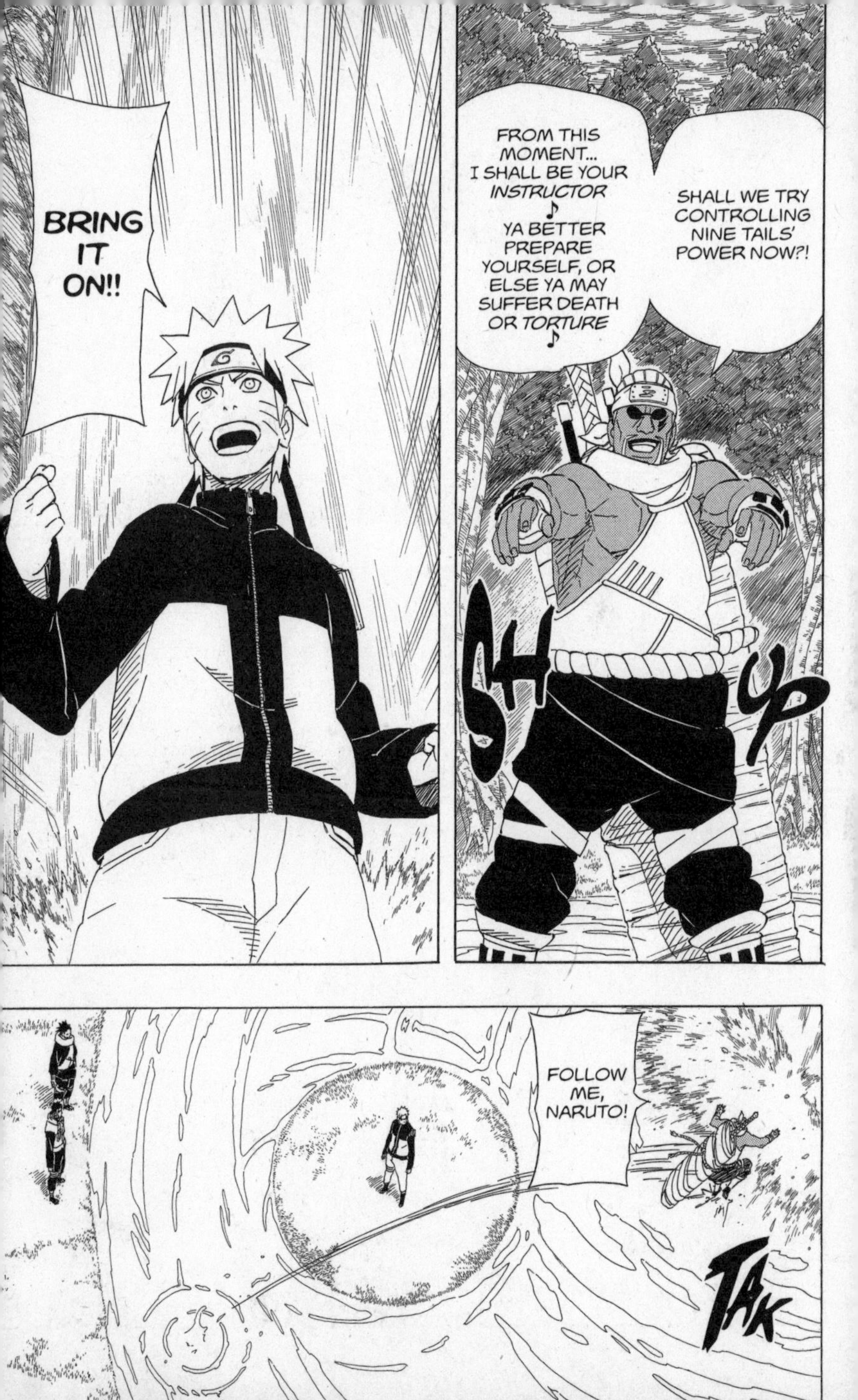
FROM THIS MOMENT... I SHALL BE YOUR INSTRUCTOR ♪ YA BETTER PREPARE YOURSELF, OR ELSE YA MAY SUFFER DEATH OR TORTURE ♪
SHALL WE TRY CONTROLLING NINE TAILS' POWER NOW?!
SHUP
BRING IT ON!!
FOLLOW ME, NARUTO!
TAK

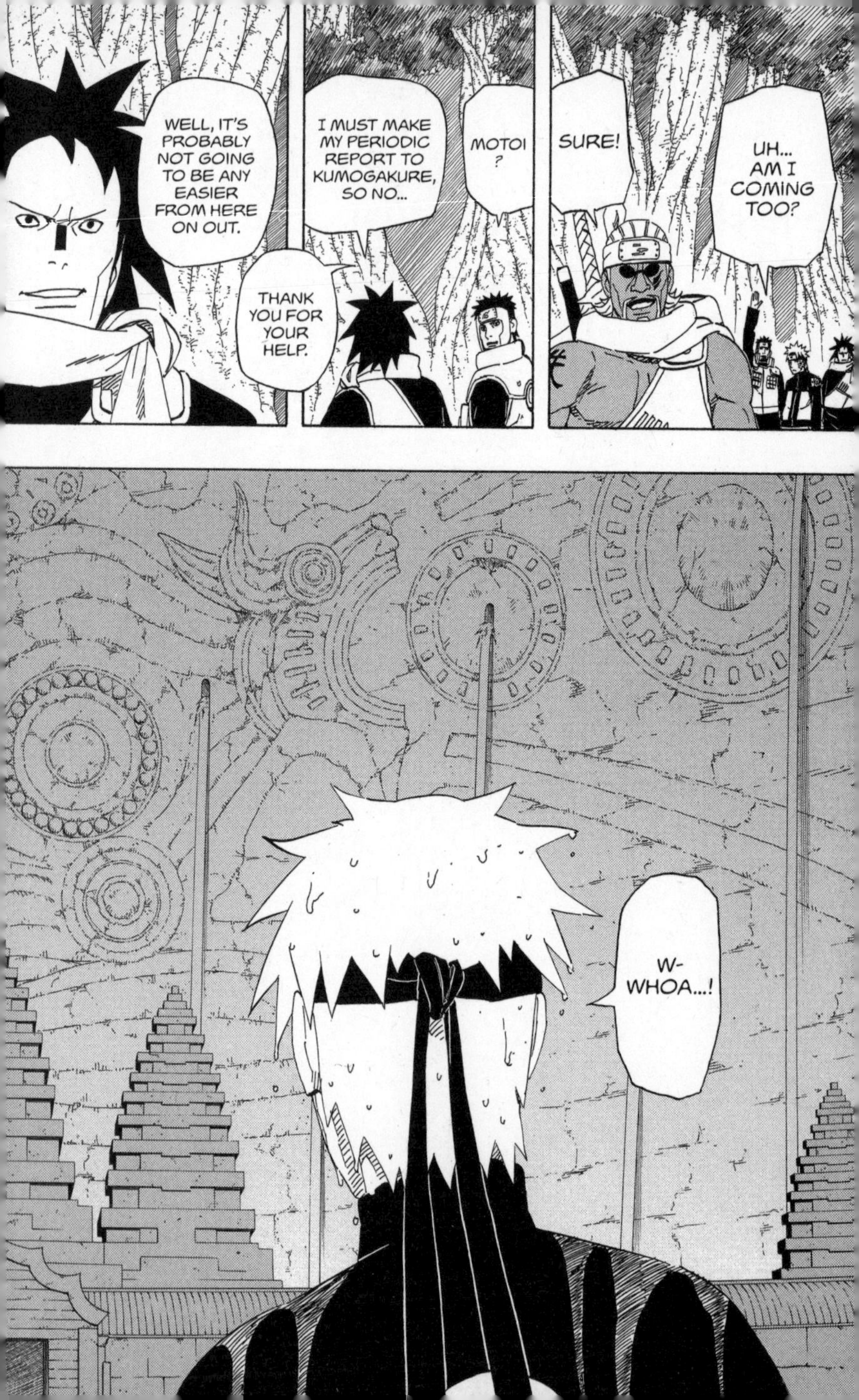
UH... AM I COMING TOO?
SURE!
MOTOI?
I MUST MAKE MY PERIODIC REPORT TO KUMOGAKURE, SO NO...
THANK YOU FOR YOUR HELP.
WELL, IT'S PROBABLY NOT GOING TO BE ANY EASIER FROM HERE ON OUT.
W- WHOA...!

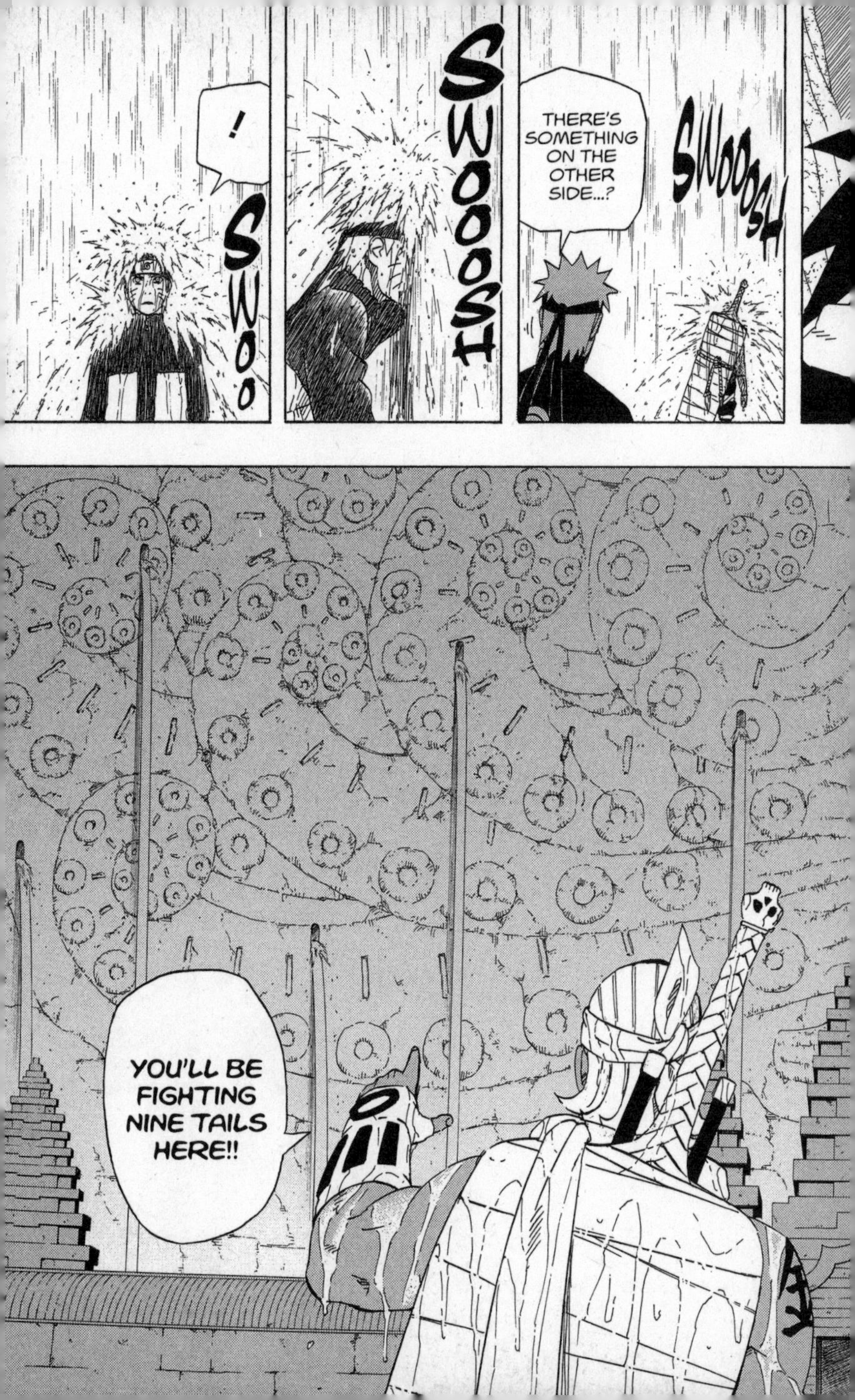
THERE'S SOMETHING ON THE OTHER SIDE...?
SWOOOSH
SWOOOOSH
!
SWOO
YOU'LL BE FIGHTING NINE TAILS HERE!!

Number 496: Reunion with Nine Tails!!

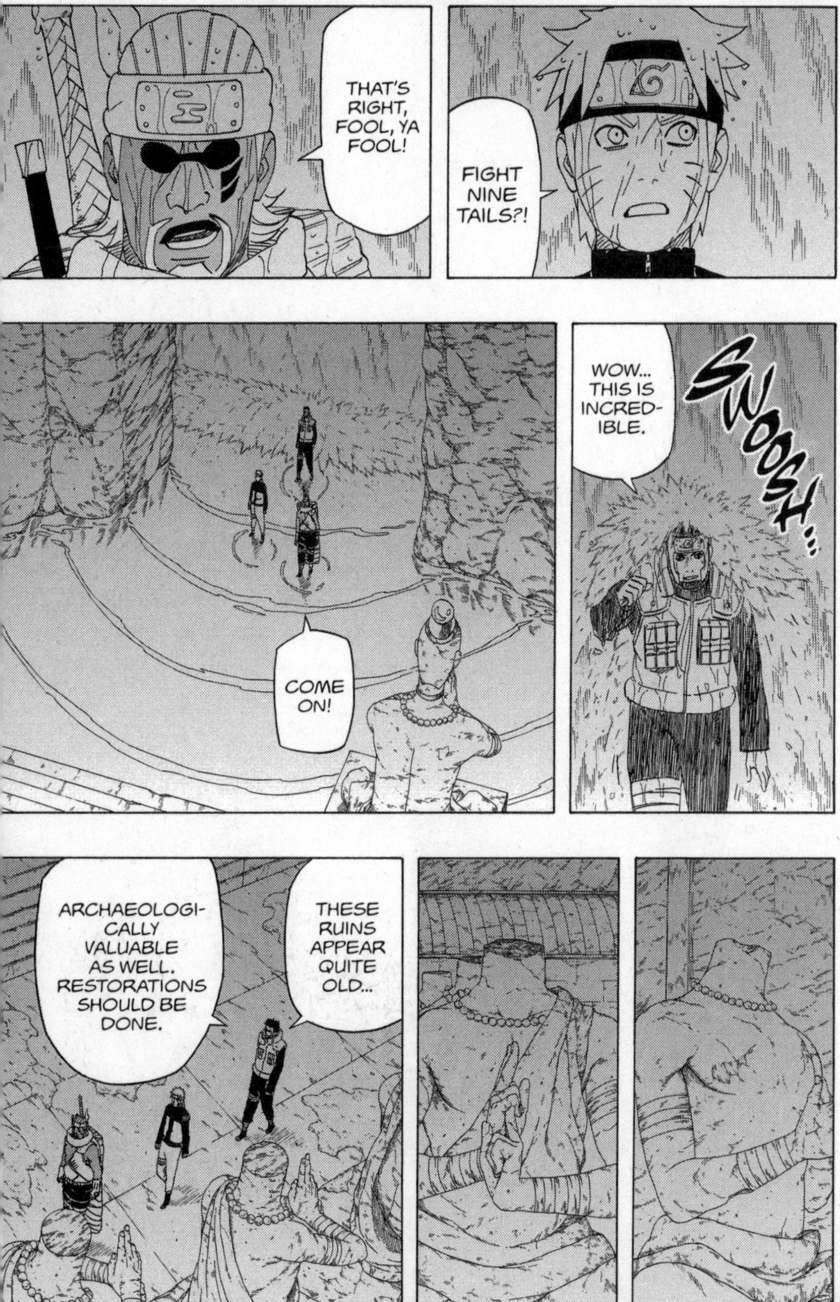
FIGHT NINE TAILS?!
THAT'S RIGHT, FOOL, YA FOOL!
WOW... THIS IS INCREDIBLE.
SWOOSH...
COME ON!
THESE RUINS APPEAR QUITE OLD...
ARCHAEOLOGICALLY VALUABLE AS WELL. RESTORATIONS SHOULD BE DONE.

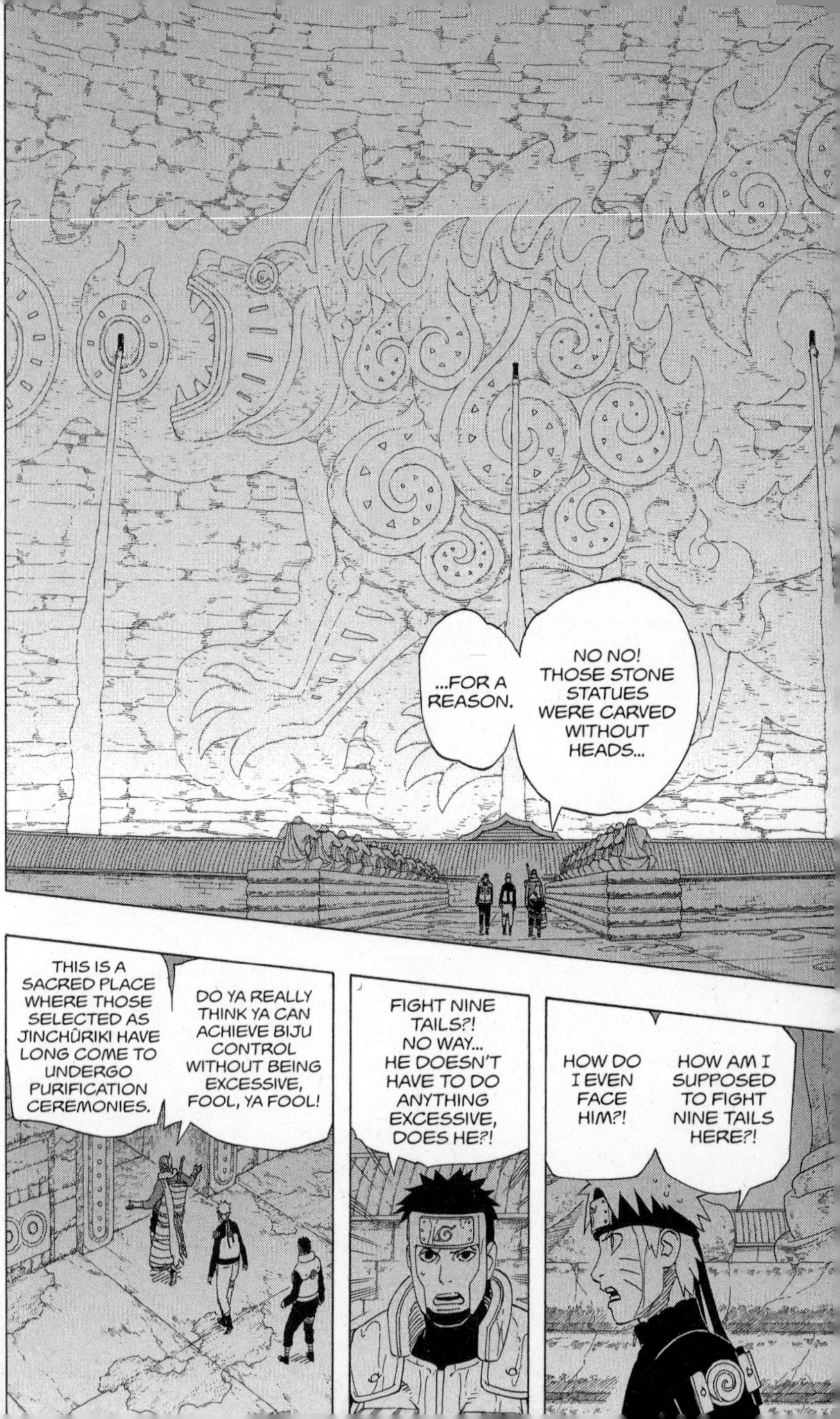
NO NO! THOSE STONE STATUES WERE CARVED WITHOUT HEADS...
...FOR A REASON.
HOW AM I SUPPOSED TO FIGHT NINE TAILS HERE?!
HOW DO I EVEN FACE HIM?!
FIGHT NINE TAILS?! NO WAY... HE DOESN'T HAVE TO DO ANYTHING EXCESSIVE, DOES HE?!
DO YA REALLY THINK YA CAN ACHIEVE BIJU CONTROL WITHOUT BEING EXCESSIVE, FOOL, YA FOOL!
THIS IS A SACRED PLACE WHERE THOSE SELECTED AS JINCHŪRIKI HAVE LONG COME TO UNDERGO PURIFICATION CEREMONIES.

READ THIS WAY

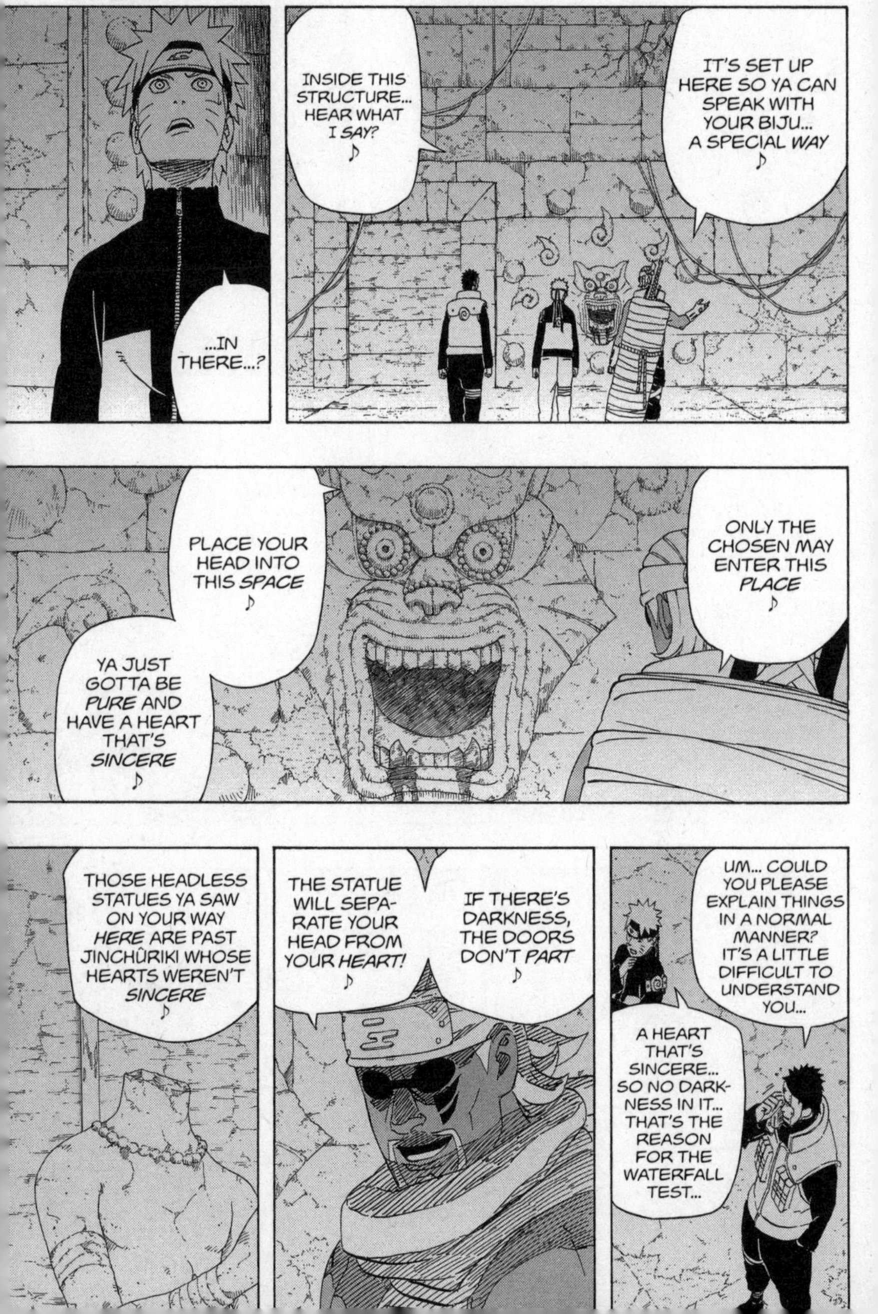
IT'S SET UP HERE SO YA CAN SPEAK WITH YOUR BIJU... A SPECIAL *WAY* ♪
INSIDE THIS STRUCTURE... HEAR WHAT I *SAY?* ♪
...IN THERE...?
ONLY THE CHOSEN MAY ENTER THIS *PLACE* ♪
PLACE YOUR HEAD INTO THIS *SPACE* ♪
YA JUST GOTTA BE *PURE* AND HAVE A HEART THAT'S *SINCERE* ♪
UM... COULD YOU PLEASE EXPLAIN THINGS IN A NORMAL MANNER? IT'S A LITTLE DIFFICULT TO UNDERSTAND YOU...
A HEART THAT'S SINCERE... SO NO DARK-NESS IN IT... THAT'S THE REASON FOR THE WATERFALL TEST...
IF THERE'S DARKNESS, THE DOORS DON'T *PART* ♪
THE STATUE WILL SEPA-RATE YOUR HEAD FROM YOUR *HEART!* ♪
THOSE HEADLESS STATUES YA SAW ON YOUR WAY *HERE* ARE PAST JINCHÛRIKI WHOSE HEARTS WEREN'T *SINCERE* ♪

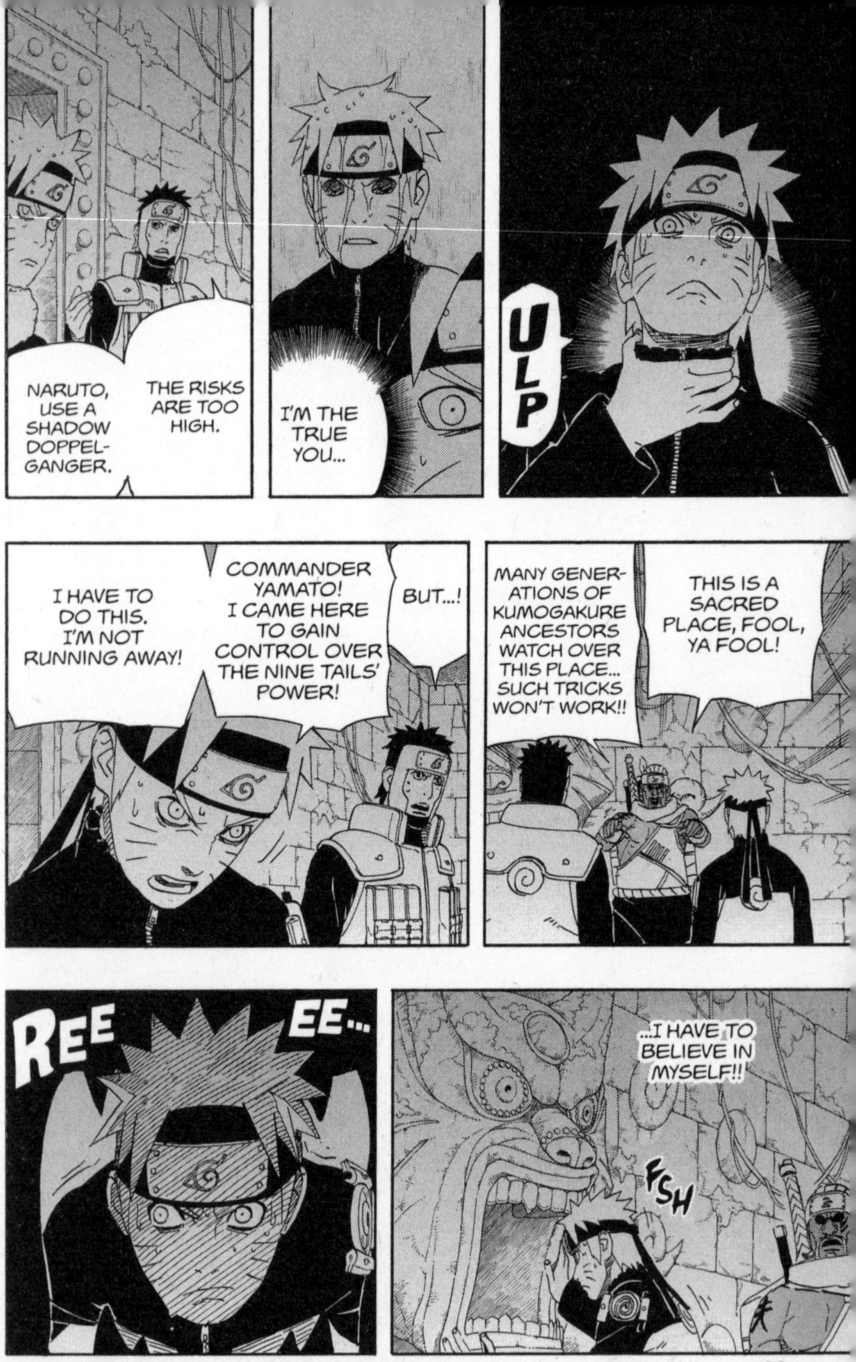
ULP
I'M THE TRUE YOU...
NARUTO, USE A SHADOW DOPPEL-GANGER.
THE RISKS ARE TOO HIGH.
THIS IS A SACRED PLACE, FOOL, YA FOOL!
MANY GENER-ATIONS OF KUMOGAKURE ANCESTORS WATCH OVER THIS PLACE... SUCH TRICKS WON'T WORK!!
BUT...!
COMMANDER YAMATO! I CAME HERE TO GAIN CONTROL OVER THE NINE TAILS' POWER!
I HAVE TO DO THIS. I'M NOT RUNNING AWAY!
...I HAVE TO BELIEVE IN MYSELF!!
FSH
REE
EE...

READ THIS WAY

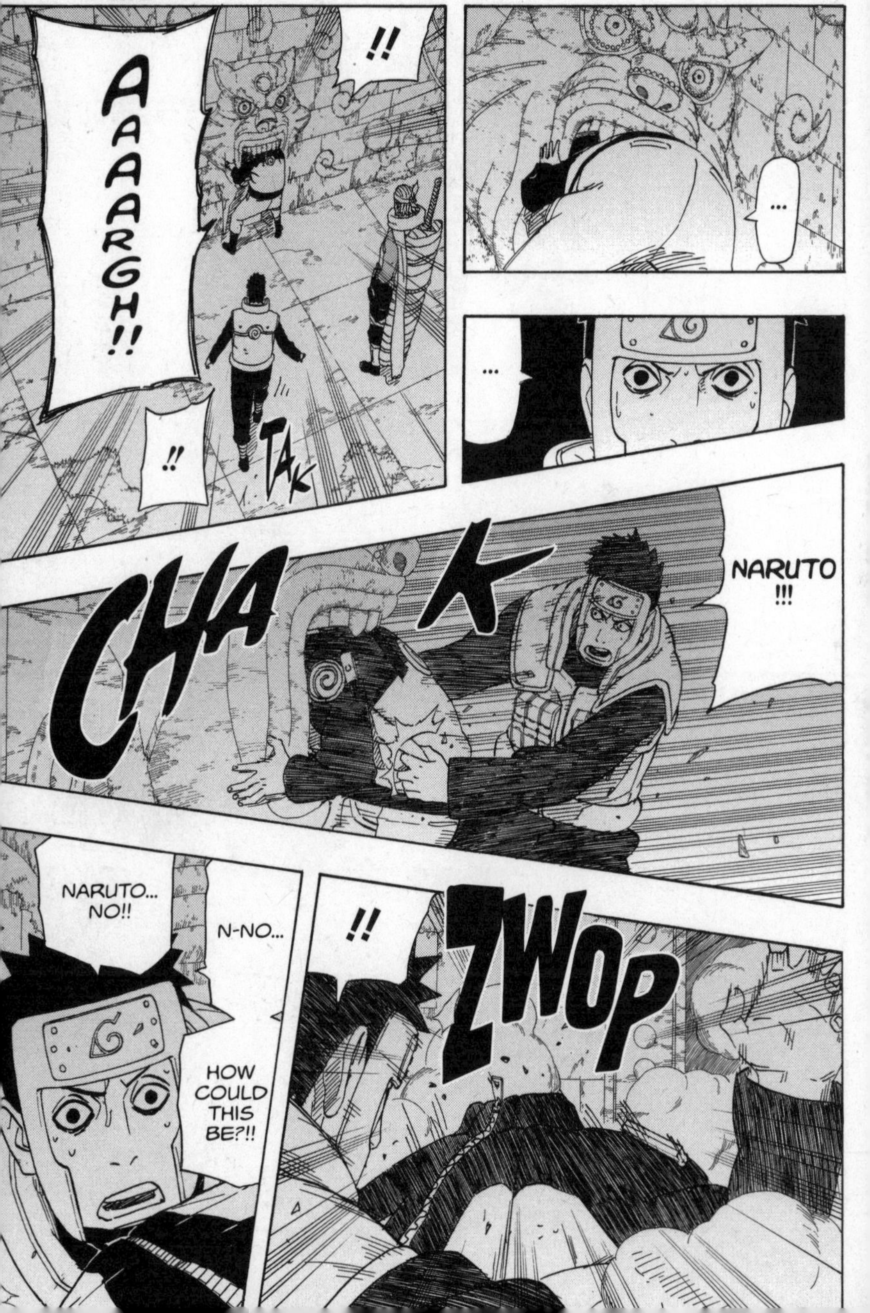
...
...
!!
AAAAARGH!!
!!
TAK
NARUTO !!!
CHAK
!!
ZWOP
NARUTO... NO!!
N-NO...
HOW COULD THIS BE?!!

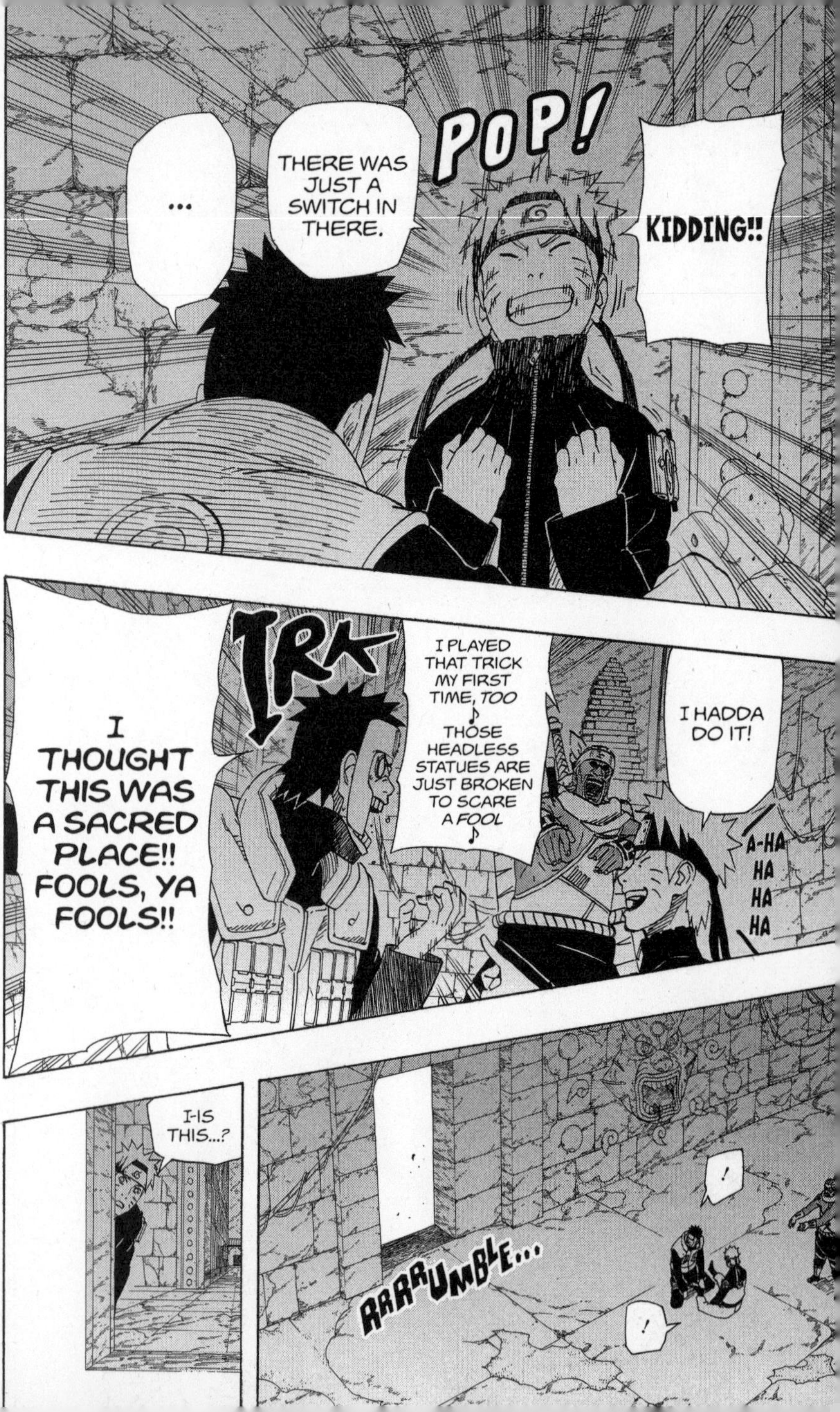
KIDDING!!
POP!
THERE WAS JUST A SWITCH IN THERE.
...
I HADDA DO IT!
A-HA HA HA HA
I PLAYED THAT TRICK MY FIRST TIME, *TOO* ♪ THOSE HEADLESS STATUES ARE JUST BROKEN TO SCARE A *FOOL* ♪
TRK
I THOUGHT THIS WAS A SACRED PLACE!! FOOLS, YA FOOLS!!
!
!
RRRRUMBLE...
I-IS THIS...?

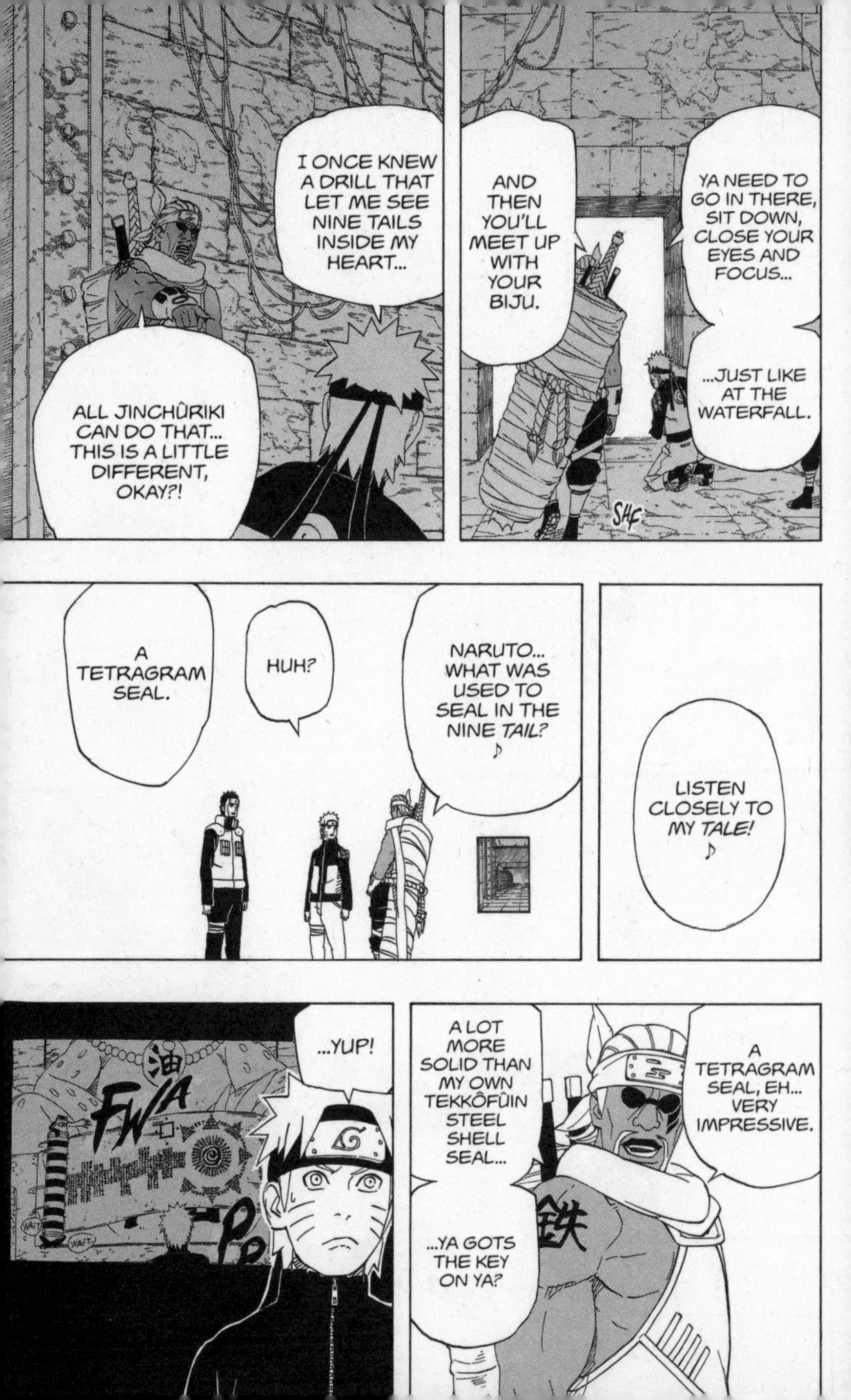
YA NEED TO GO IN THERE, SIT DOWN, CLOSE YOUR EYES AND FOCUS...
...JUST LIKE AT THE WATERFALL.
AND THEN YOU'LL MEET UP WITH YOUR BIJU.
SHF
I ONCE KNEW A DRILL THAT LET ME SEE NINE TAILS INSIDE MY HEART...
ALL JINCHÛRIKI CAN DO THAT... THIS IS A LITTLE DIFFERENT, OKAY?!
LISTEN CLOSELY TO MY *TALE!* ♪
NARUTO... WHAT WAS USED TO SEAL IN THE NINE *TAIL?* ♪
HUH?
A TETRAGRAM SEAL.
A TETRAGRAM SEAL, EH... VERY IMPRESSIVE.
A LOT MORE SOLID THAN MY OWN TEKKÔFÛIN STEEL SHELL SEAL...
...YA GOTS THE KEY ON YA?
...YUP!
FWA

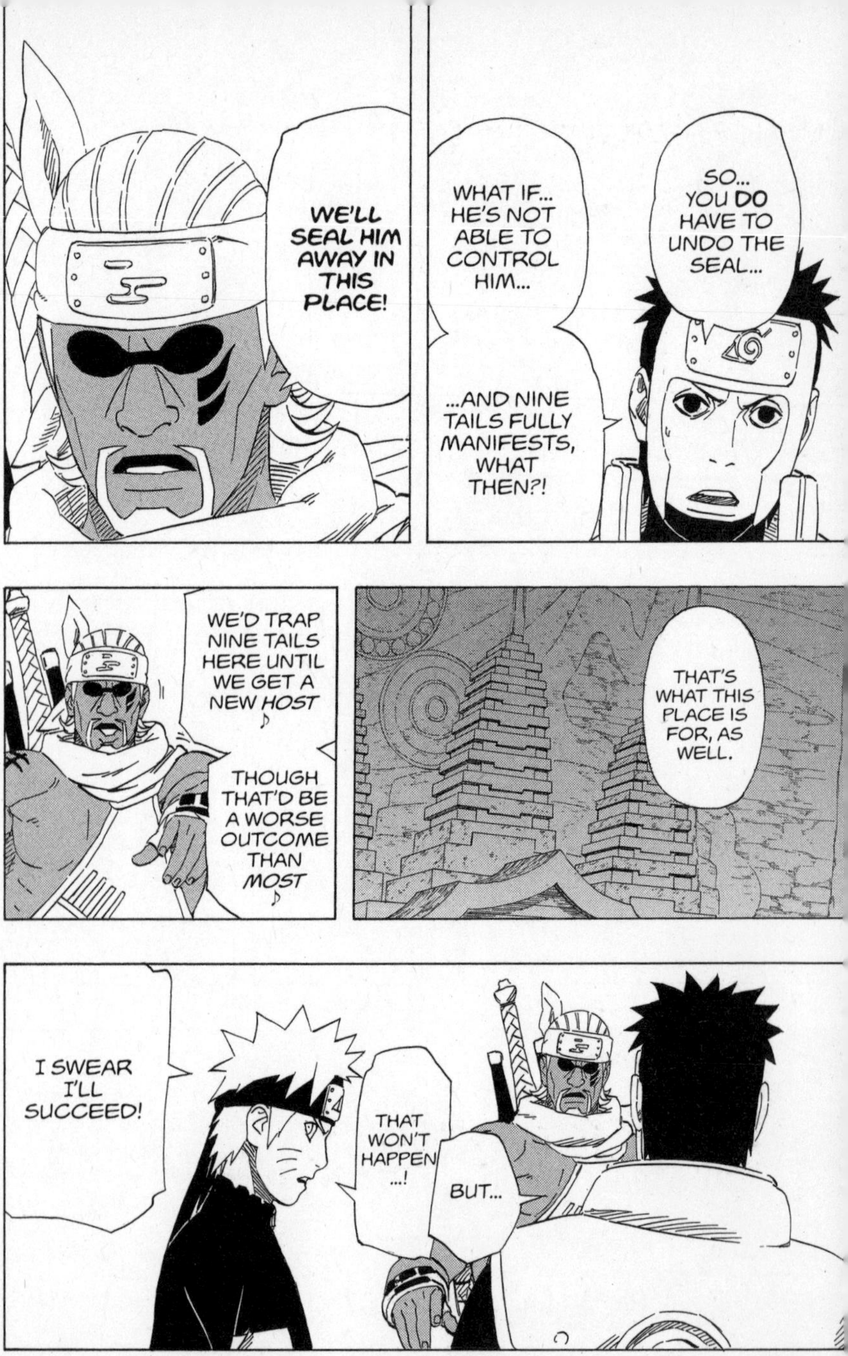

SO... YOU DO HAVE TO UNDO THE SEAL...
WHAT IF... HE'S NOT ABLE TO CONTROL HIM...
...AND NINE TAILS FULLY MANIFESTS, WHAT THEN?!
WE'LL SEAL HIM AWAY IN THIS PLACE!
THAT'S WHAT THIS PLACE IS FOR, AS WELL.
WE'D TRAP NINE TAILS HERE UNTIL WE GET A NEW *HOST* ♪
THOUGH THAT'D BE A WORSE OUTCOME THAN *MOST* ♪
BUT...
THAT WON'T HAPPEN ...!
I SWEAR I'LL SUCCEED!

READ THIS WAY

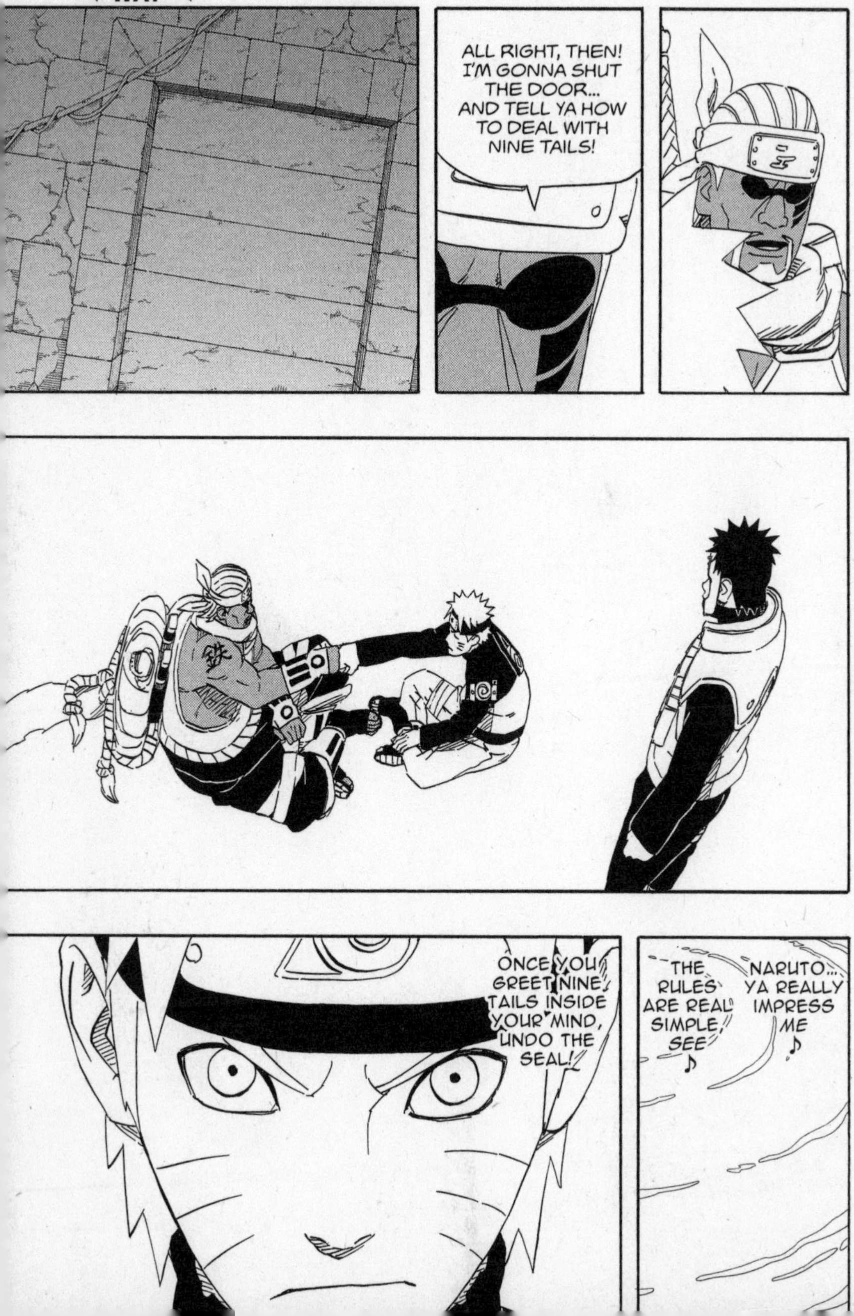
ALL RIGHT, THEN! I'M GONNA SHUT THE DOOR... AND TELL YA HOW TO DEAL WITH NINE TAILS!
NARUTO... YA REALLY IMPRESS ME ♪
THE RULES ARE REAL SIMPLE, SEE ♪
ONCE YOU GREET NINE TAILS INSIDE YOUR MIND, UNDO THE SEAL!

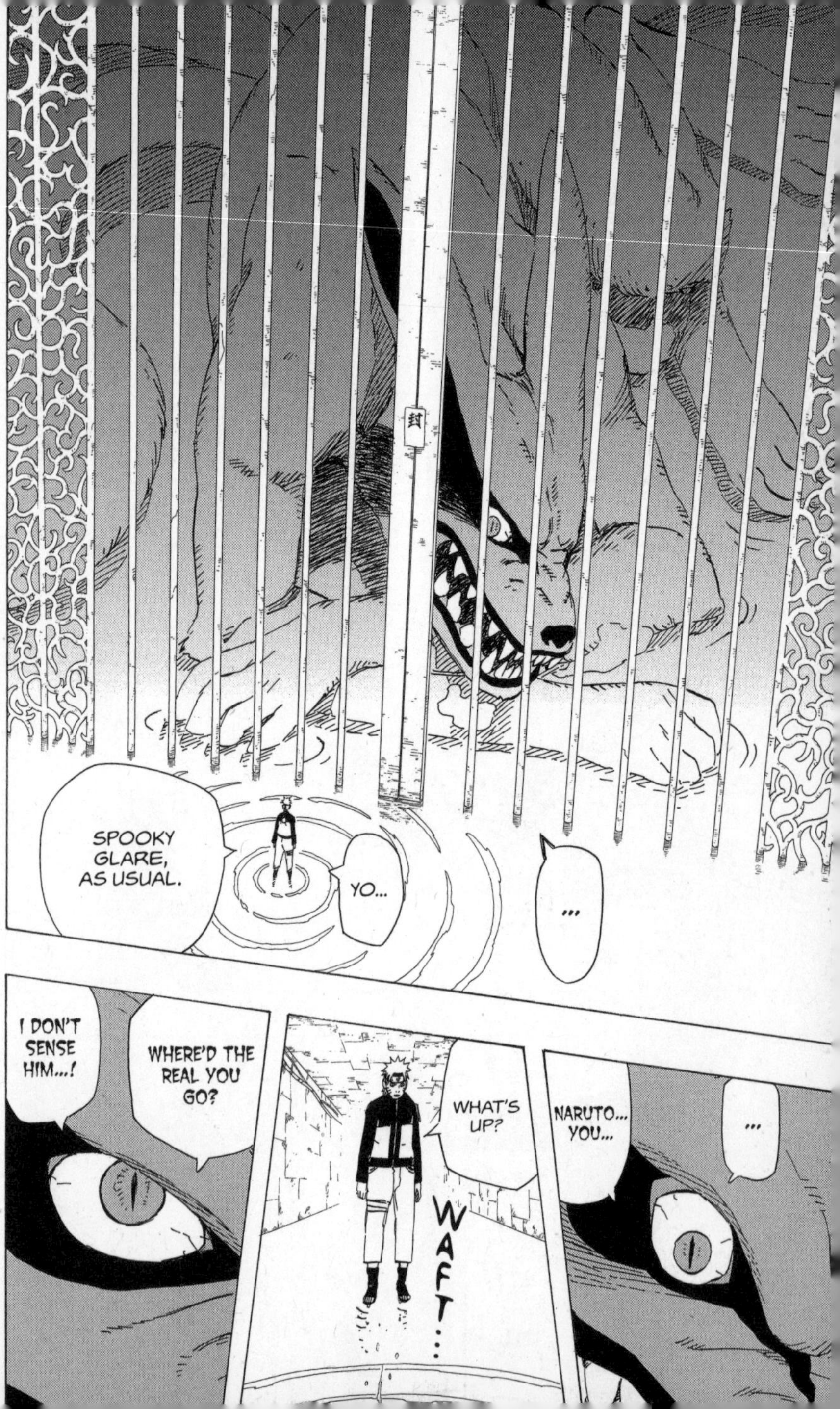
...
YO...
SPOOKY GLARE, AS USUAL.
...
NARUTO... YOU...
WHAT'S UP?
WAFT...
WHERE'D THE REAL YOU GO?
I DON'T SENSE HIM...!

READ THIS WAY

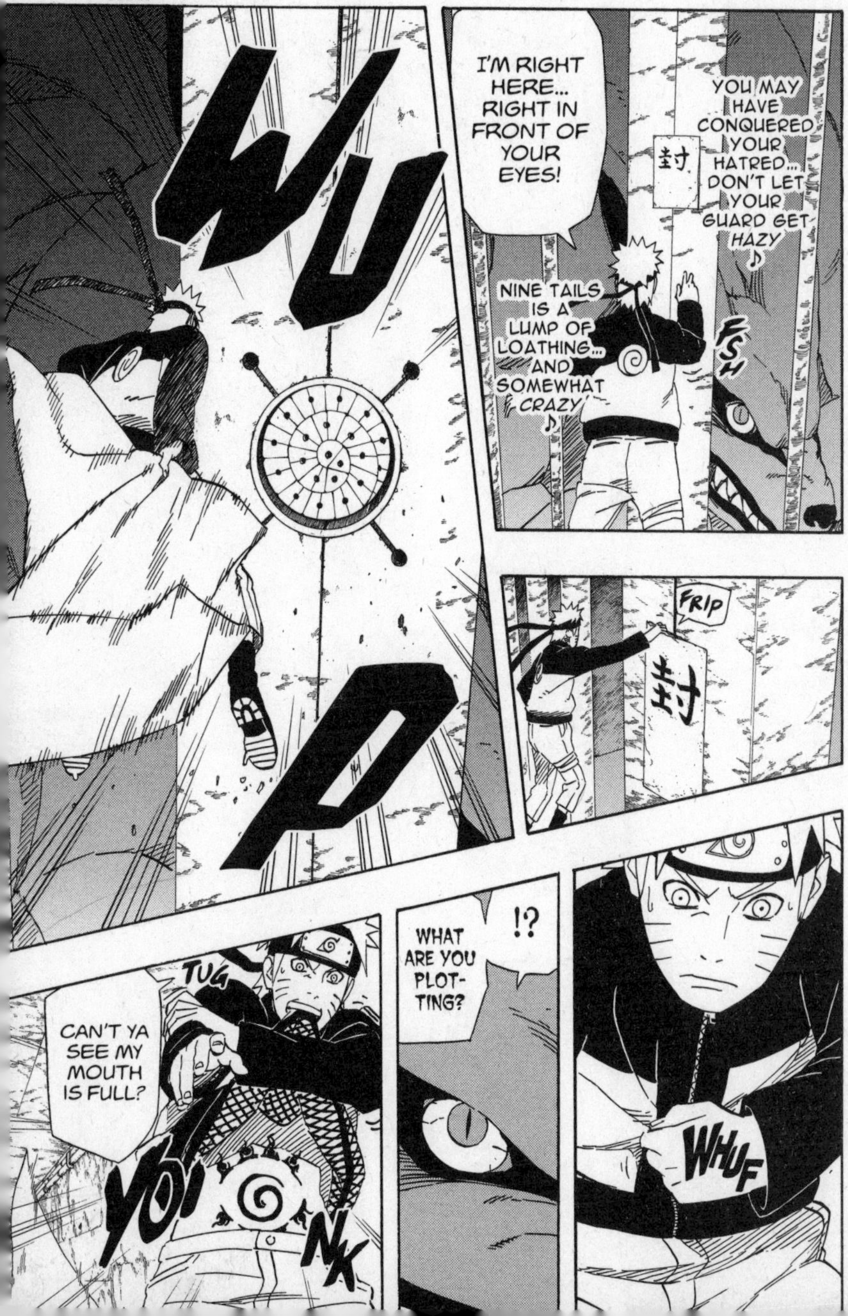
YOU MAY HAVE CONQUERED YOUR HATRED... DON'T LET YOUR GUARD GET HAZY ♪
I'M RIGHT HERE... RIGHT IN FRONT OF YOUR EYES!
封
FSH
NINE TAILS IS A LUMP OF LOATHING... AND SOMEWHAT CRAZY ♪
FRIP
封
WUD
WHUF
!?
WHAT ARE YOU PLOT-TING?
TUG
CAN'T YA SEE MY MOUTH IS FULL?
YOINK

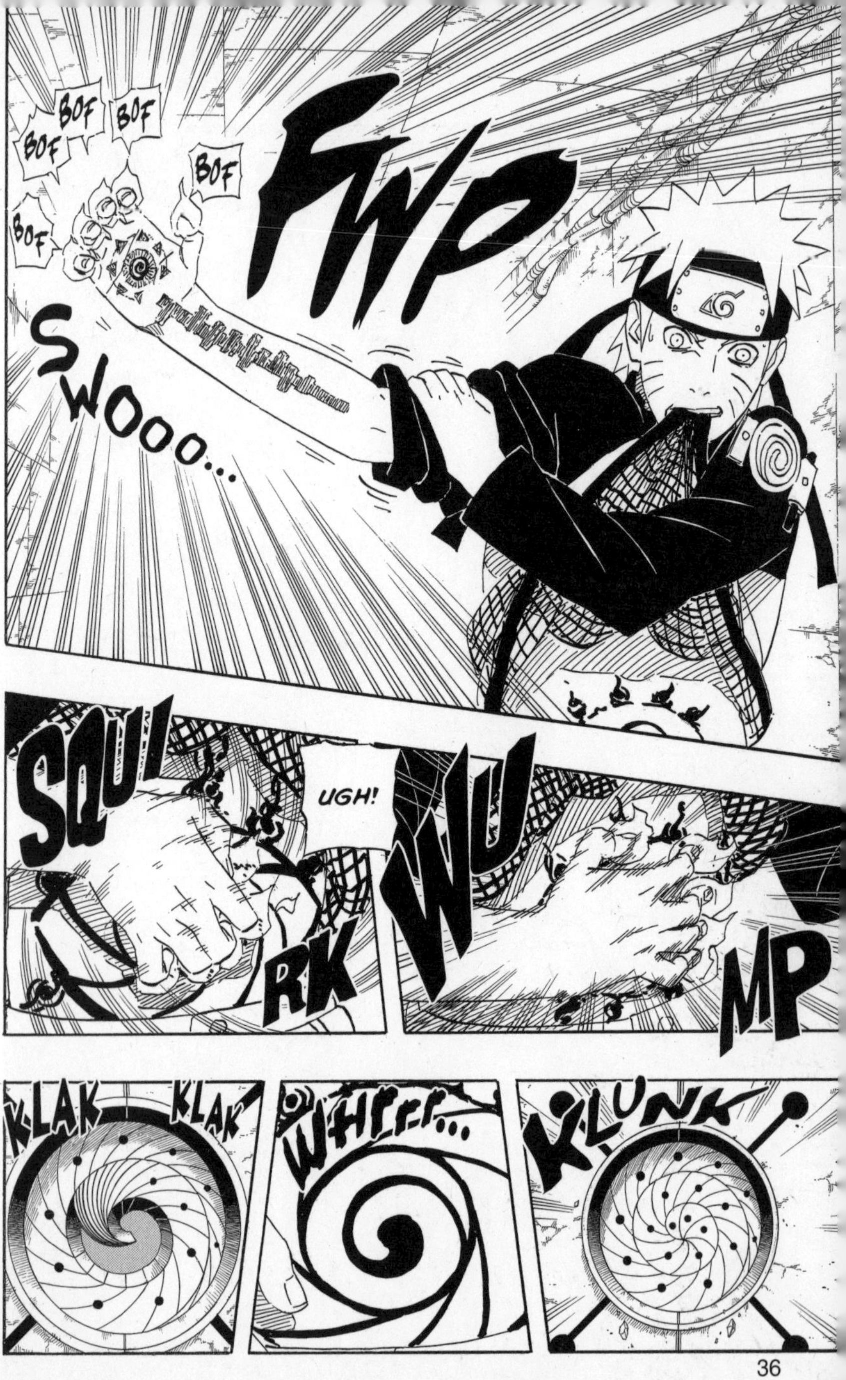
FWP
BOF
BOF
BOF
BOF
BOF
BOF
SWOOO...
WUMP
UGH!
SQUIRK
K-LUNK
WHrrr...
K-LAK K-LAK

READ THIS WAY

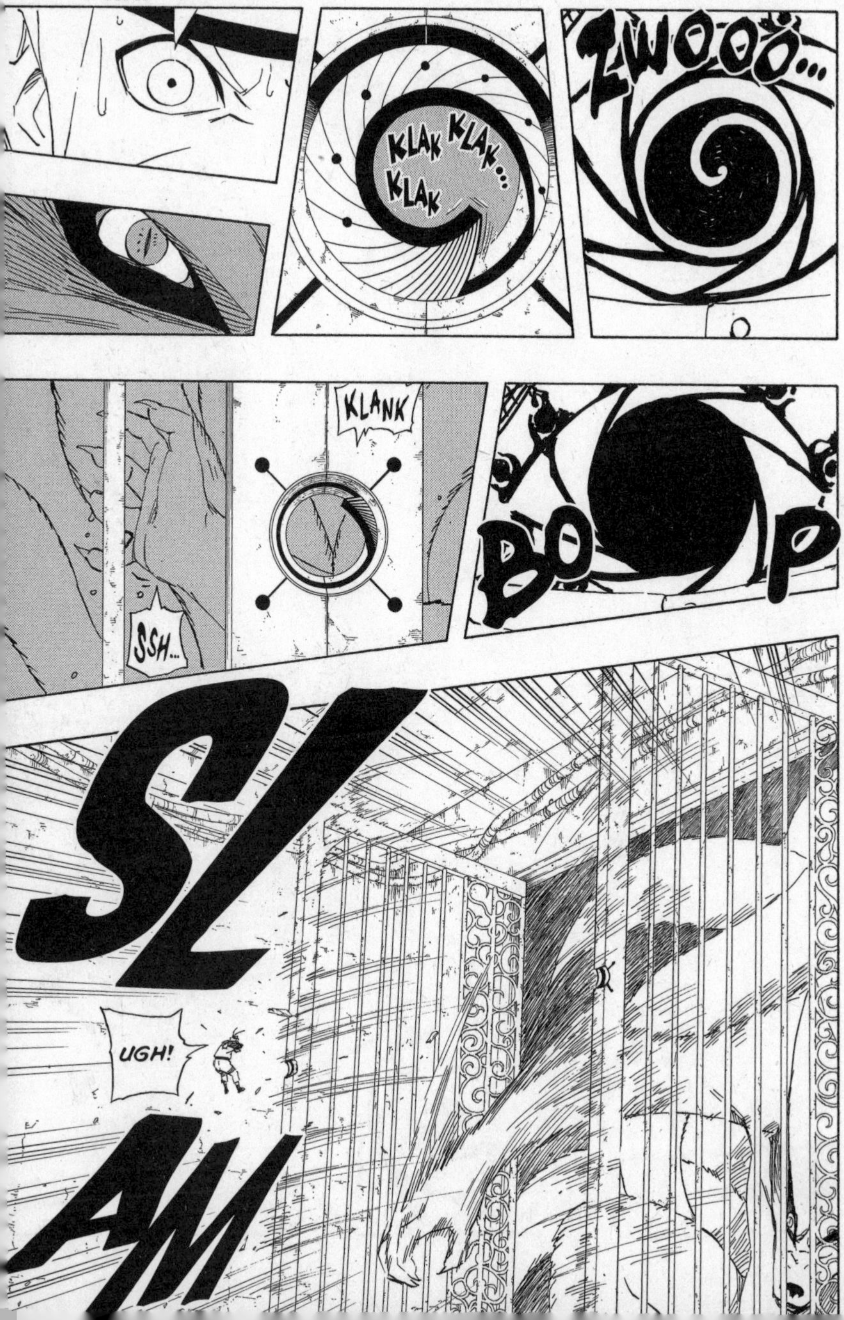
ZWOOO...
KLAK KLAK... KLAK
BOP
KLANK
SSH...
SLAM
UGH!

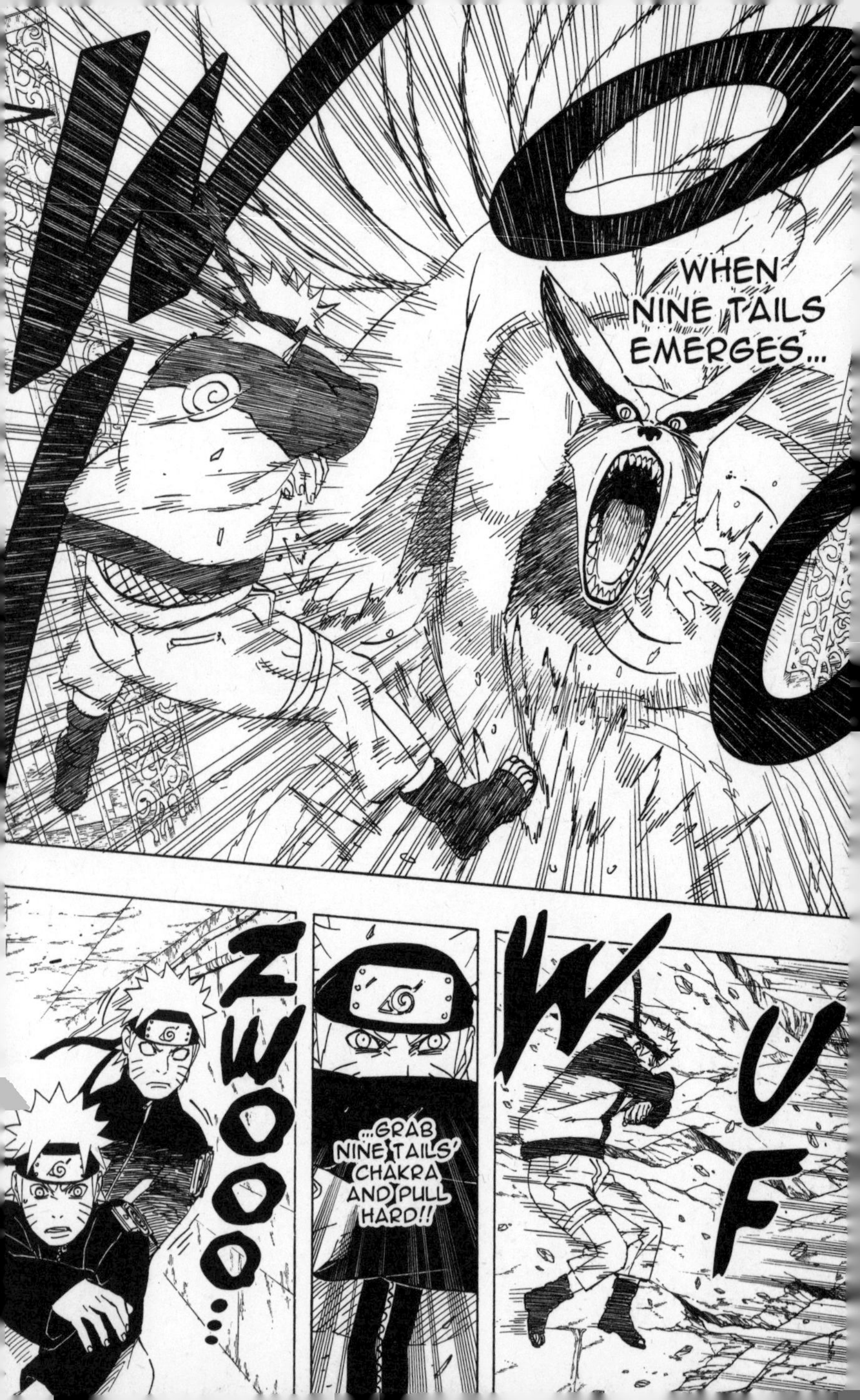
WHEN NINE TAILS EMERGES...
WUF
...GRAB NINE TAILS' CHAKRA AND PULL HARD!!
ZWOOO...

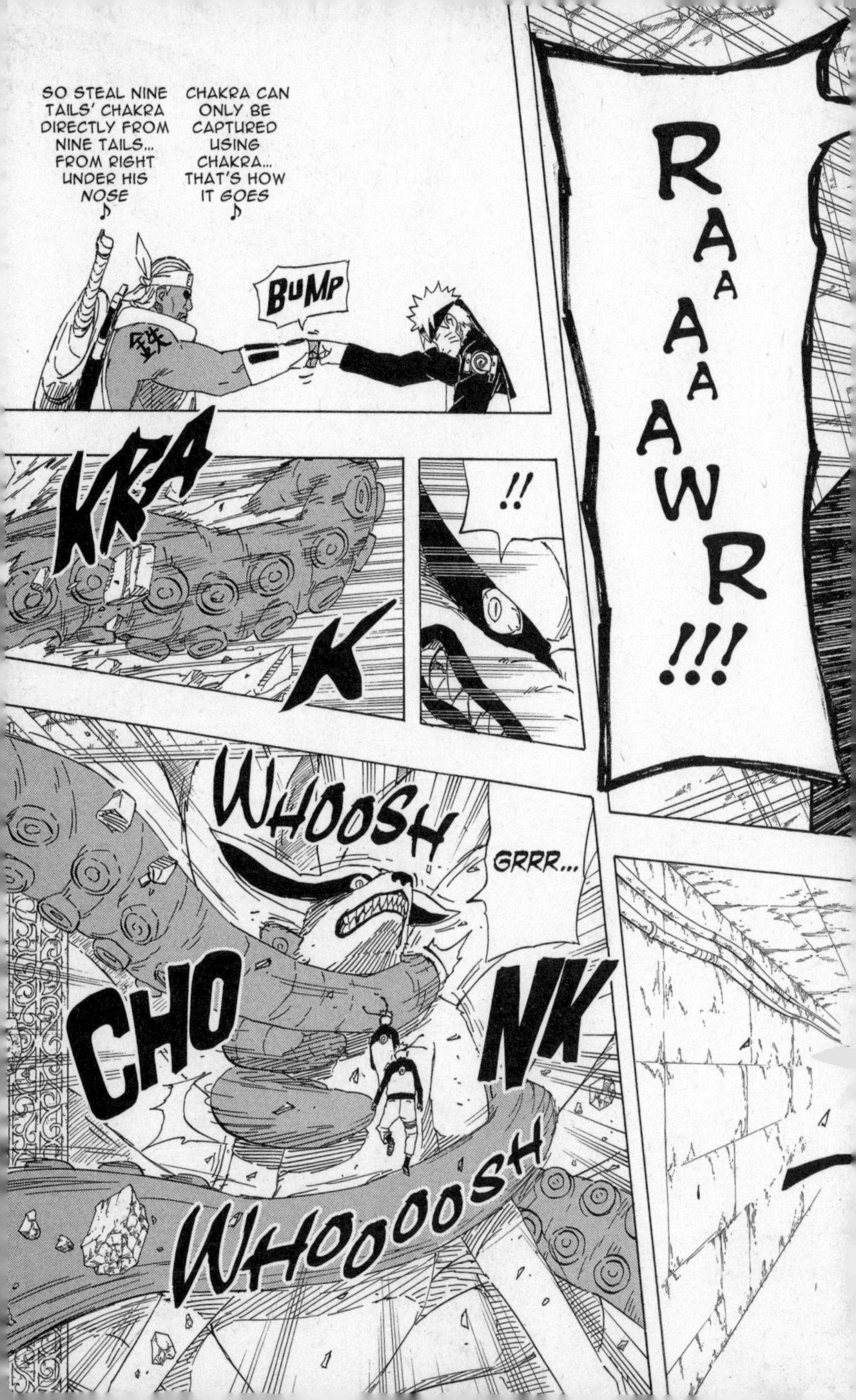
RAAAAAWR!!!
CHAKRA CAN ONLY BE CAPTURED USING CHAKRA... THAT'S HOW IT GOES ♪
SO STEAL NINE TAILS' CHAKRA DIRECTLY FROM NINE TAILS... FROM RIGHT UNDER HIS NOSE ♪
BUMP
!!
KRAAK
WHOOSH
GRRR...
CHONK
WHOOOOOSH

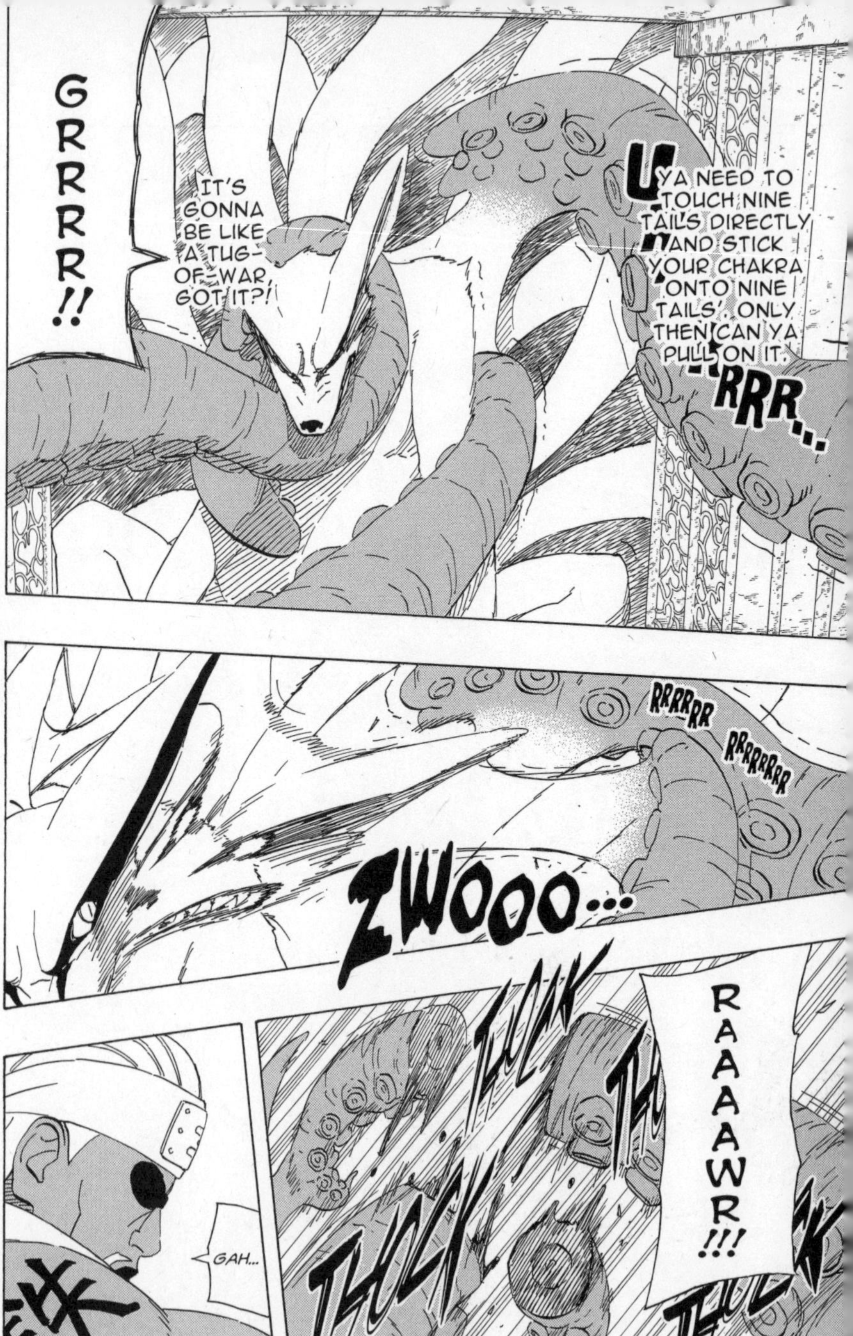

YA NEED TO TOUCH NINE TAILS DIRECTLY AND STICK YOUR CHAKRA ONTO NINE TAILS'. ONLY THEN CAN YA PULL ON IT.
U...RRR...
IT'S GONNA BE LIKE A TUG-OF-WAR GOT IT?!
GRRRRR!!
RRRRRR
RRRRRRRR
ZWOOO...
RAAAAAWR!!!
THUCK
THUCK
THUCK
GAH...

READ THIS WAY

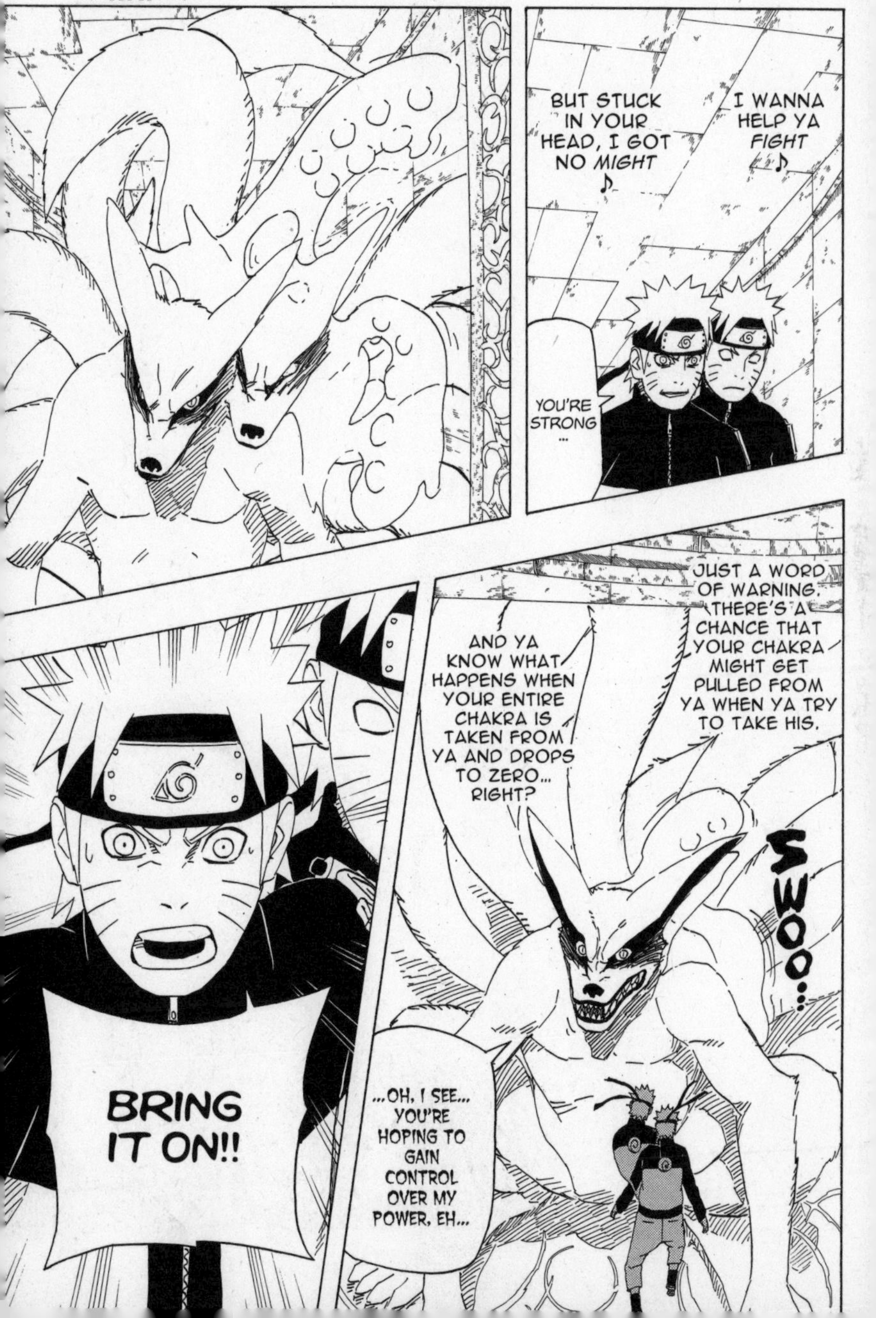
I WANNA HELP YA FIGHT ♪
BUT STUCK IN YOUR HEAD, I GOT NO MIGHT ♪
YOU'RE STRONG ...
JUST A WORD OF WARNING. THERE'S A CHANCE THAT YOUR CHAKRA MIGHT GET PULLED FROM YA WHEN YA TRY TO TAKE HIS.
AND YA KNOW WHAT HAPPENS WHEN YOUR ENTIRE CHAKRA IS TAKEN FROM YA AND DROPS TO ZERO... RIGHT?
SWOO...
...OH, I SEE... YOU'RE HOPING TO GAIN CONTROL OVER MY POWER, EH...
BRING IT ON!!

NARUTO

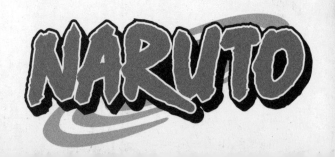

Number 497: Nine Tails vs. Naruto!!

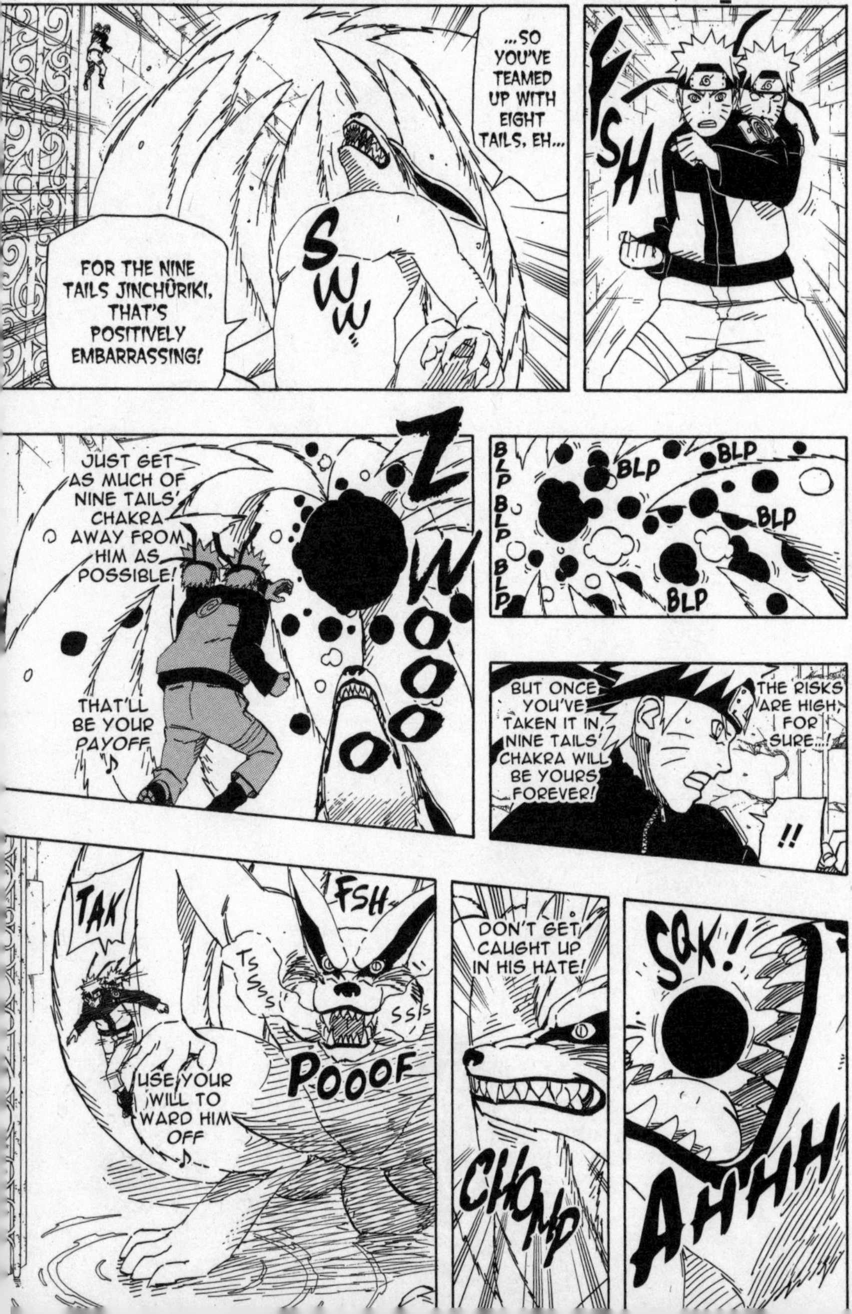

YSH
...SO YOU'VE TEAMED UP WITH EIGHT TAILS, EH...
FOR THE NINE TAILS JINCHŪRIKI, THAT'S POSITIVELY EMBARRASSING!
SWW
BLP BLP BLP BLP BLP BLP BLP
THE RISKS ARE HIGH, FOR SURE...!
BUT ONCE YOU'VE TAKEN IT IN, NINE TAILS' CHAKRA WILL BE YOURS FOREVER!
!!
ZWOOOOO
JUST GET AS MUCH OF NINE TAILS' CHAKRA AWAY FROM HIM AS POSSIBLE!
THAT'LL BE YOUR PAYOFF ♪
SQK!
AHHHH
DON'T GET CAUGHT UP IN HIS HATE!
CHOMP
FSH
TAK
TSSSS
SSSS
POOOF
USE YOUR WILL TO WARD HIM OFF ♪

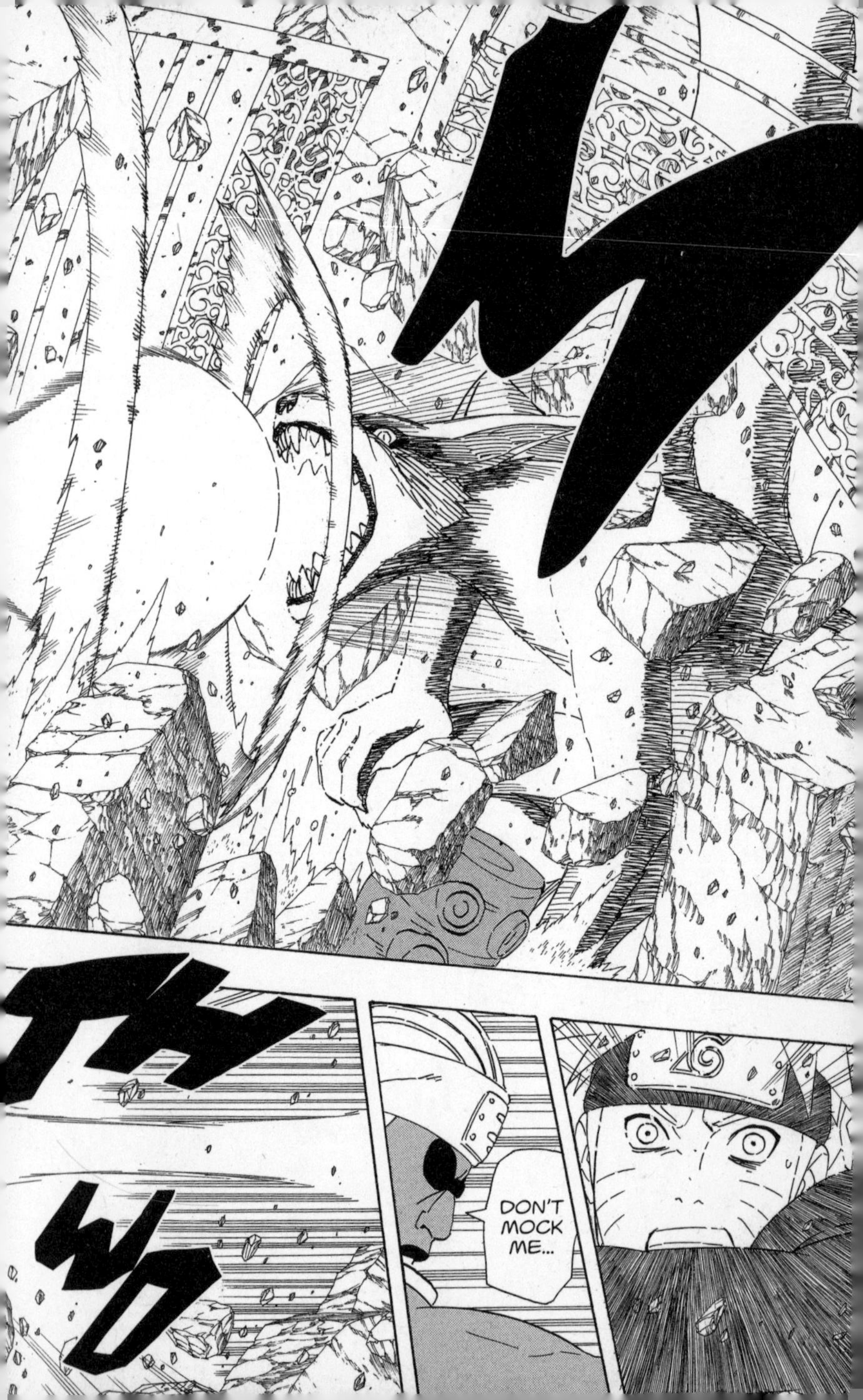
DON'T MOCK ME...

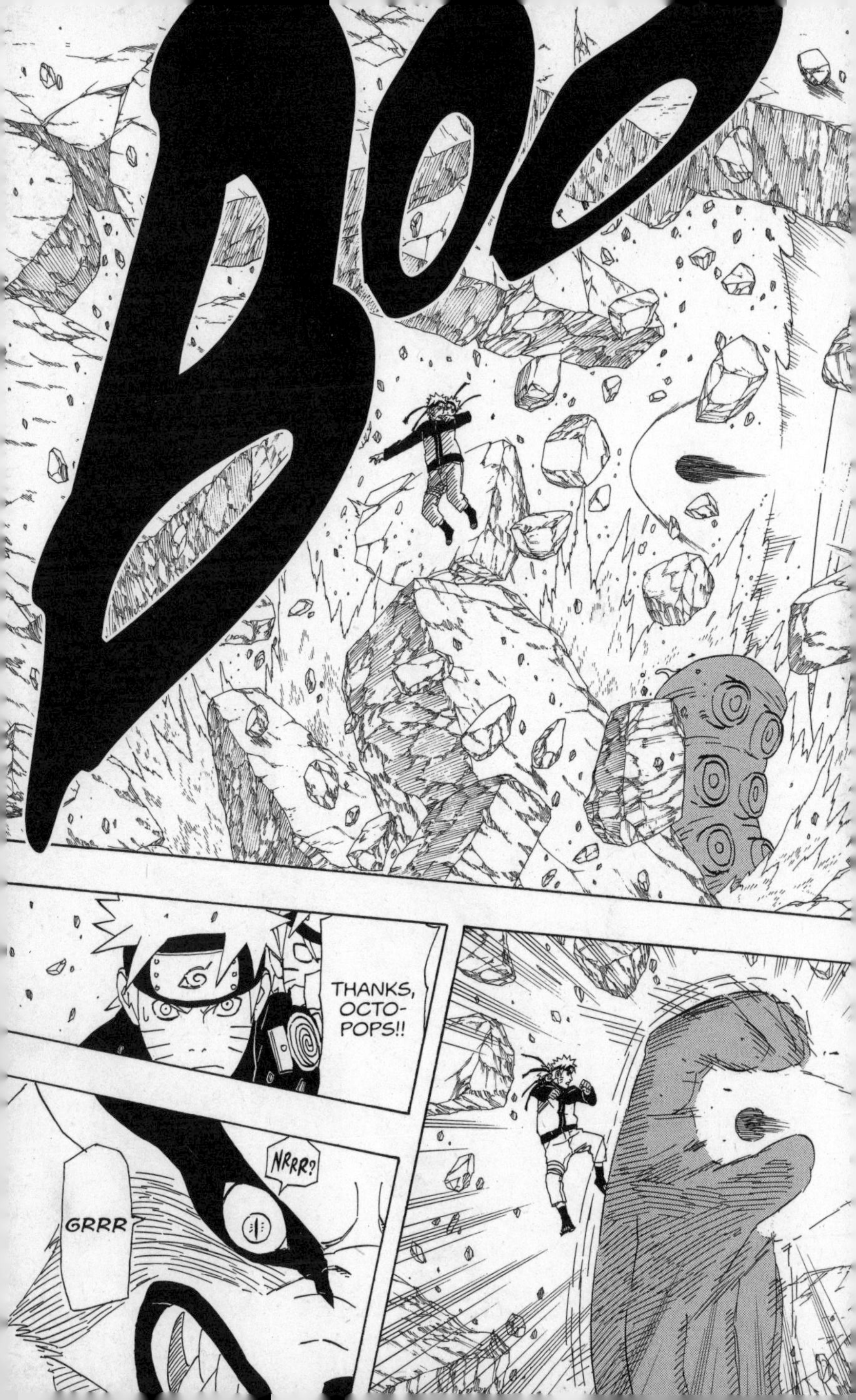
THANKS, OCTO-POPS!!
NRRR?
GRRR

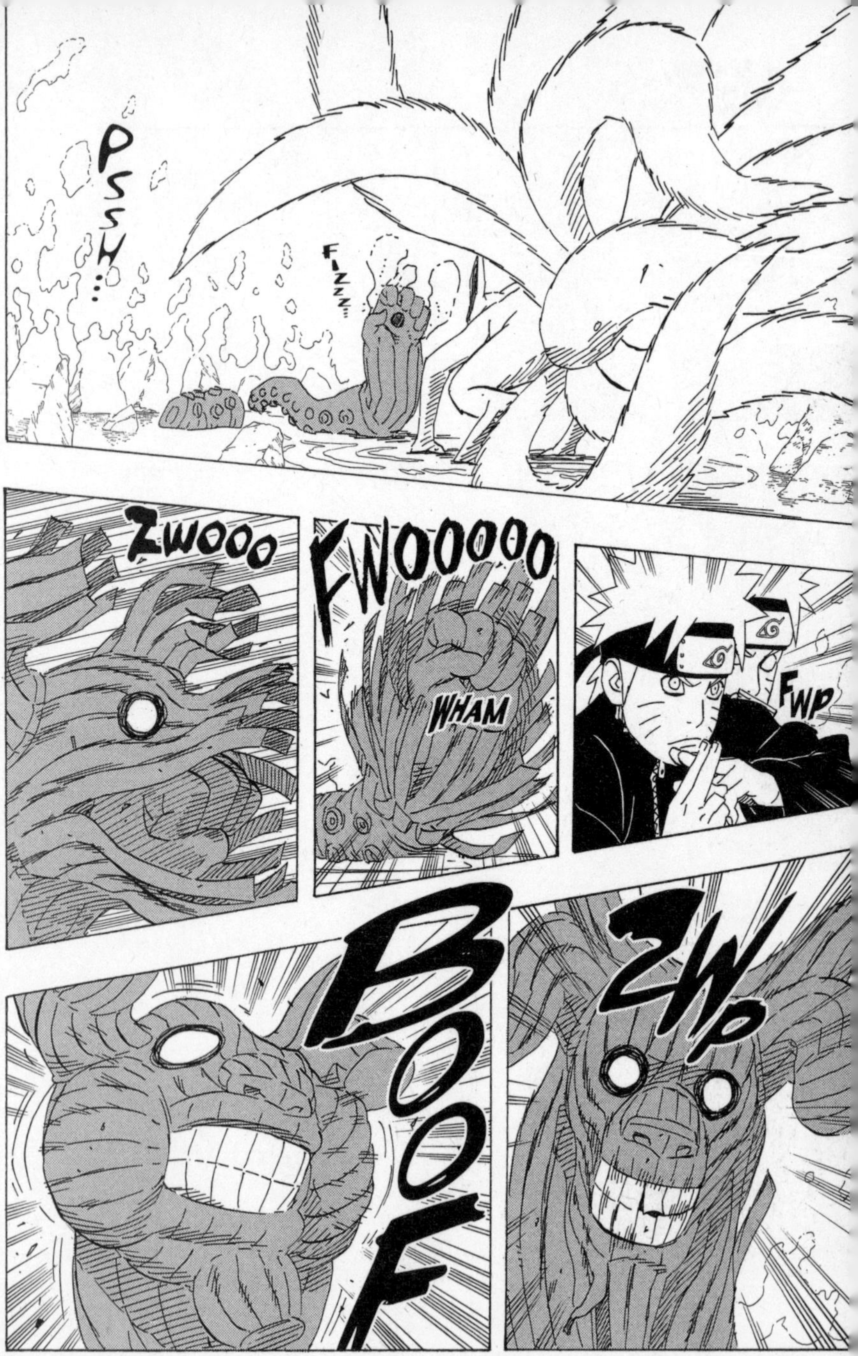
FIZZZ...
PSSH...
FWP
FWOOOOO
WHAM
ZWOOO
ZWP
BOOOF

READ THIS WAY

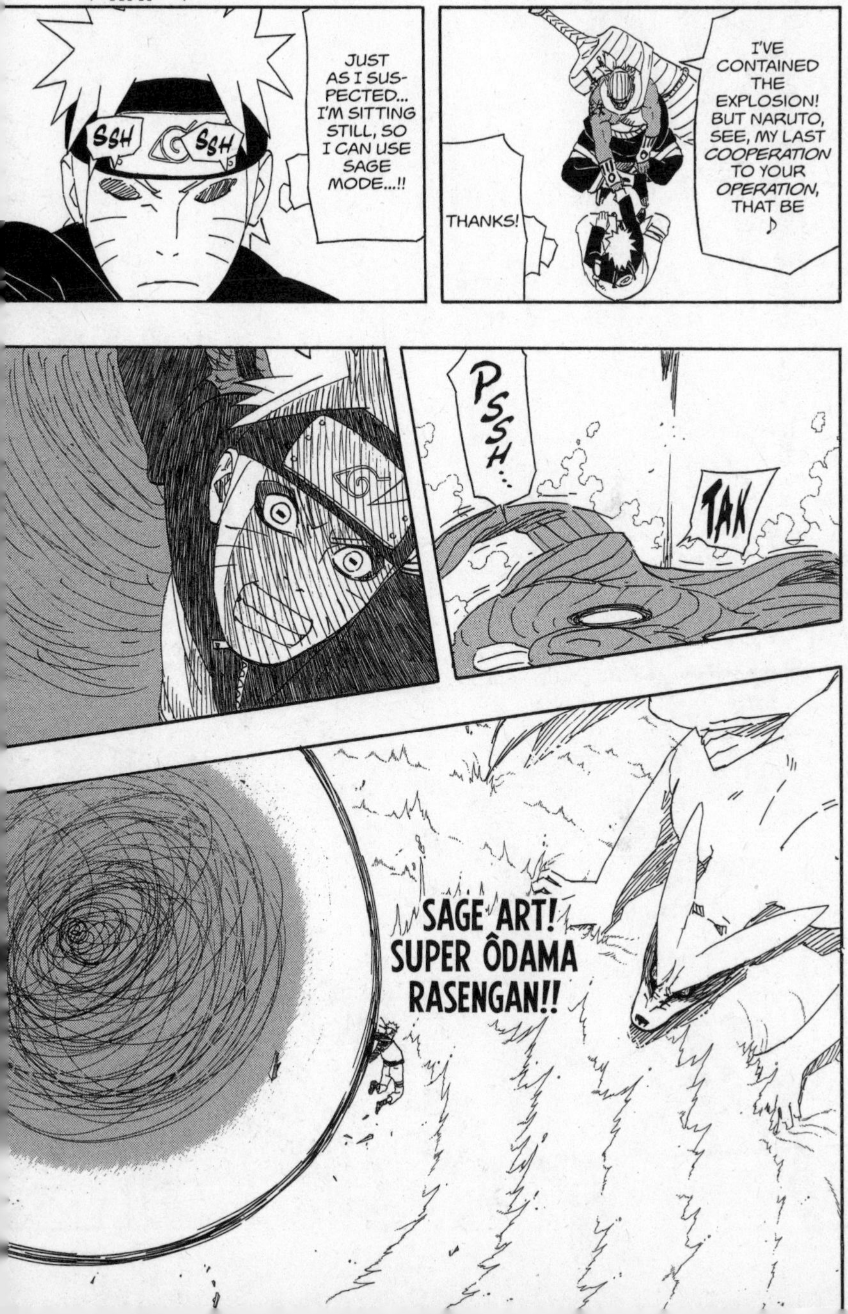
I'VE CONTAINED THE EXPLOSION! BUT NARUTO, SEE, MY LAST COOPERATION TO YOUR OPERATION, THAT BE ♪
THANKS!
SSH
SSH
JUST AS I SUSPECTED... I'M SITTING STILL, SO I CAN USE SAGE MODE...!!
PSSH...
TAK
SAGE ART! SUPER ÔDAMA RASENGAN!!

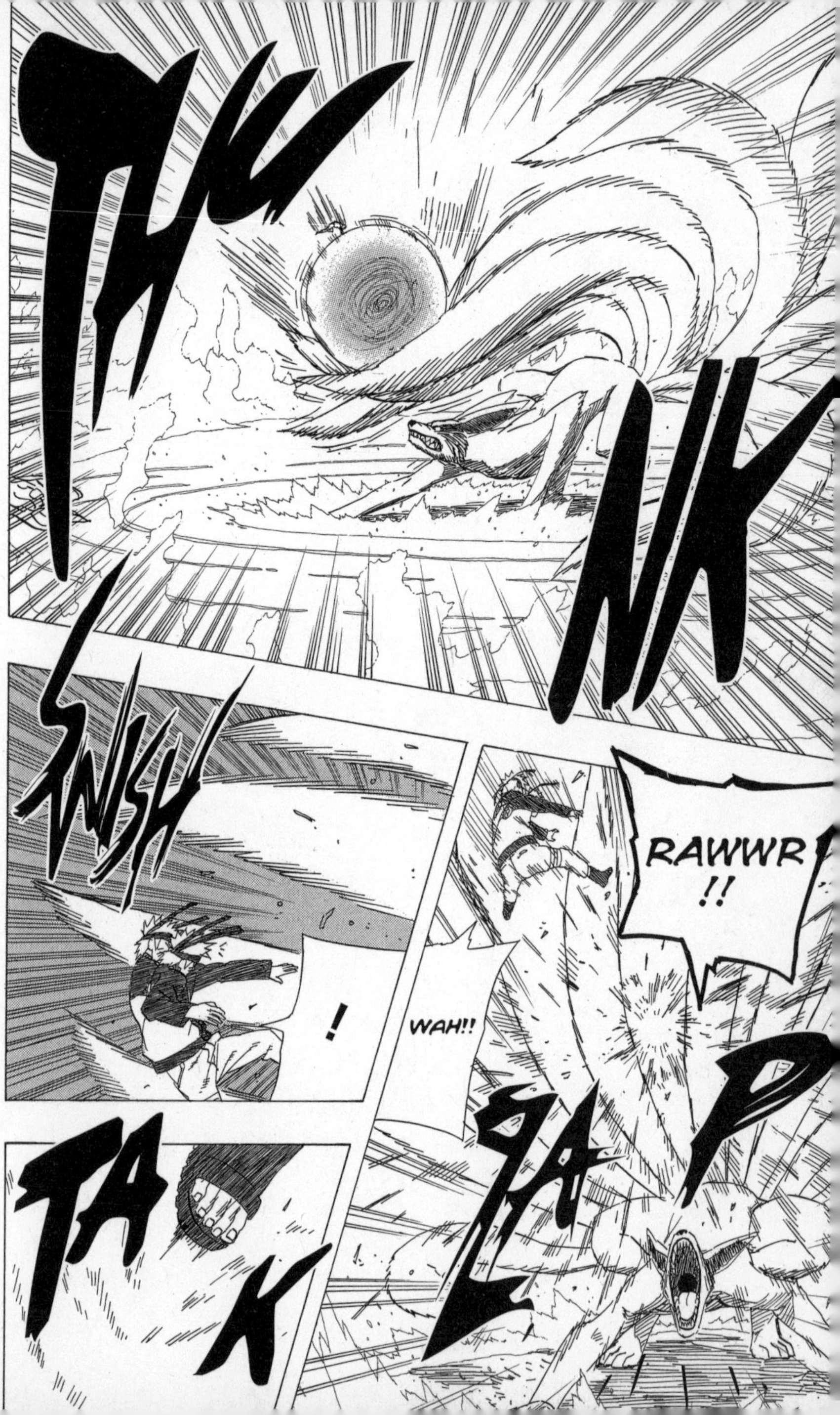
THUNK
RAWWR !!
WAH!!
SWISH
!
ZAP
TAK

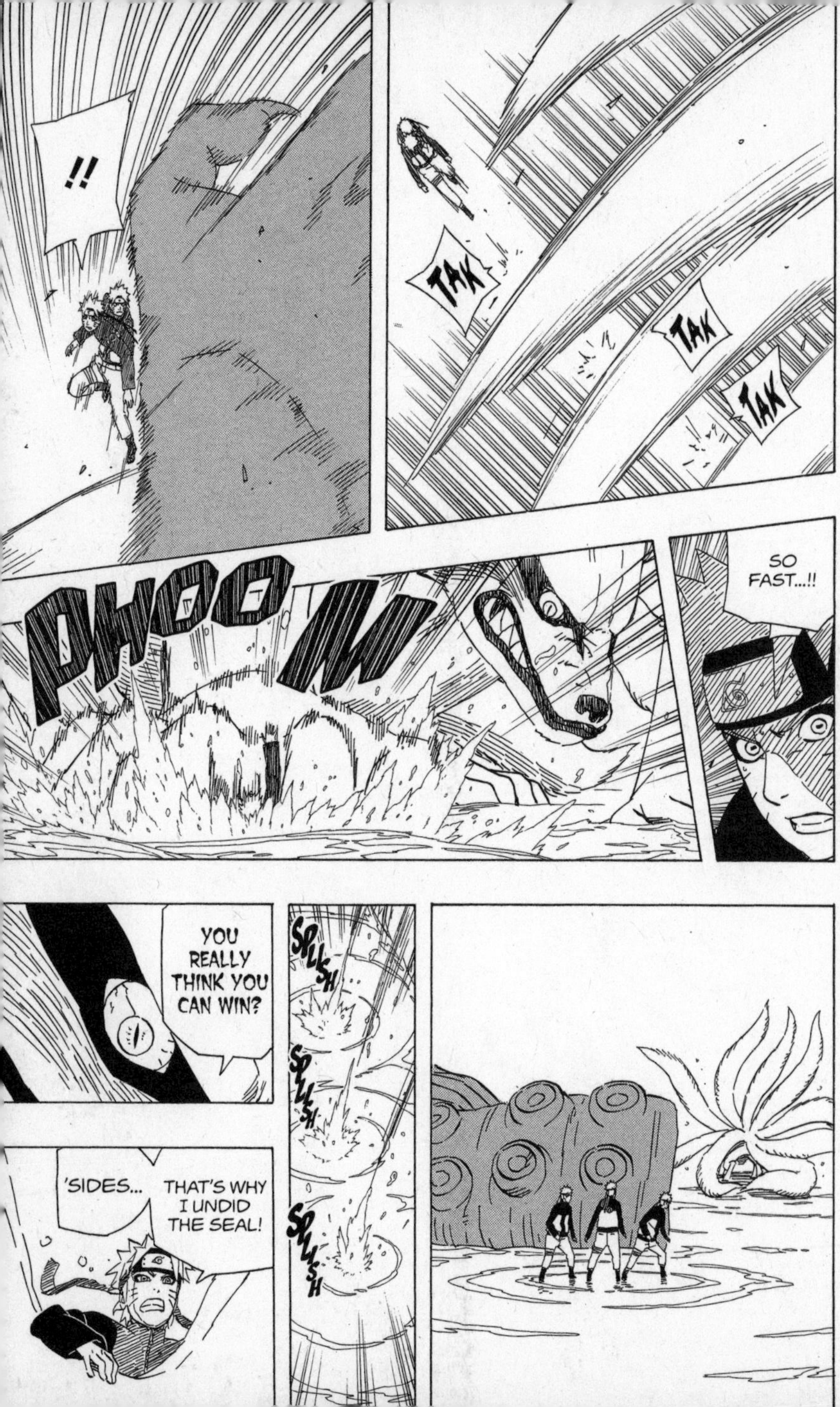
TAK
TAK
TAK
!!
SO FAST...!!
PHOOM
SPLISH
SPLISH
SPLISH
YOU REALLY THINK YOU CAN WIN?
'SIDES...
THAT'S WHY I UNDID THE SEAL!

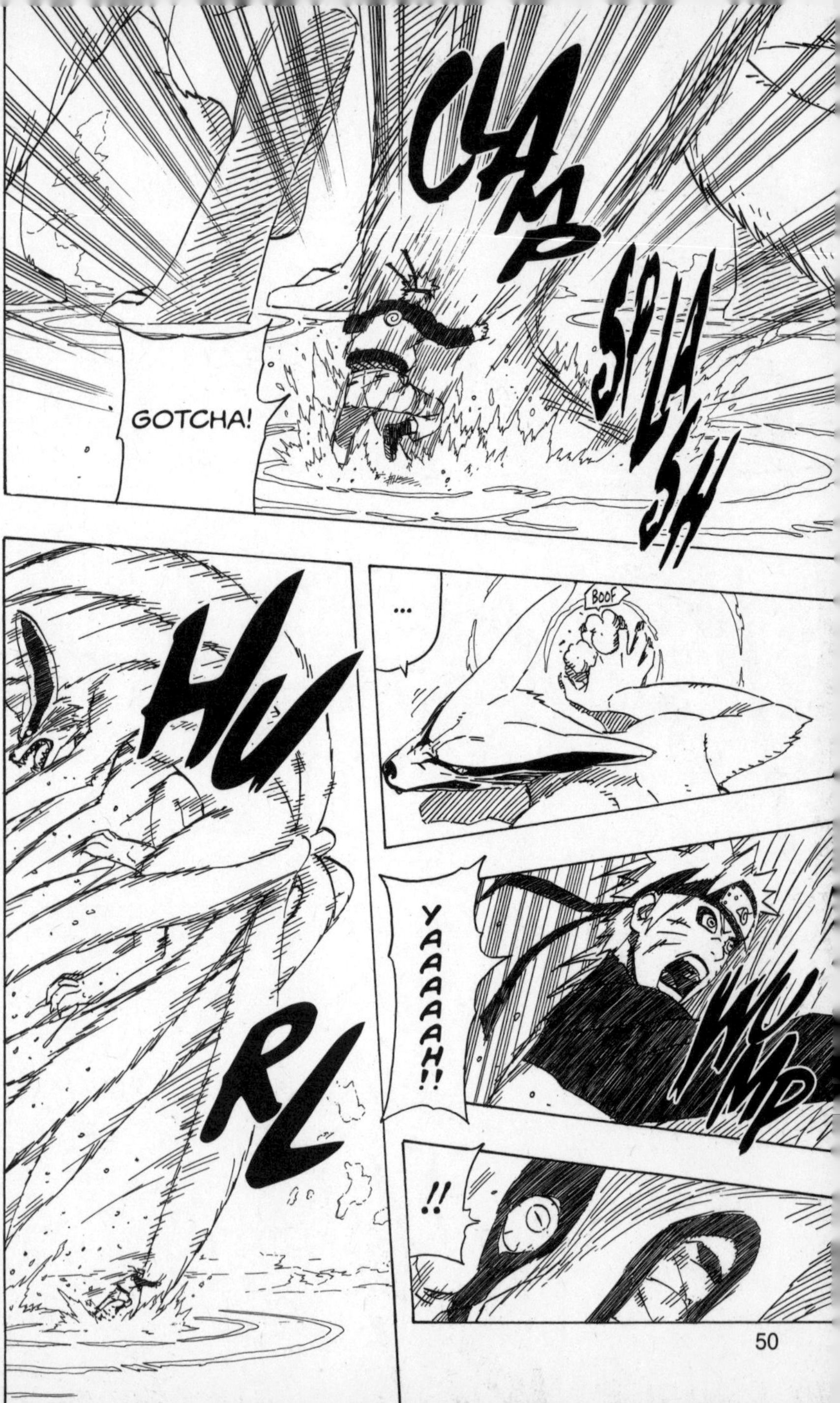
CLAMP
SPLASH
GOTCHA!
...
BOOF
YAAAAAAH!!
WHUMP
!!
HURL

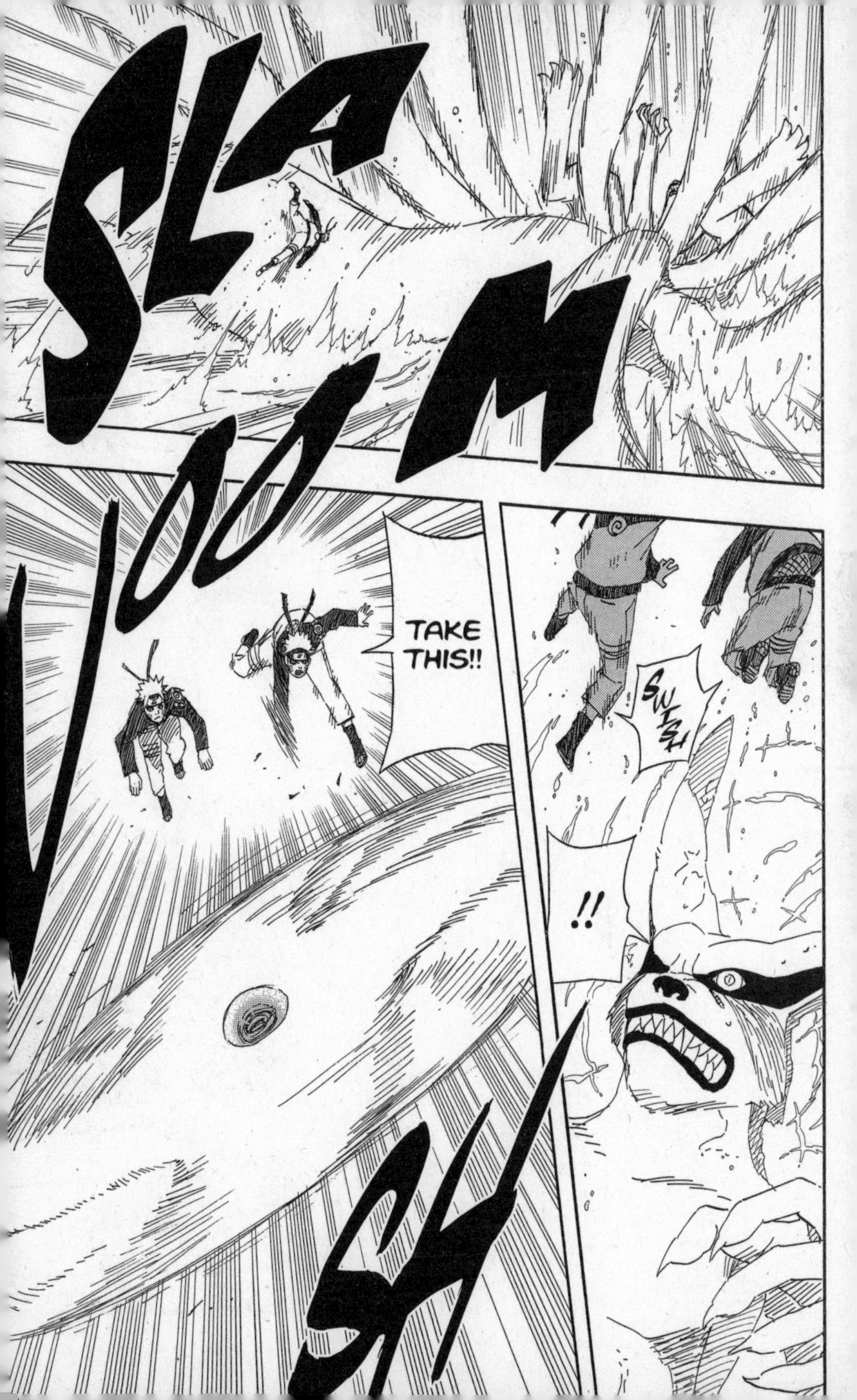
SLAM
TAKE THIS!!
SWISH
!!
WOOSH

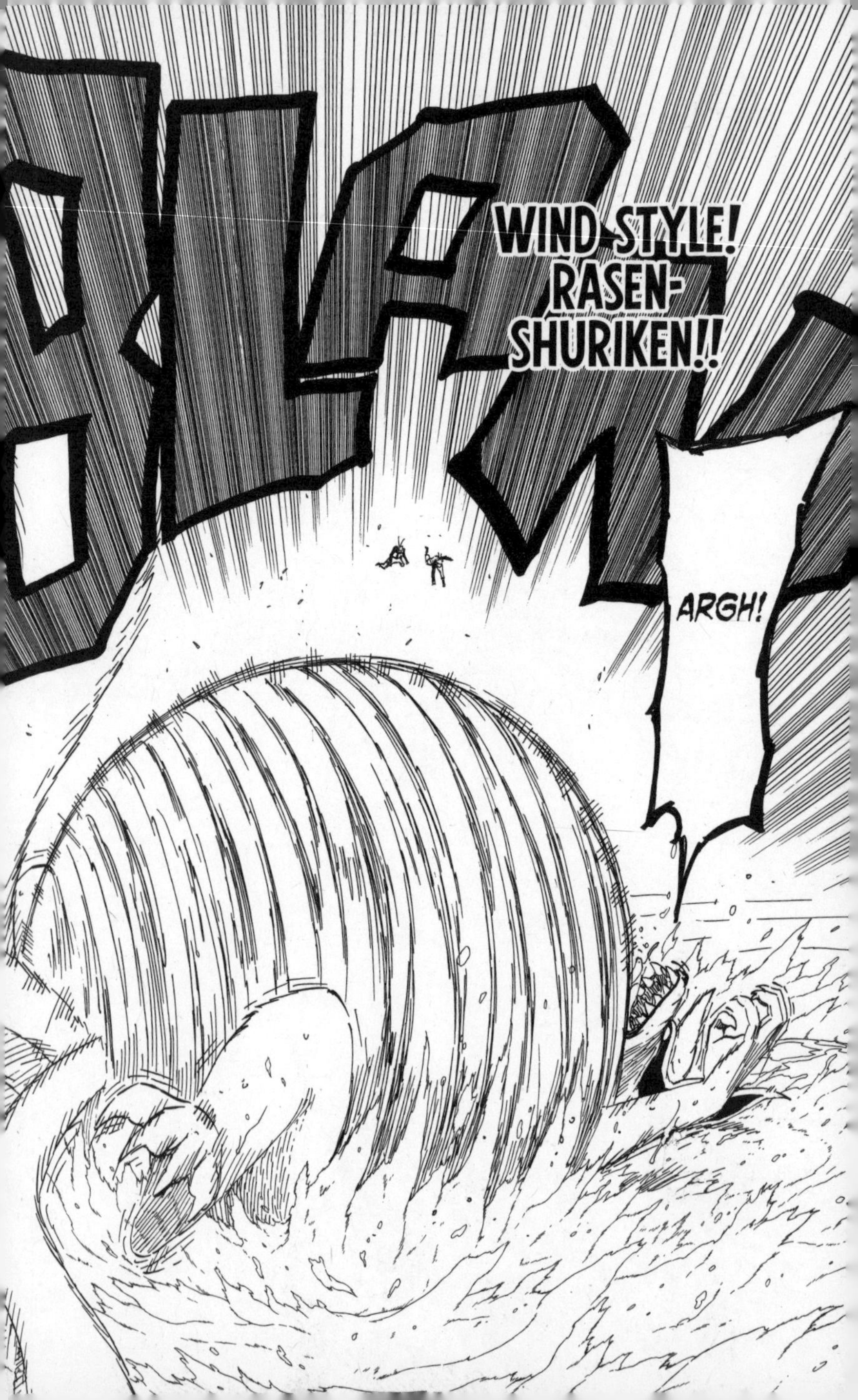
WIND STYLE! RASEN-SHURIKEN!!
ARGH!

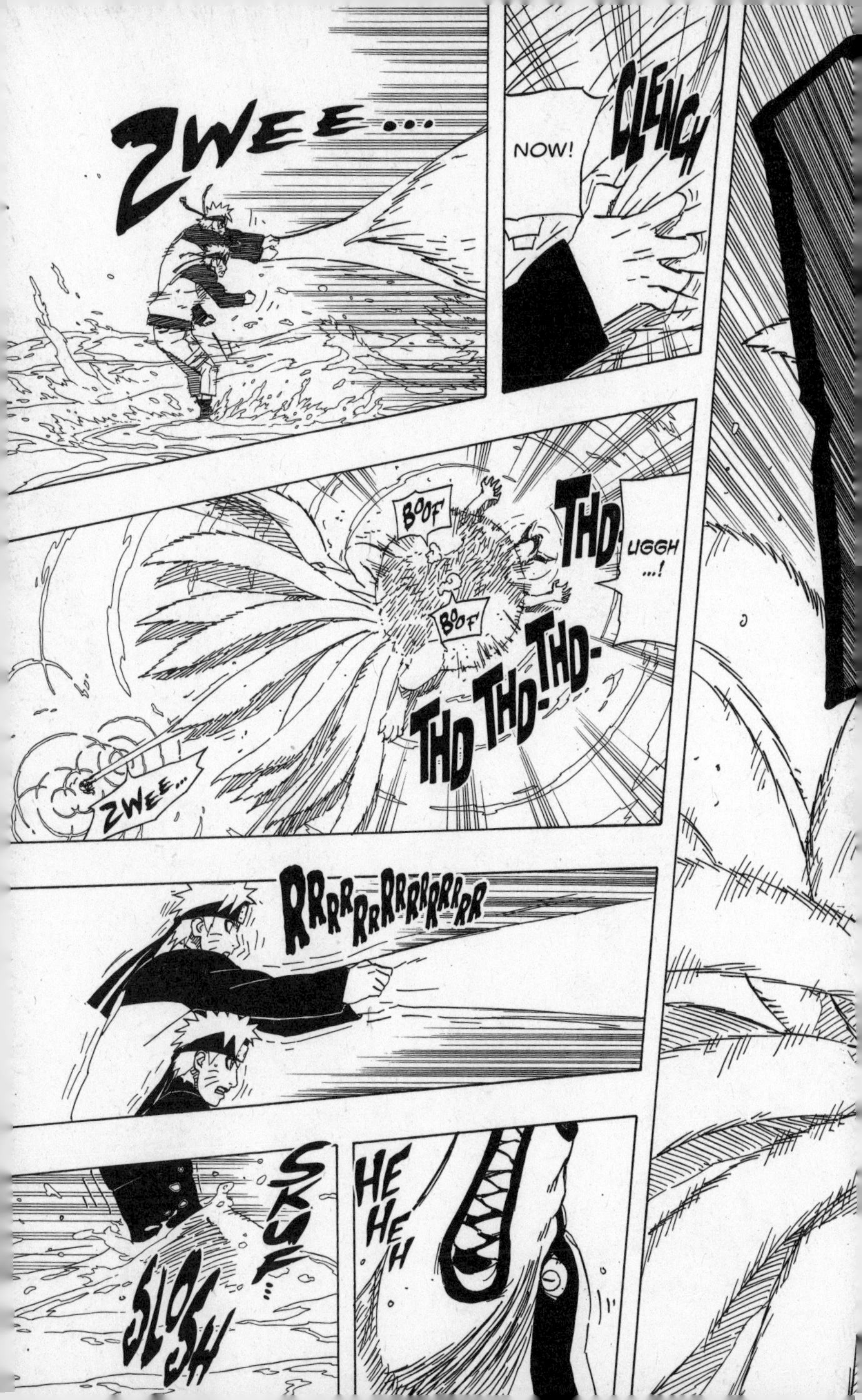
NOW!
CLENCH
ZWEE...
THD-
UGGH ...!
BOOF
BOOF
THD THD-THD-
ZWEE...
RRRRRRRRRRRRRR
HEHEHEH
SKUF...
SLOSH

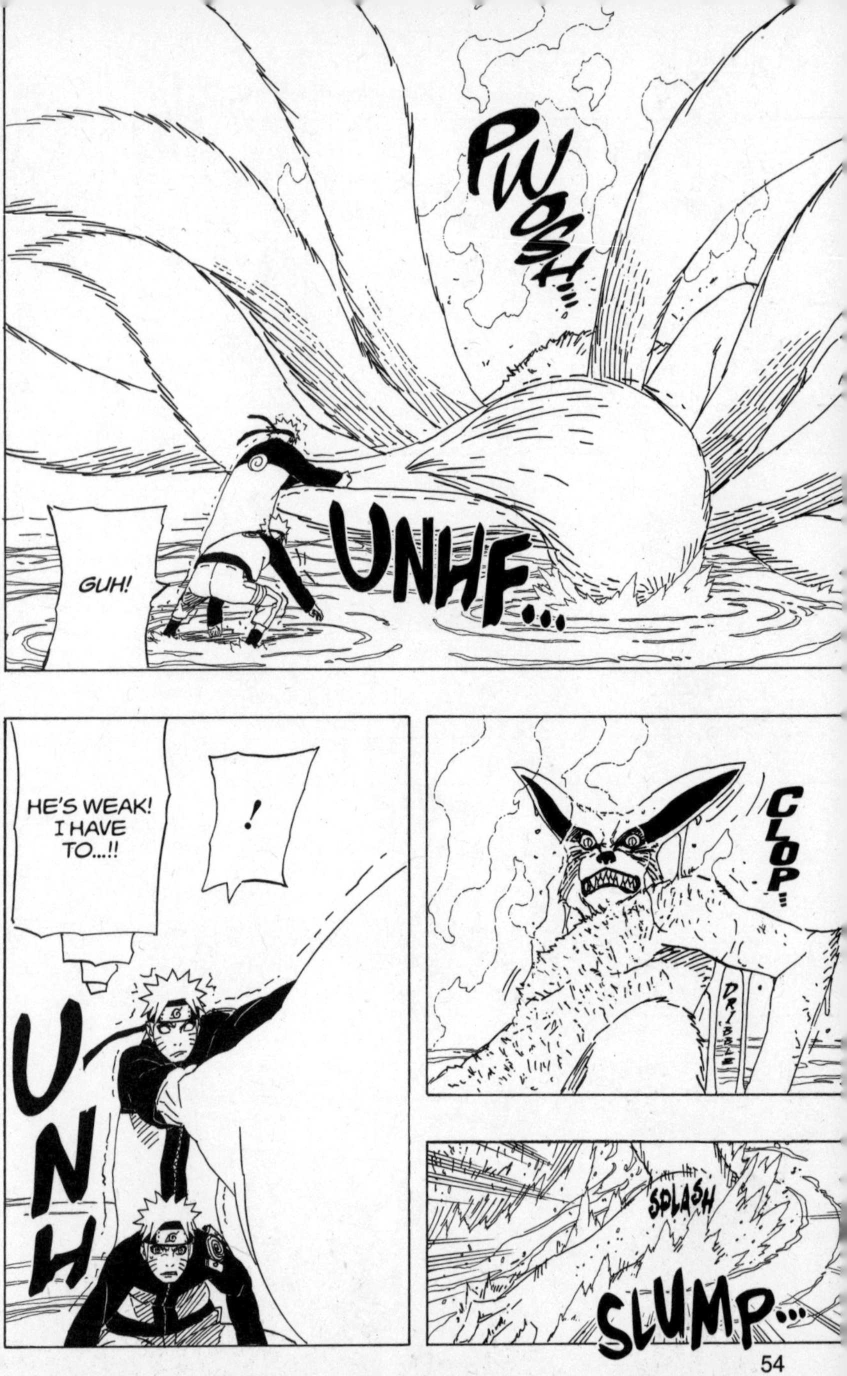
PWOSH!!!
UNHF...
GUH!
CLOP...
DRIBBLE
SPLASH
SLUMP...
!
HE'S WEAK! I HAVE TO...!!
UNH

READ THIS WAY

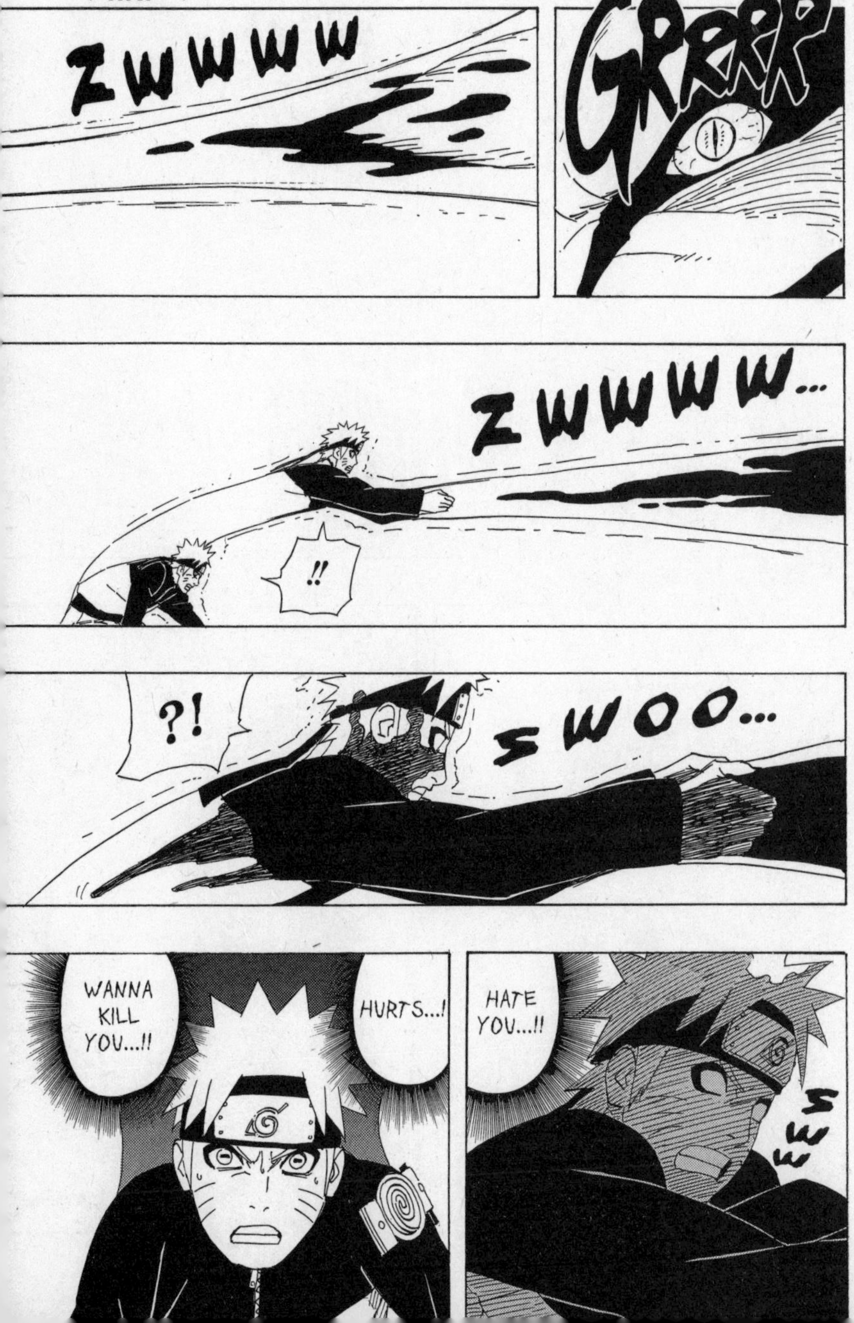
GRRRP
ZWWWW
ZWWWW...
!!
SWOO...
?!
HATE YOU...!!
SWW
HURTS...!
WANNA KILL YOU...!!

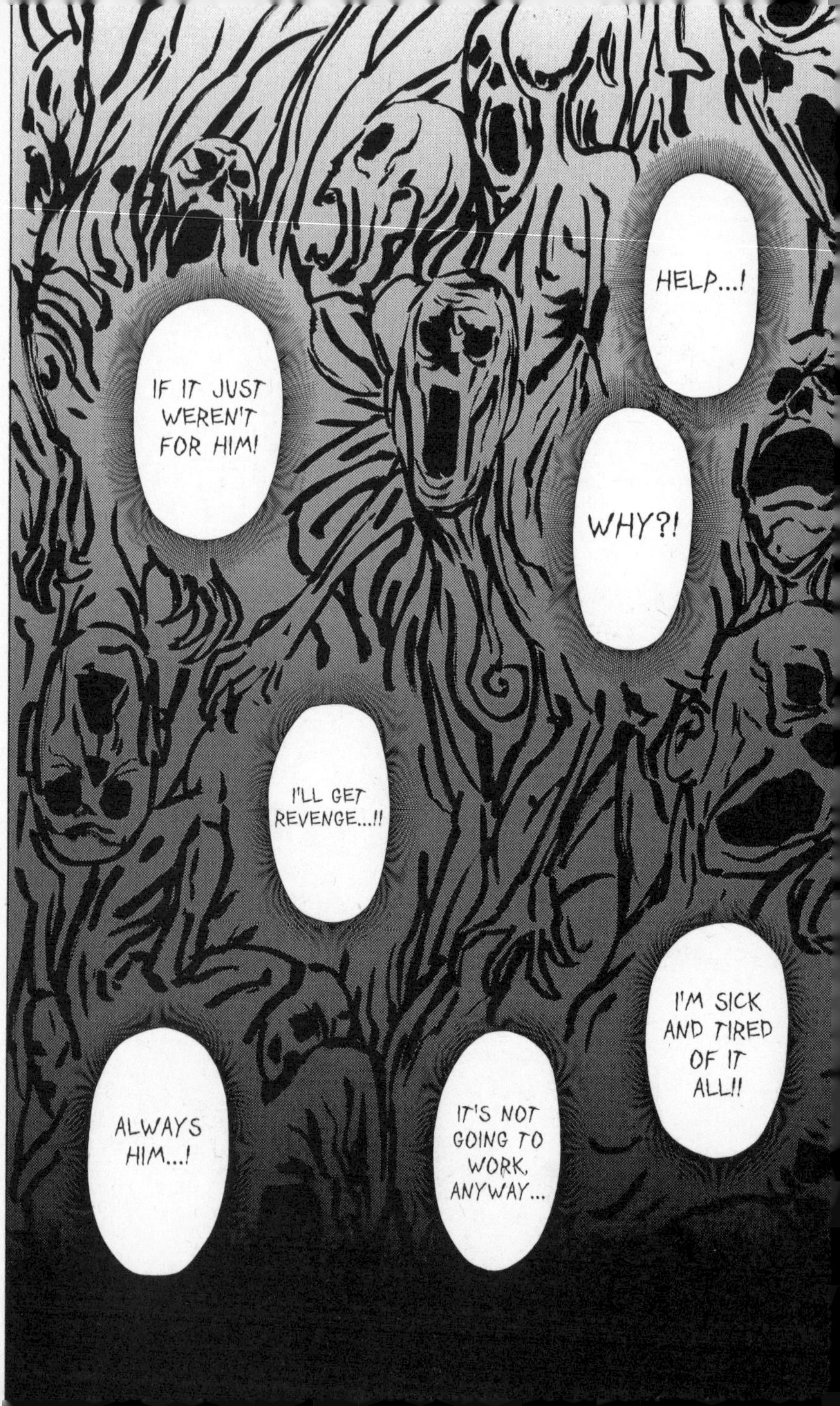
HELP...!
IF IT JUST WEREN'T FOR HIM!
WHY?!
I'LL GET REVENGE...!!
I'M SICK AND TIRED OF IT ALL!!
IT'S NOT GOING TO WORK, ANYWAY...
ALWAYS HIM...!

READ THIS WAY

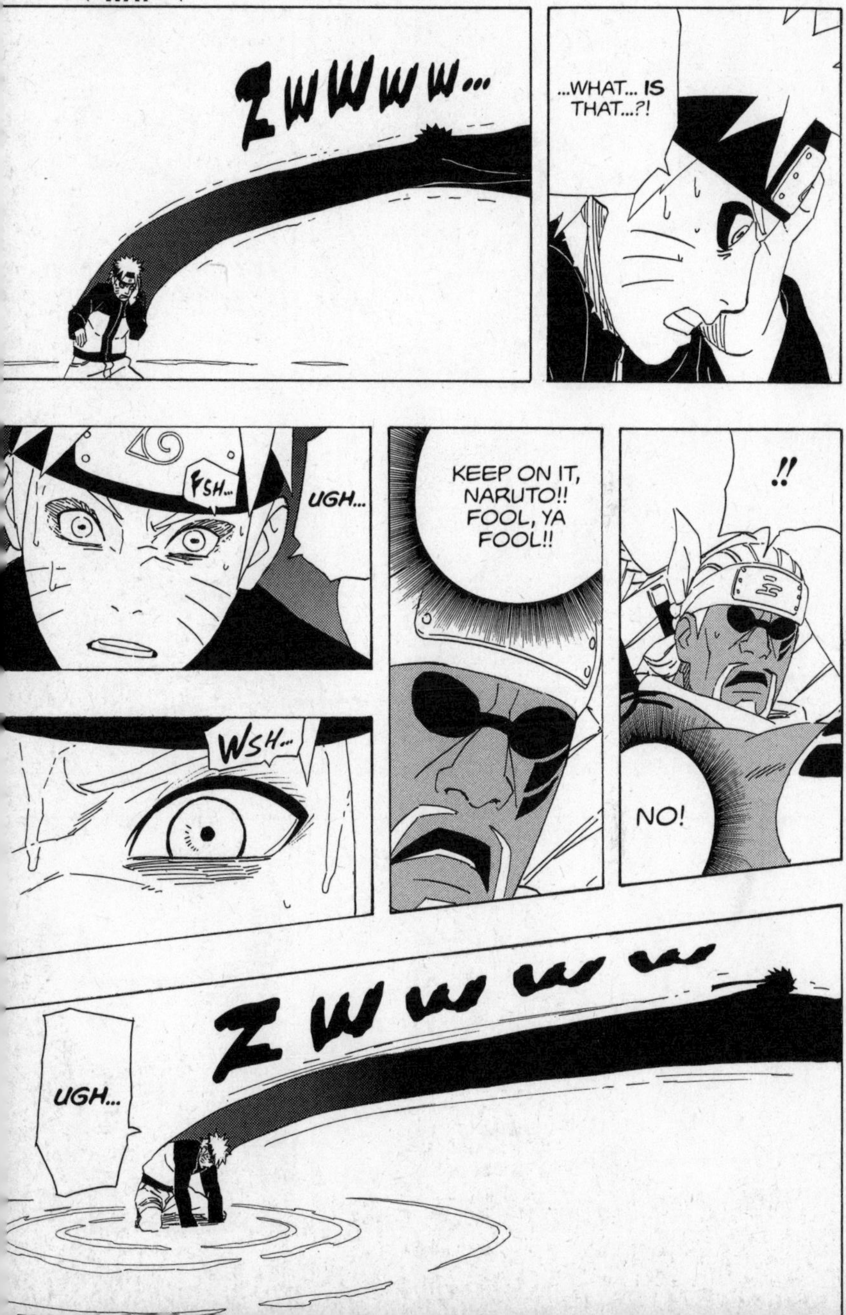
...WHAT... IS THAT...?!
ZWWWW...
!!
NO!
KEEP ON IT, NARUTO!! FOOL, YA FOOL!!
YSH...
UGH...
WSH...
ZWWWWW
UGH...

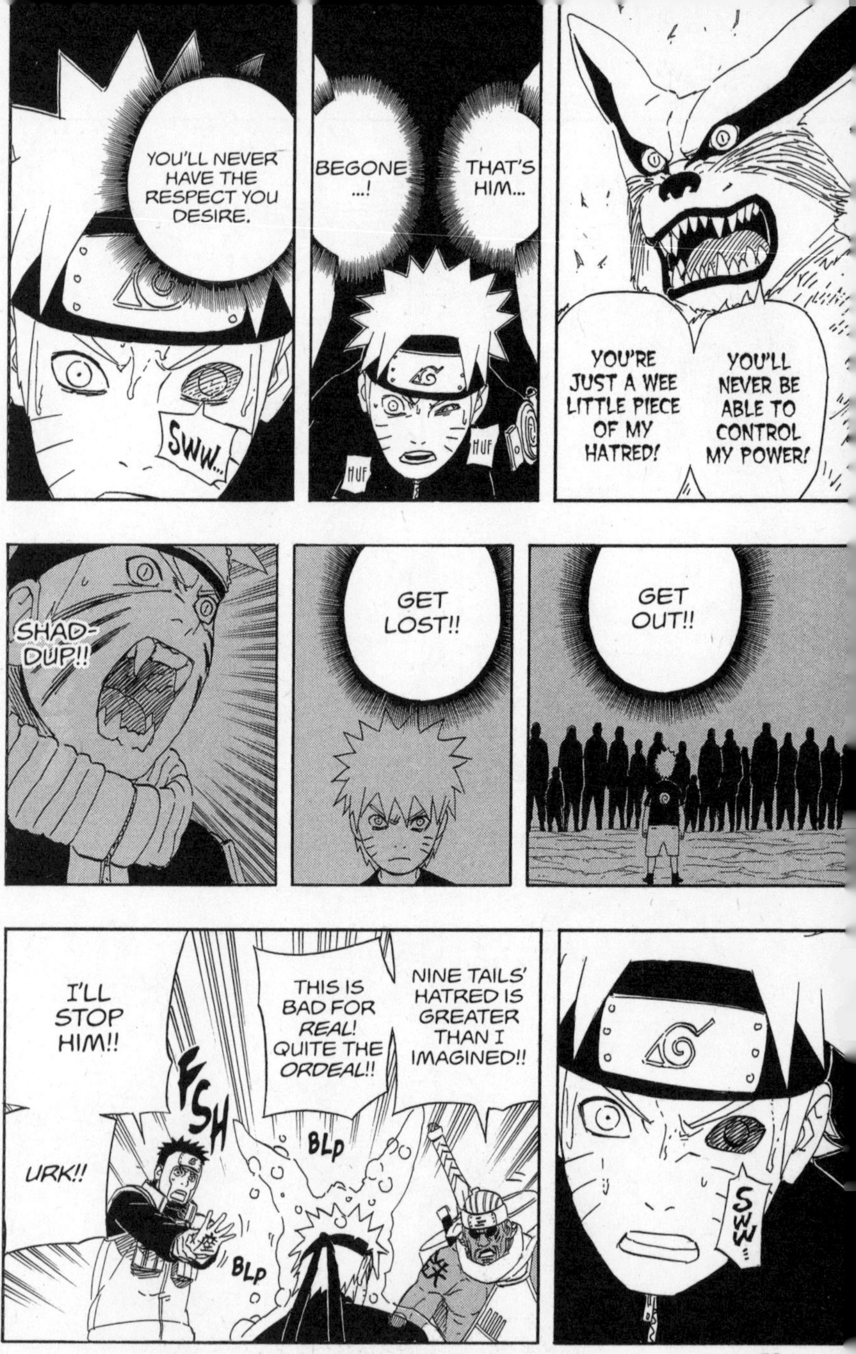
YOU'LL NEVER BE ABLE TO CONTROL MY POWER!
YOU'RE JUST A WEE LITTLE PIECE OF MY HATRED!
THAT'S HIM...
BEGONE ...!
HUF
HUF
YOU'LL NEVER HAVE THE RESPECT YOU DESIRE.
SWW...
GET OUT!!
GET LOST!!
SHAD-DUP!!
SWW...
NINE TAILS' HATRED IS GREATER THAN I IMAGINED!!
THIS IS BAD FOR REAL! QUITE THE ORDEAL!!
FSH
BLP
I'LL STOP HIM!!
URK!!
BLP

READ THIS WAY

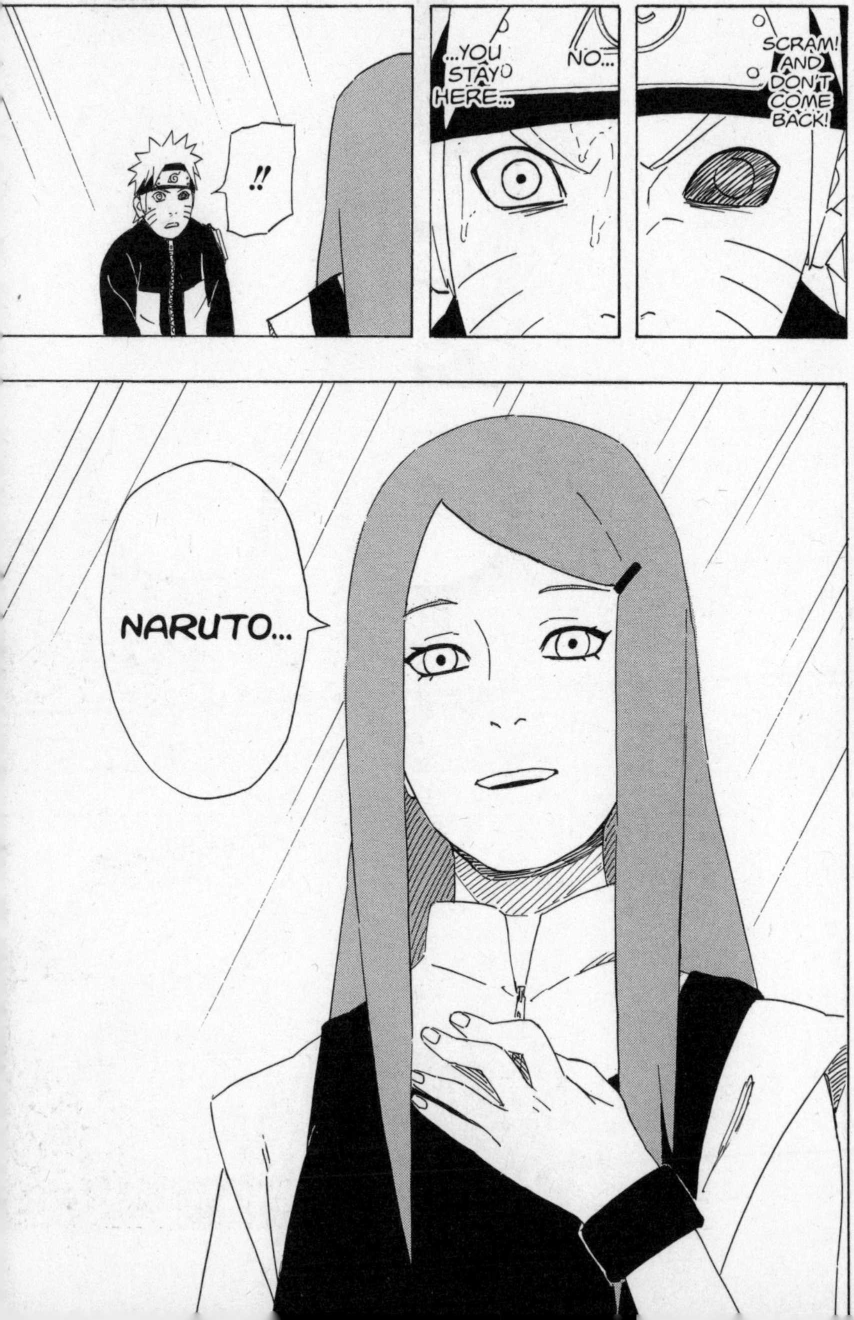
SCRAM! AND DON'T COME BACK!
NO...
...YOU STAY HERE...
!!
NARUTO...

NARUTO

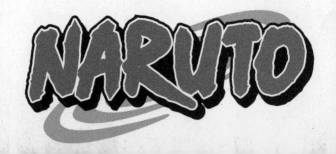

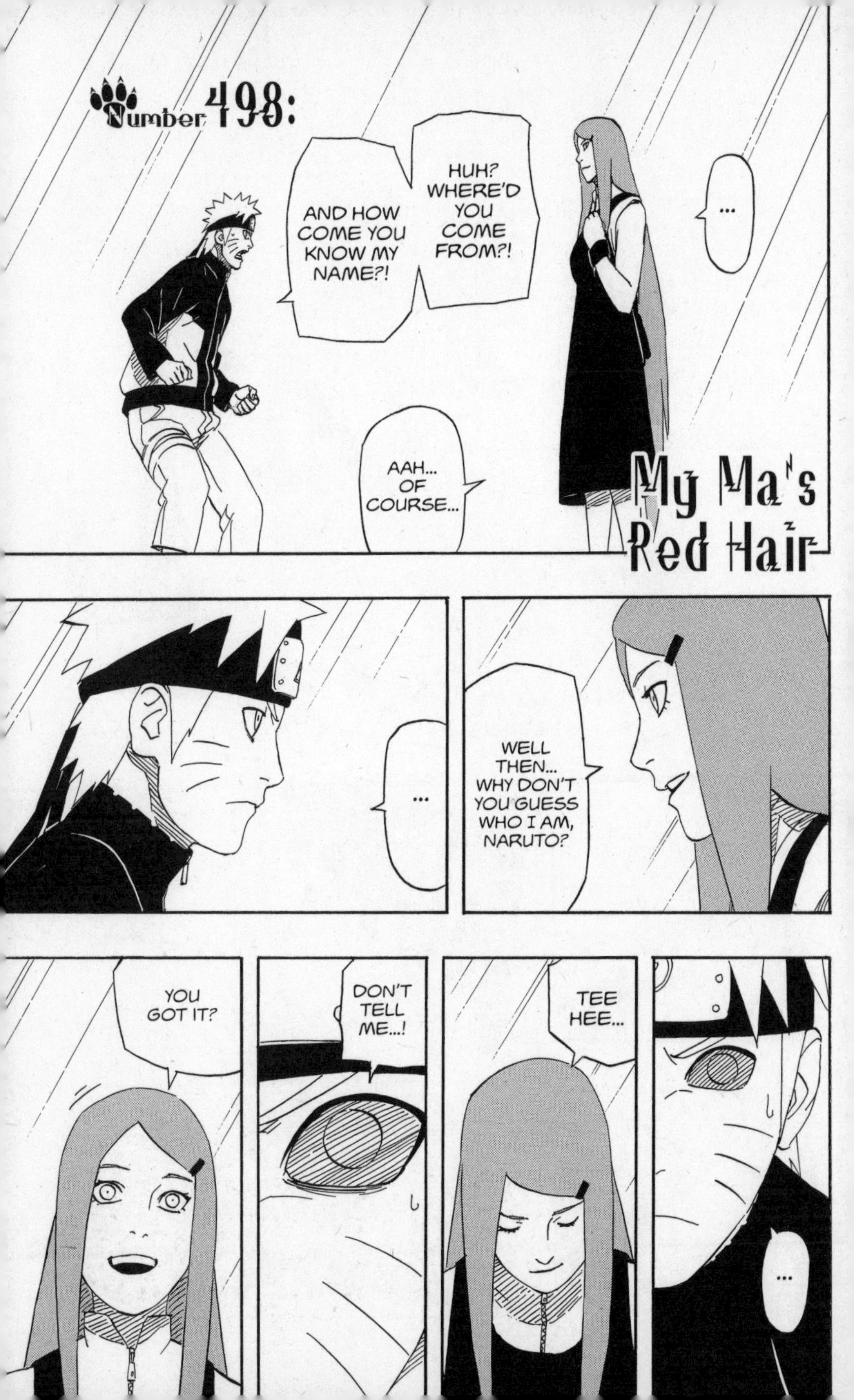
Number 498:
My Ma's Red Hair
...
HUH? WHERE'D YOU COME FROM?!
AND HOW COME YOU KNOW MY NAME?!
AAH... OF COURSE...
WELL THEN... WHY DON'T YOU GUESS WHO I AM, NARUTO?
...
...
TEE HEE...
DON'T TELL ME...!
YOU GOT IT?

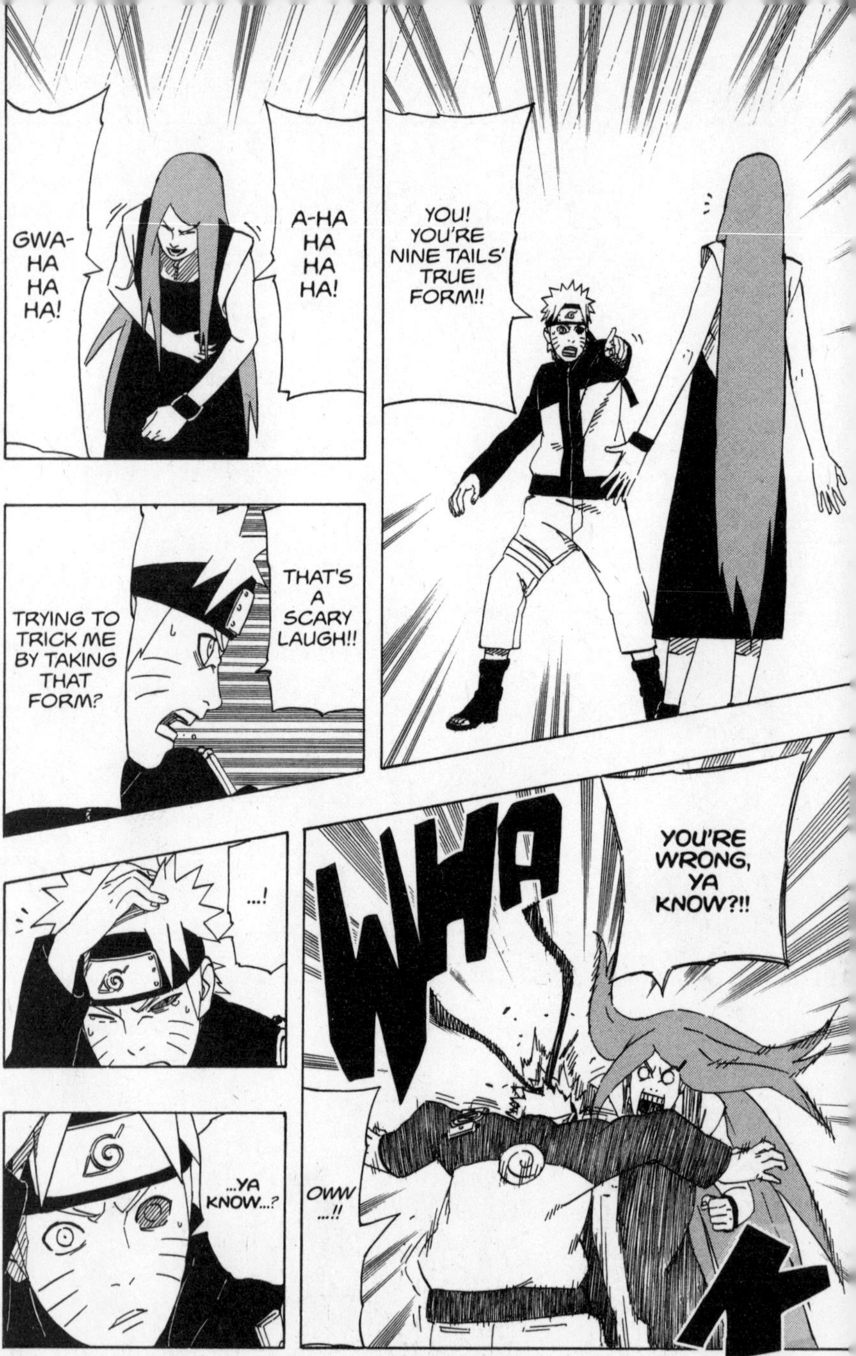
YOU! YOU'RE NINE TAILS' TRUE FORM!!
A-HA HA HA HA!
GWA-HA HA HA!
THAT'S A SCARY LAUGH!!
TRYING TO TRICK ME BY TAKING THAT FORM?
YOU'RE WRONG, YA KNOW?!!
WHA
OWW ...!!
...!
...YA KNOW...?

READ THIS WAY

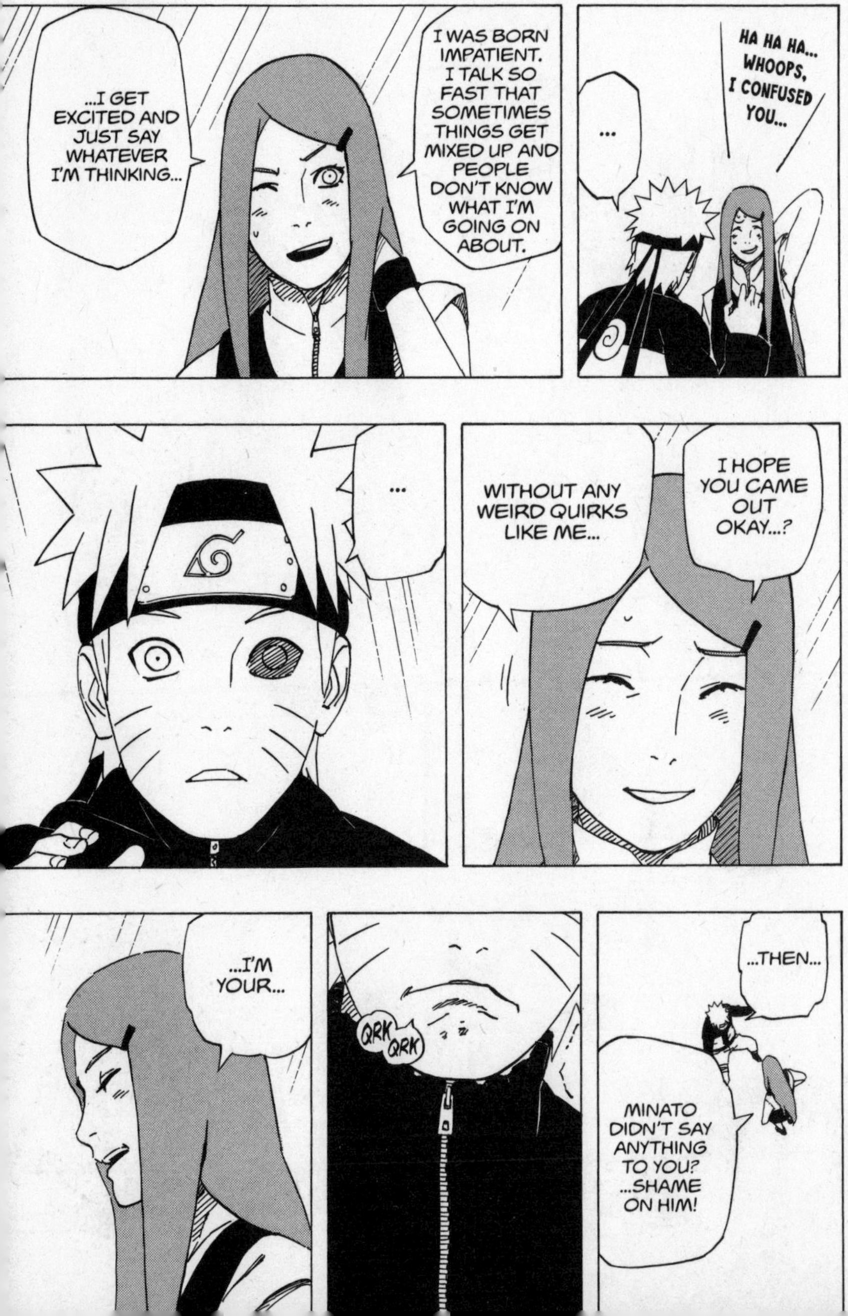
HA HA HA... WHOOPS, I CONFUSED YOU...
...
I WAS BORN IMPATIENT. I TALK SO FAST THAT SOMETIMES THINGS GET MIXED UP AND PEOPLE DON'T KNOW WHAT I'M GOING ON ABOUT.
...I GET EXCITED AND JUST SAY WHATEVER I'M THINKING...
I HOPE YOU CAME OUT OKAY...?
WITHOUT ANY WEIRD QUIRKS LIKE ME...
...
...THEN...
MINATO DIDN'T SAY ANYTHING TO YOU? ...SHAME ON HIM!
QRK QRK
...I'M YOUR...

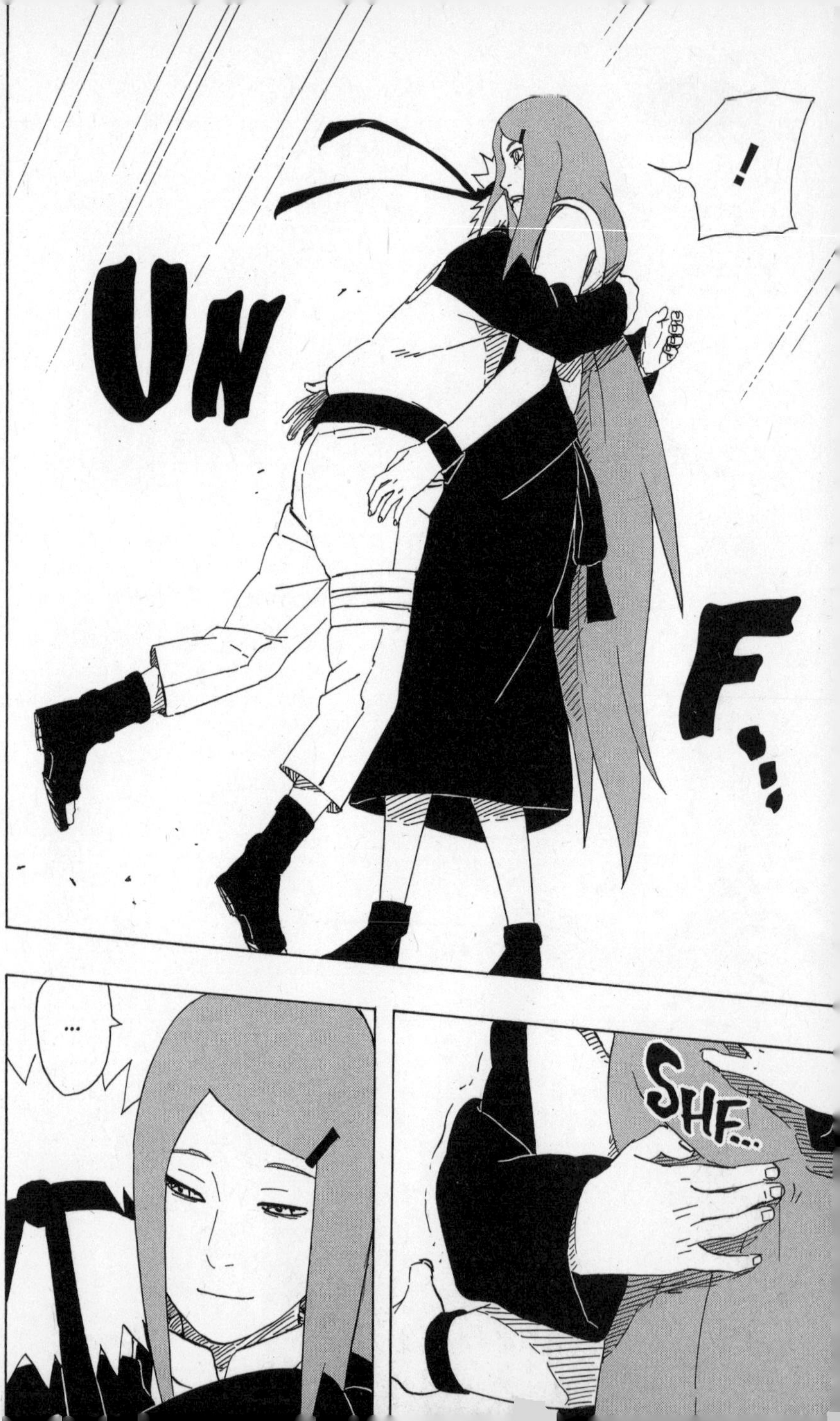
!
UN
F...
SHF...
...

READ THIS WAY

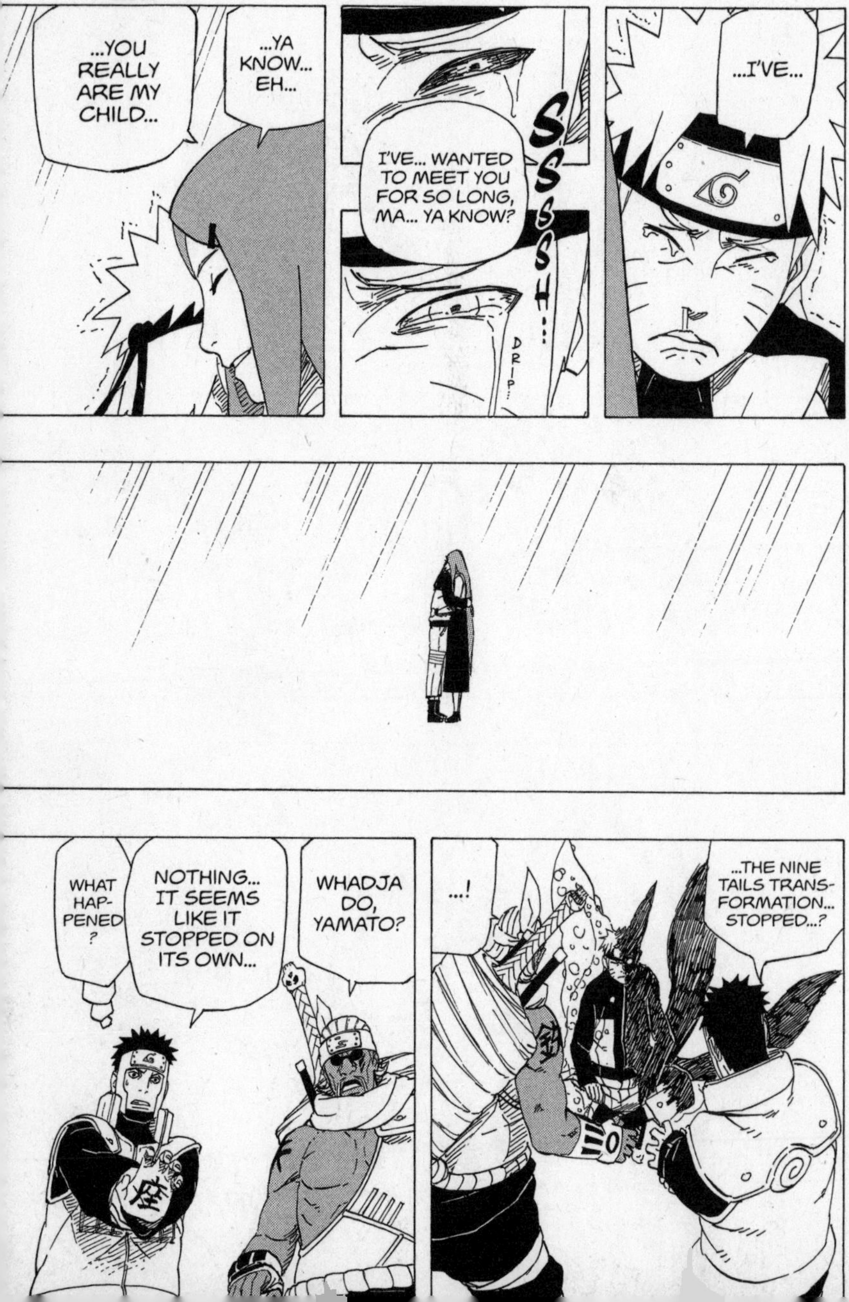
...I'VE...
I'VE... WANTED TO MEET YOU FOR SO LONG, MA... YA KNOW?
SSSSSH...
DRIP...
...YA KNOW... EH...
...YOU REALLY ARE MY CHILD...
...THE NINE TAILS TRANS-FORMATION... STOPPED...?
...!
WHADJA DO, YAMATO?
NOTHING... IT SEEMS LIKE IT STOPPED ON ITS OWN...
WHAT HAP-PENED?

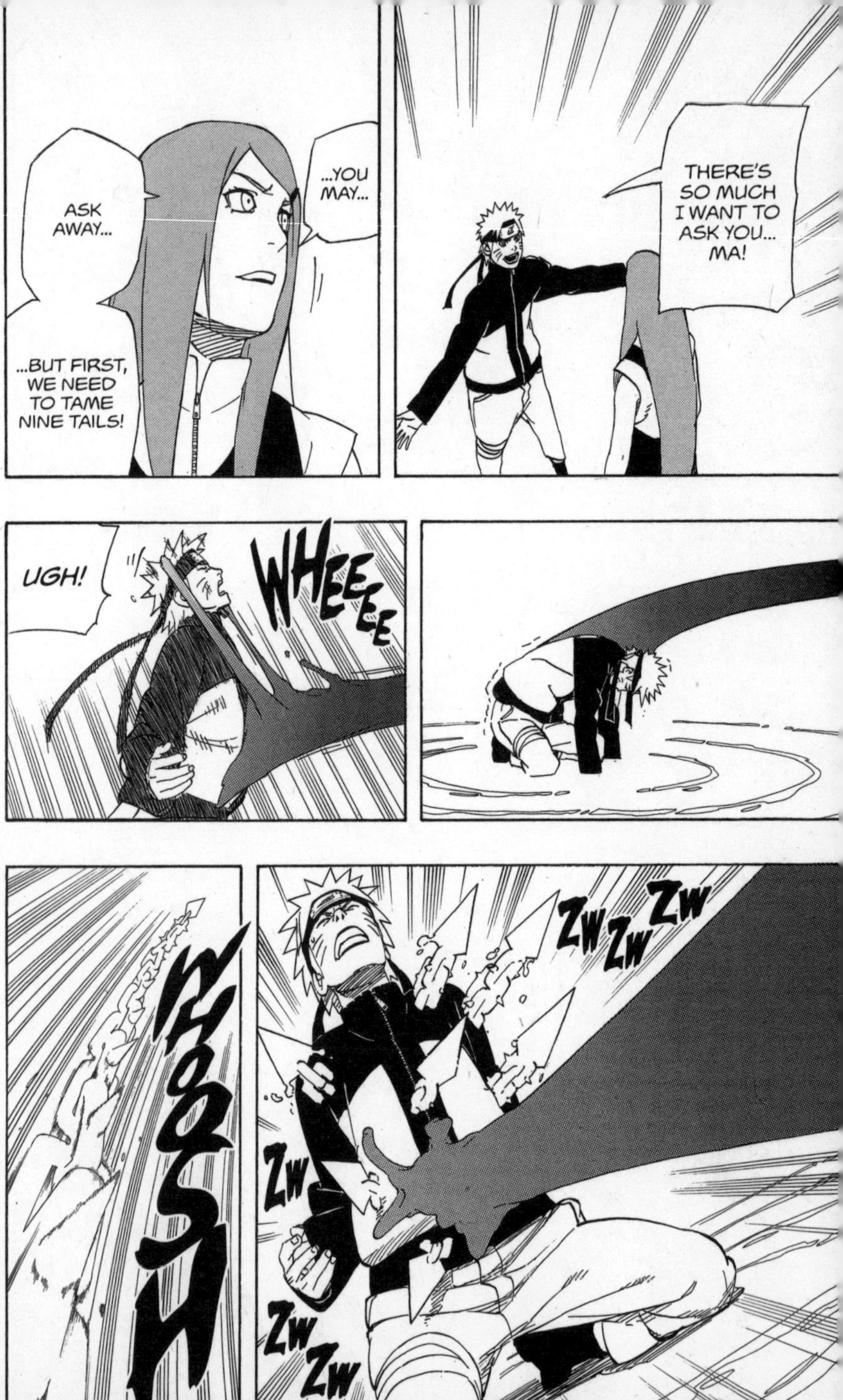
THERE'S SO MUCH I WANT TO ASK YOU... MA!
...YOU MAY...
ASK AWAY...
...BUT FIRST, WE NEED TO TAME NINE TAILS!
UGH!
WHEEEEE
ZW ZW ZW
ZW
ZW ZW
WHOOSH

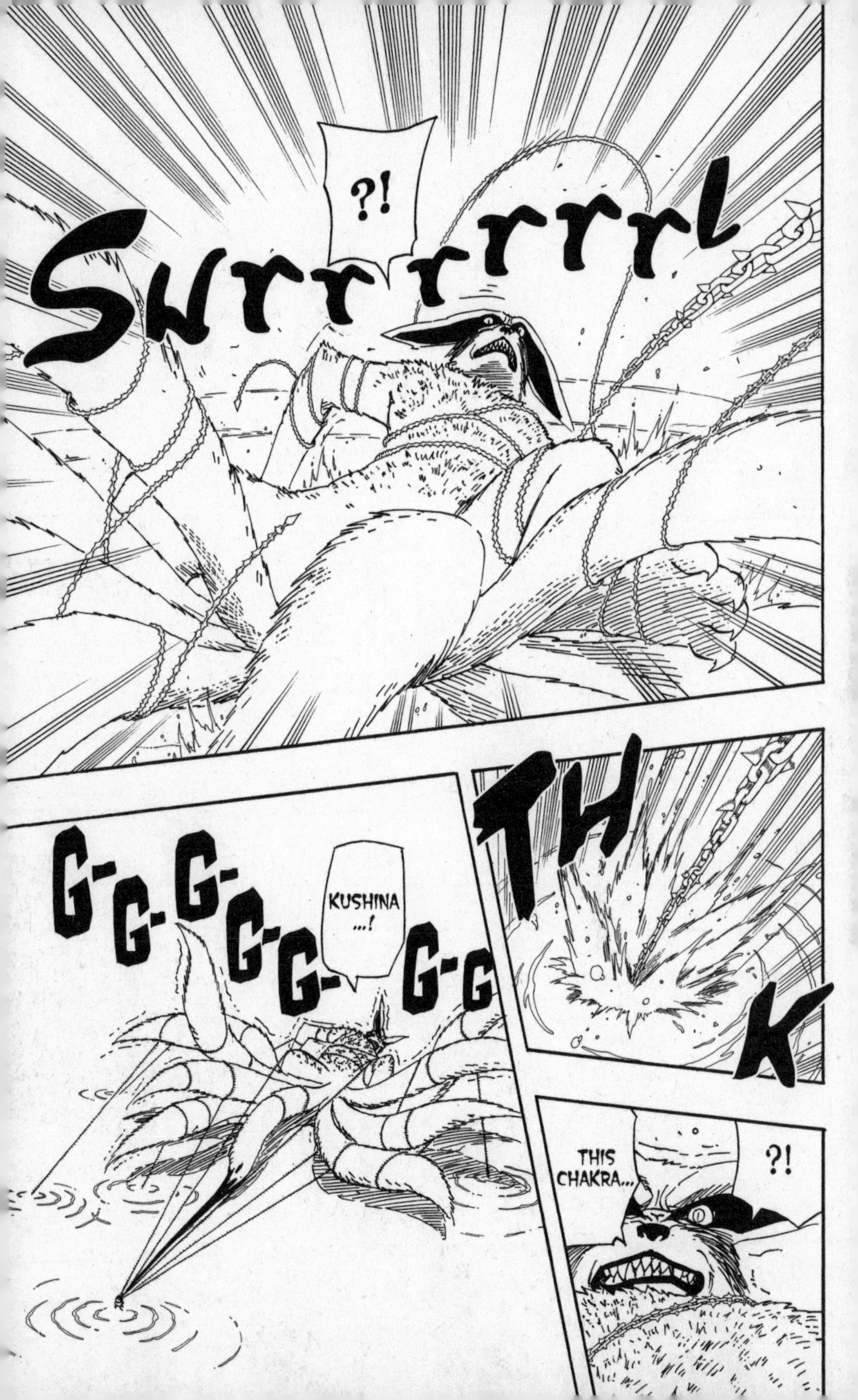
?!
Swrrrrrrl
TH
K
THIS CHAKRA...
?!
KUSHINA ...!
G-G-G-G-G-G-G

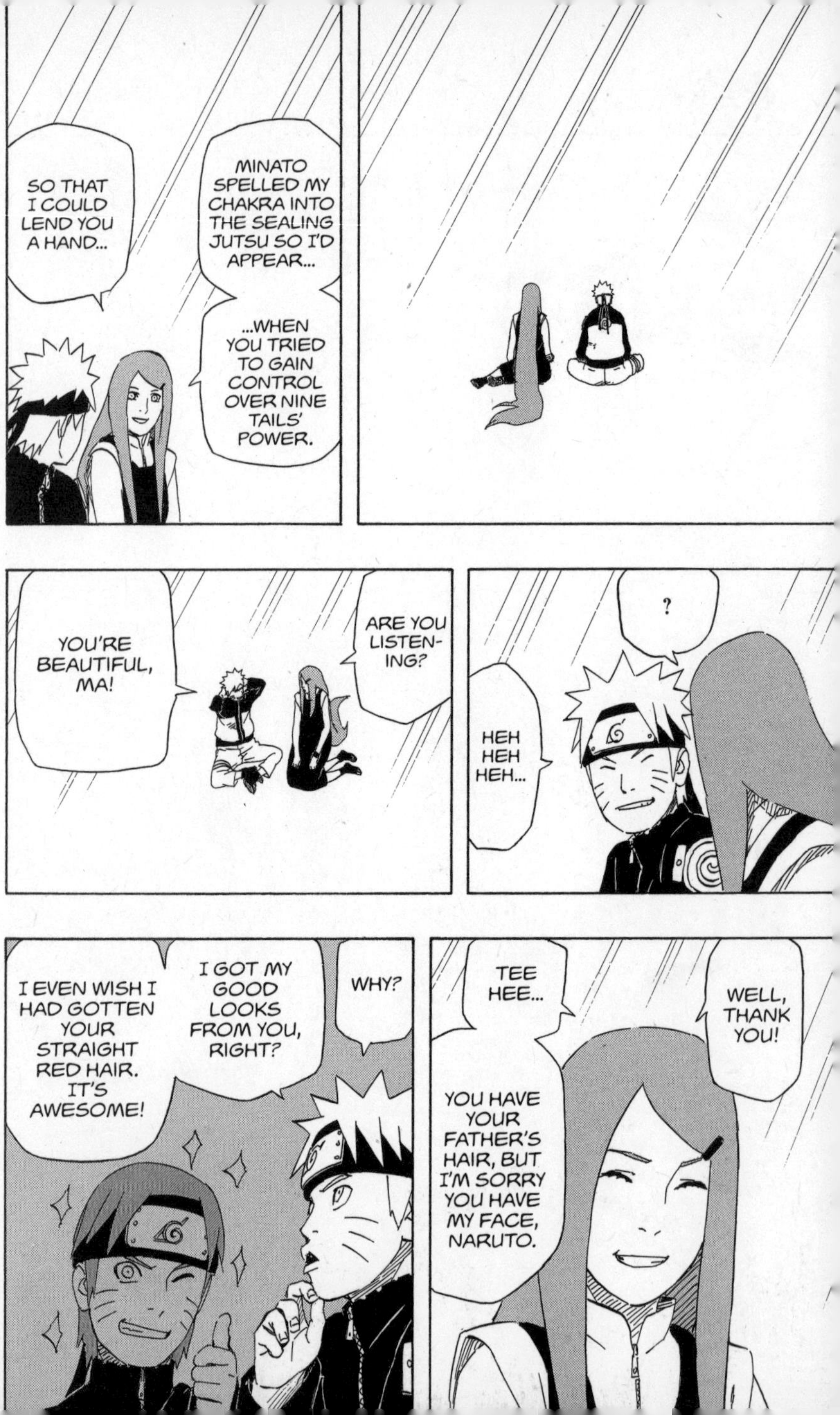
MINATO SPELLED MY CHAKRA INTO THE SEALING JUTSU SO I'D APPEAR...
...WHEN YOU TRIED TO GAIN CONTROL OVER NINE TAILS' POWER.
SO THAT I COULD LEND YOU A HAND...
?
HEH HEH HEH...
ARE YOU LISTEN-ING?
YOU'RE BEAUTIFUL, MA!
WELL, THANK YOU!
TEE HEE...
YOU HAVE YOUR FATHER'S HAIR, BUT I'M SORRY YOU HAVE MY FACE, NARUTO.
WHY?
I GOT MY GOOD LOOKS FROM YOU, RIGHT?
I EVEN WISH I HAD GOTTEN YOUR STRAIGHT RED HAIR. IT'S AWESOME!

READ THIS WAY

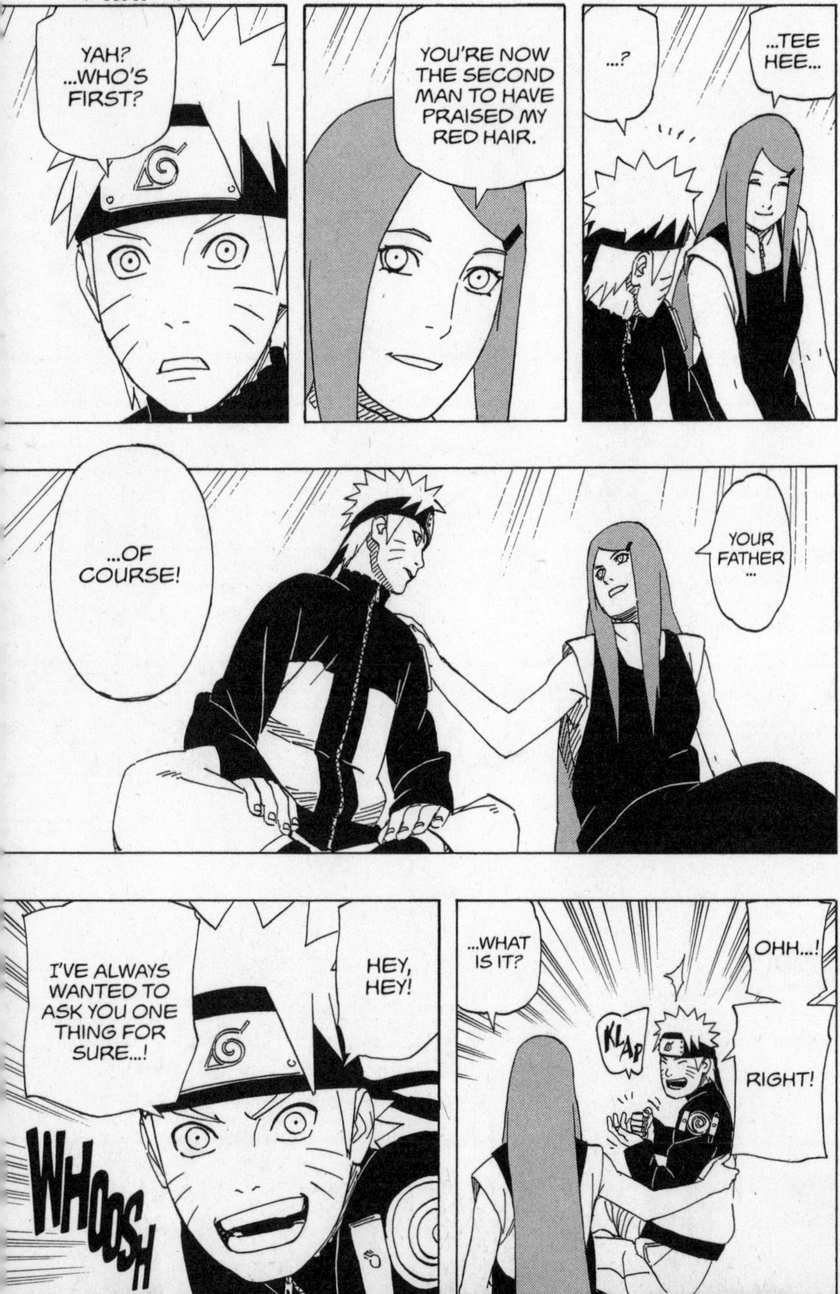
...TEE HEE...
...?
YOU'RE NOW THE SECOND MAN TO HAVE PRAISED MY RED HAIR.
YAH? ...WHO'S FIRST?
YOUR FATHER...
...OF COURSE!
OHH...!
RIGHT!
KLAP
...WHAT IS IT?
HEY, HEY!
I'VE ALWAYS WANTED TO ASK YOU ONE THING FOR SURE...!
WHOOSH

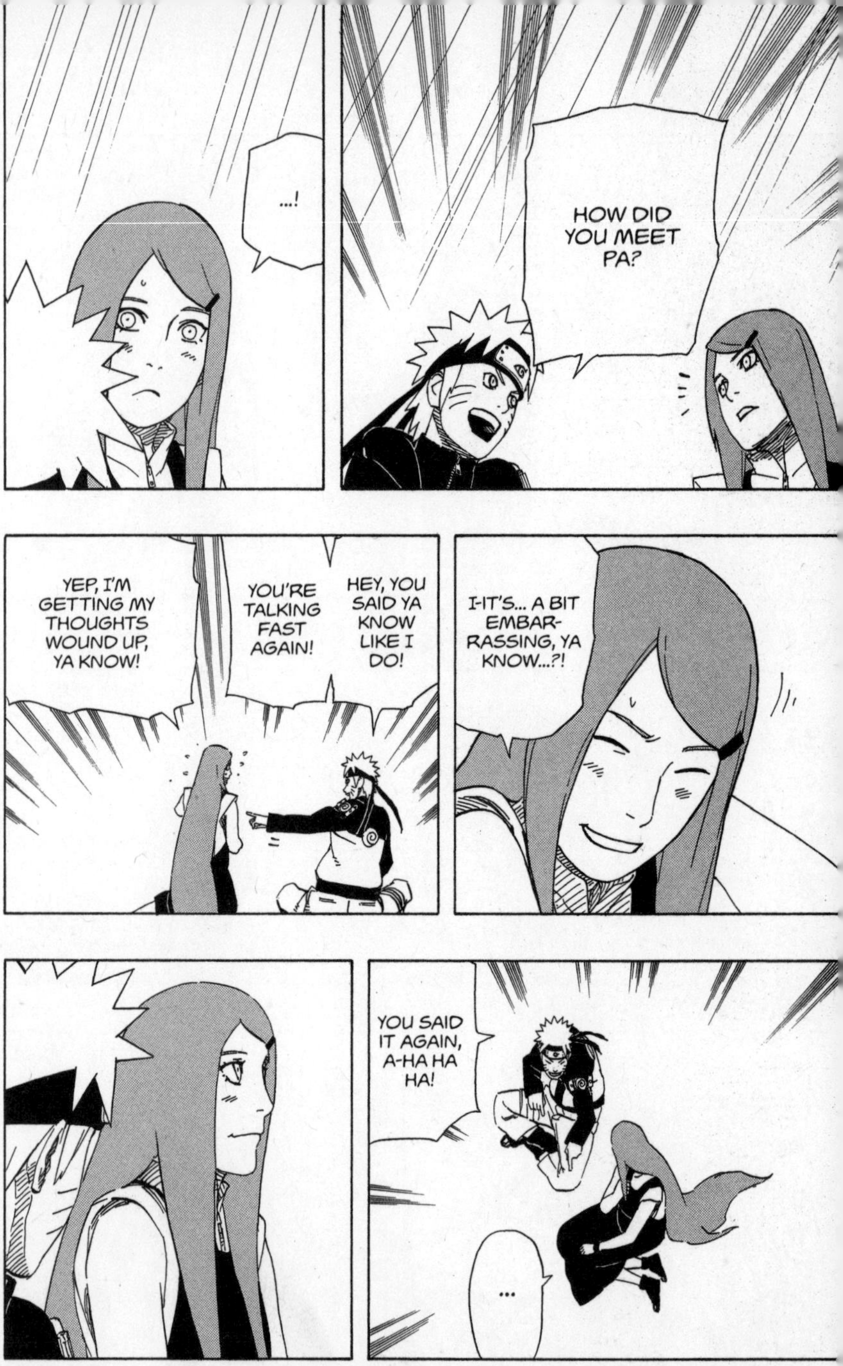
HOW DID YOU MEET PA?
...!
I-IT'S... A BIT EMBAR-RASSING, YA KNOW...?!
HEY, YOU SAID YA KNOW LIKE I DO!
YOU'RE TALKING FAST AGAIN!
YEP, I'M GETTING MY THOUGHTS WOUND UP, YA KNOW!
YOU SAID IT AGAIN, A-HA HA HA!
...

READ THIS WAY

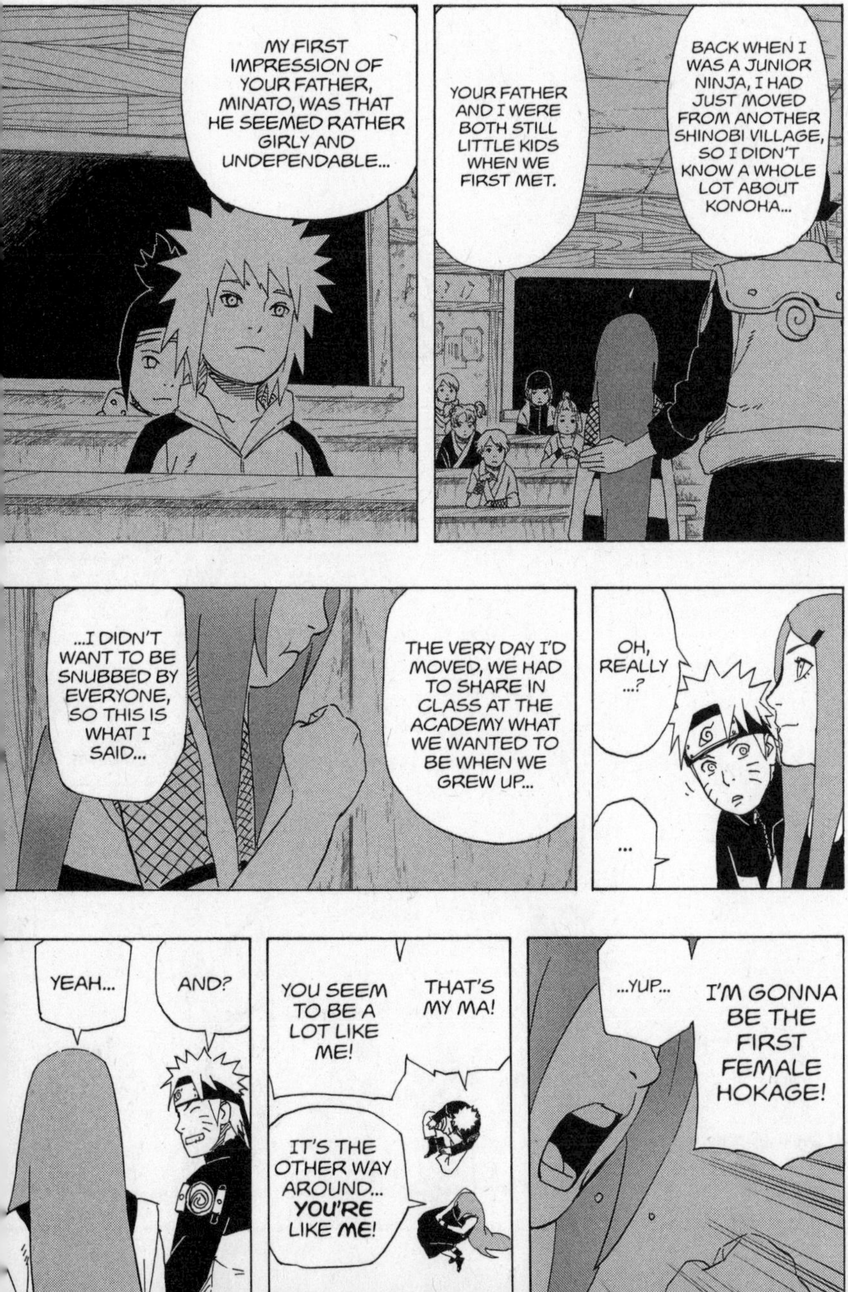
BACK WHEN I WAS A JUNIOR NINJA, I HAD JUST MOVED FROM ANOTHER SHINOBI VILLAGE, SO I DIDN'T KNOW A WHOLE LOT ABOUT KONOHA...
YOUR FATHER AND I WERE BOTH STILL LITTLE KIDS WHEN WE FIRST MET.
MY FIRST IMPRESSION OF YOUR FATHER, MINATO, WAS THAT HE SEEMED RATHER GIRLY AND UNDEPENDABLE...
OH, REALLY ...?
...
THE VERY DAY I'D MOVED, WE HAD TO SHARE IN CLASS AT THE ACADEMY WHAT WE WANTED TO BE WHEN WE GREW UP...
...I DIDN'T WANT TO BE SNUBBED BY EVERYONE, SO THIS IS WHAT I SAID...
I'M GONNA BE THE FIRST FEMALE HOKAGE!
...YUP...
THAT'S MY MA!
YOU SEEM TO BE A LOT LIKE ME!
IT'S THE OTHER WAY AROUND... **YOU'RE** LIKE **ME**!
AND?
YEAH...

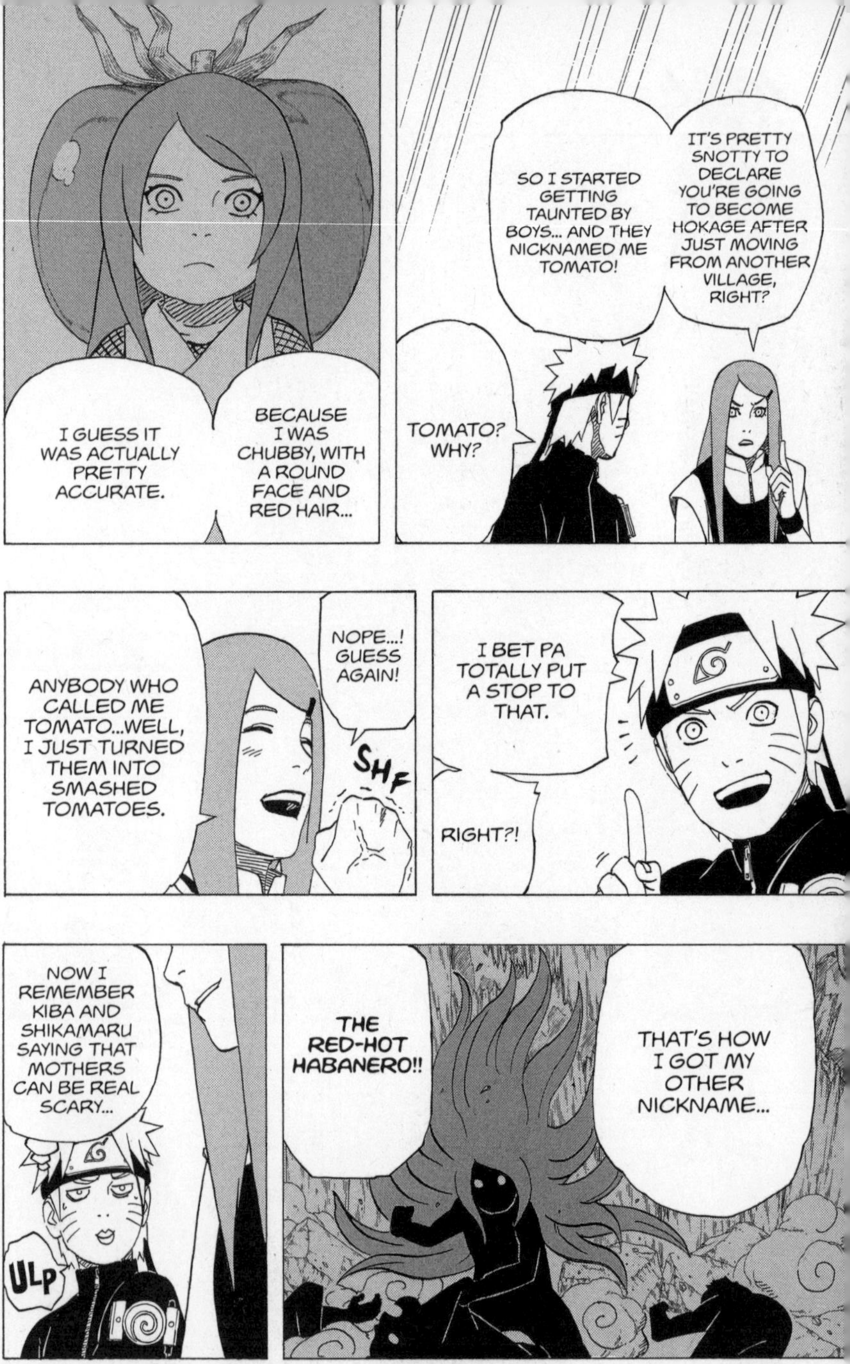
IT'S PRETTY SNOTTY TO DECLARE YOU'RE GOING TO BECOME HOKAGE AFTER JUST MOVING FROM ANOTHER VILLAGE, RIGHT?
SO I STARTED GETTING TAUNTED BY BOYS... AND THEY NICKNAMED ME TOMATO!
TOMATO? WHY?
BECAUSE I WAS CHUBBY, WITH A ROUND FACE AND RED HAIR...
I GUESS IT WAS ACTUALLY PRETTY ACCURATE.
I BET PA TOTALLY PUT A STOP TO THAT.
RIGHT?!
NOPE...! GUESS AGAIN!
SHF
ANYBODY WHO CALLED ME TOMATO...WELL, I JUST TURNED THEM INTO SMASHED TOMATOES.
THAT'S HOW I GOT MY OTHER NICKNAME...
THE RED-HOT HABANERO!!
NOW I REMEMBER KIBA AND SHIKAMARU SAYING THAT MOTHERS CAN BE REAL SCARY...
ULP

READ THIS WAY

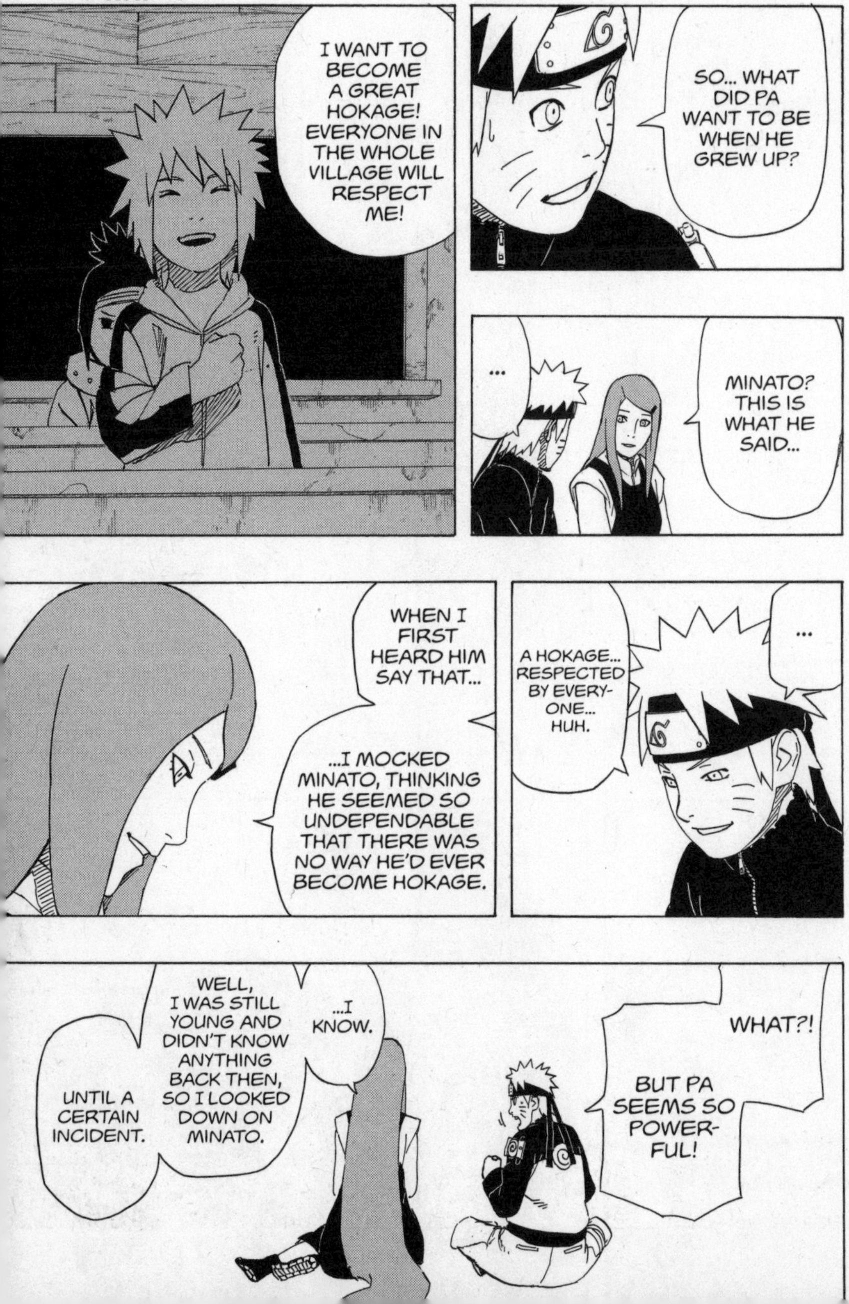
SO... WHAT DID PA WANT TO BE WHEN HE GREW UP?
MINATO? THIS IS WHAT HE SAID...
...
I WANT TO BECOME A GREAT HOKAGE! EVERYONE IN THE WHOLE VILLAGE WILL RESPECT ME!
...
A HOKAGE... RESPECTED BY EVERY-ONE... HUH.
WHEN I FIRST HEARD HIM SAY THAT...
...I MOCKED MINATO, THINKING HE SEEMED SO UNDEPENDABLE THAT THERE WAS NO WAY HE'D EVER BECOME HOKAGE.
WHAT?!
BUT PA SEEMS SO POWER-FUL!
...I KNOW.
WELL, I WAS STILL YOUNG AND DIDN'T KNOW ANYTHING BACK THEN, SO I LOOKED DOWN ON MINATO.
UNTIL A CERTAIN INCIDENT.

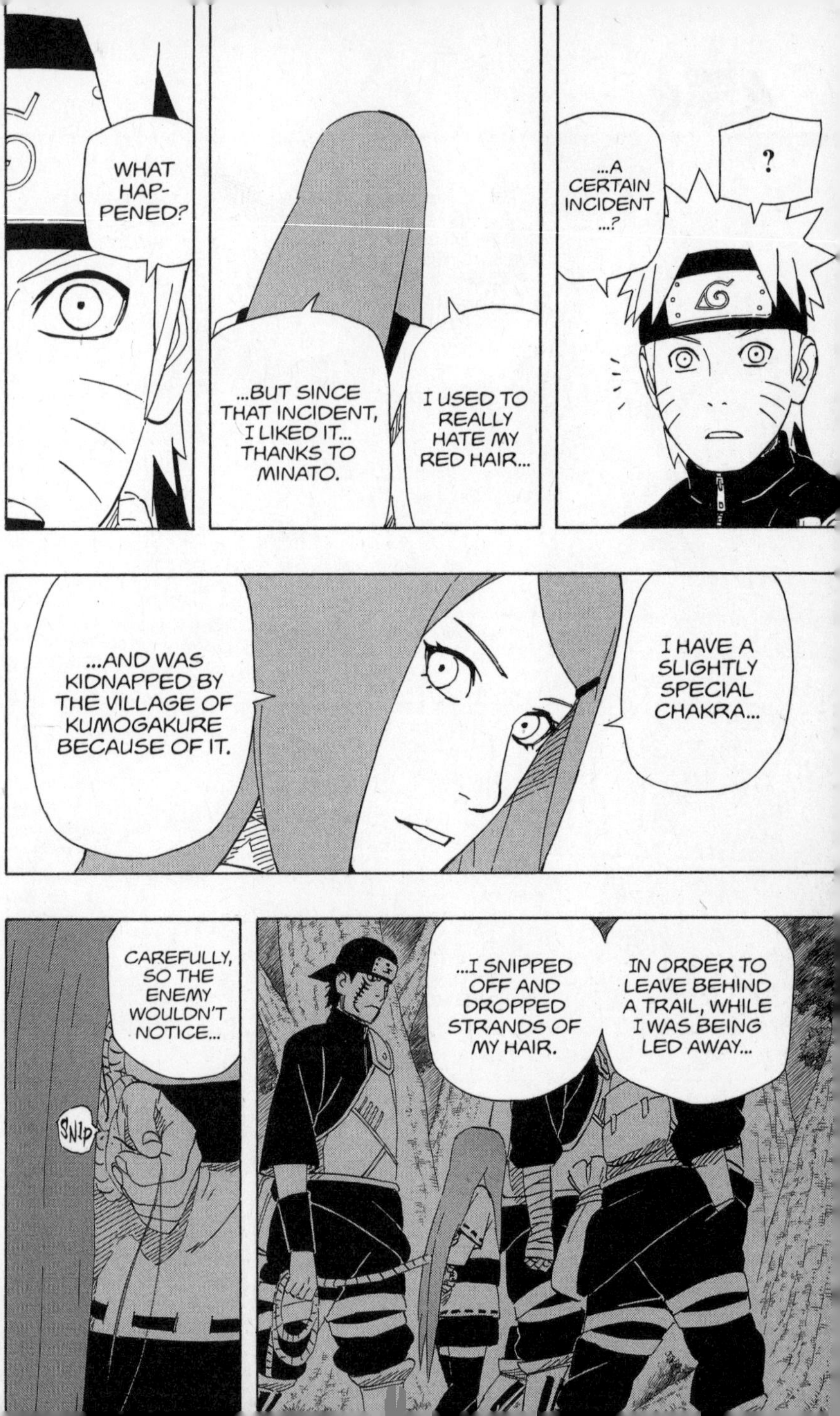
?
...A CERTAIN INCIDENT ...?
I USED TO REALLY HATE MY RED HAIR...
...BUT SINCE THAT INCIDENT, I LIKED IT... THANKS TO MINATO.
WHAT HAP-PENED?
I HAVE A SLIGHTLY SPECIAL CHAKRA...
...AND WAS KIDNAPPED BY THE VILLAGE OF KUMOGAKURE BECAUSE OF IT.
IN ORDER TO LEAVE BEHIND A TRAIL, WHILE I WAS BEING LED AWAY...
...I SNIPPED OFF AND DROPPED STRANDS OF MY HAIR.
CAREFULLY, SO THE ENEMY WOULDN'T NOTICE...
SNIP

READ THIS WAY

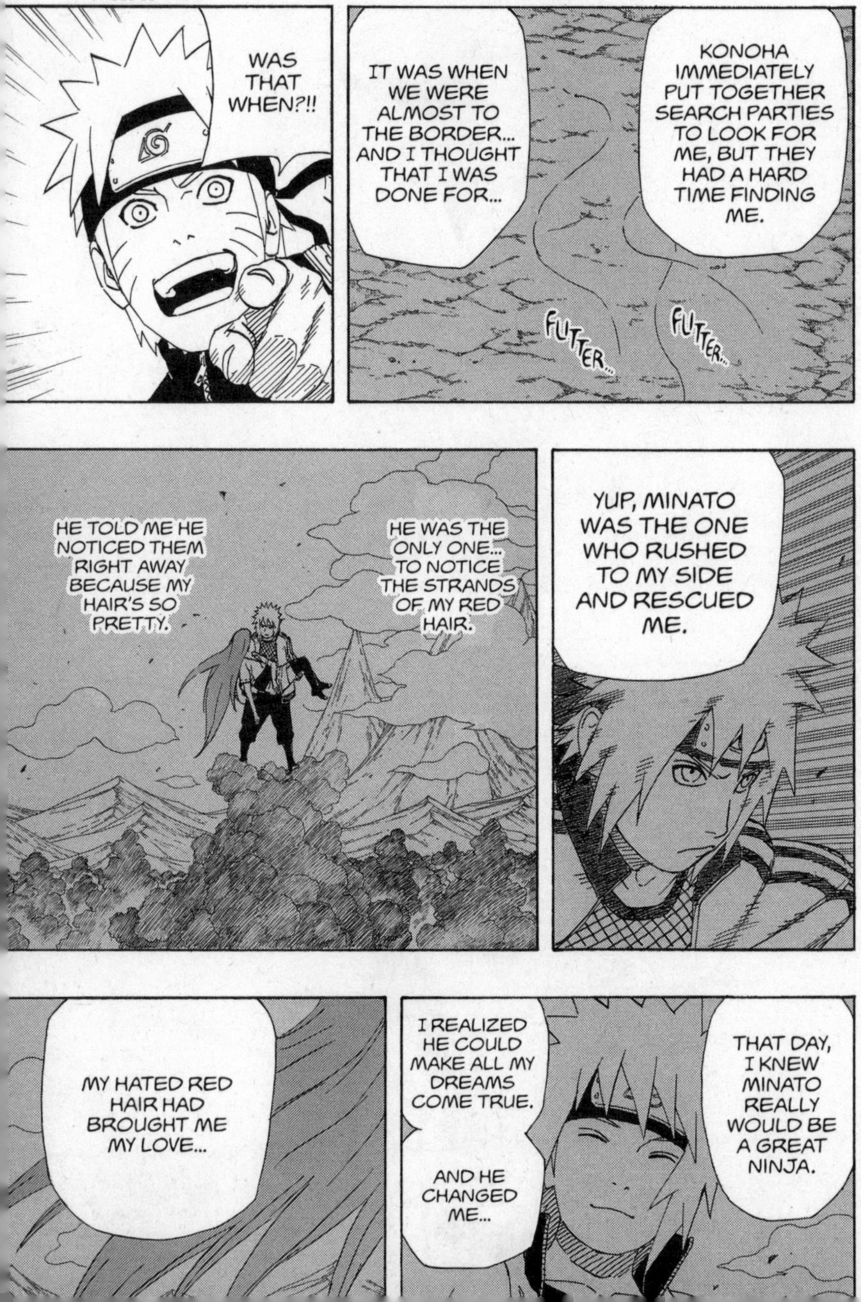
KONOHA IMMEDIATELY PUT TOGETHER SEARCH PARTIES TO LOOK FOR ME, BUT THEY HAD A HARD TIME FINDING ME.
IT WAS WHEN WE WERE ALMOST TO THE BORDER... AND I THOUGHT THAT I WAS DONE FOR...
FLUTTER...
FLUTTER...
WAS THAT WHEN?!!
YUP, MINATO WAS THE ONE WHO RUSHED TO MY SIDE AND RESCUED ME.
HE WAS THE ONLY ONE... TO NOTICE THE STRANDS OF MY RED HAIR.
HE TOLD ME HE NOTICED THEM RIGHT AWAY BECAUSE MY HAIR'S SO PRETTY.
THAT DAY, I KNEW MINATO REALLY WOULD BE A GREAT NINJA.
I REALIZED HE COULD MAKE ALL MY DREAMS COME TRUE.
AND HE CHANGED ME...
MY HATED RED HAIR HAD BROUGHT ME MY LOVE...

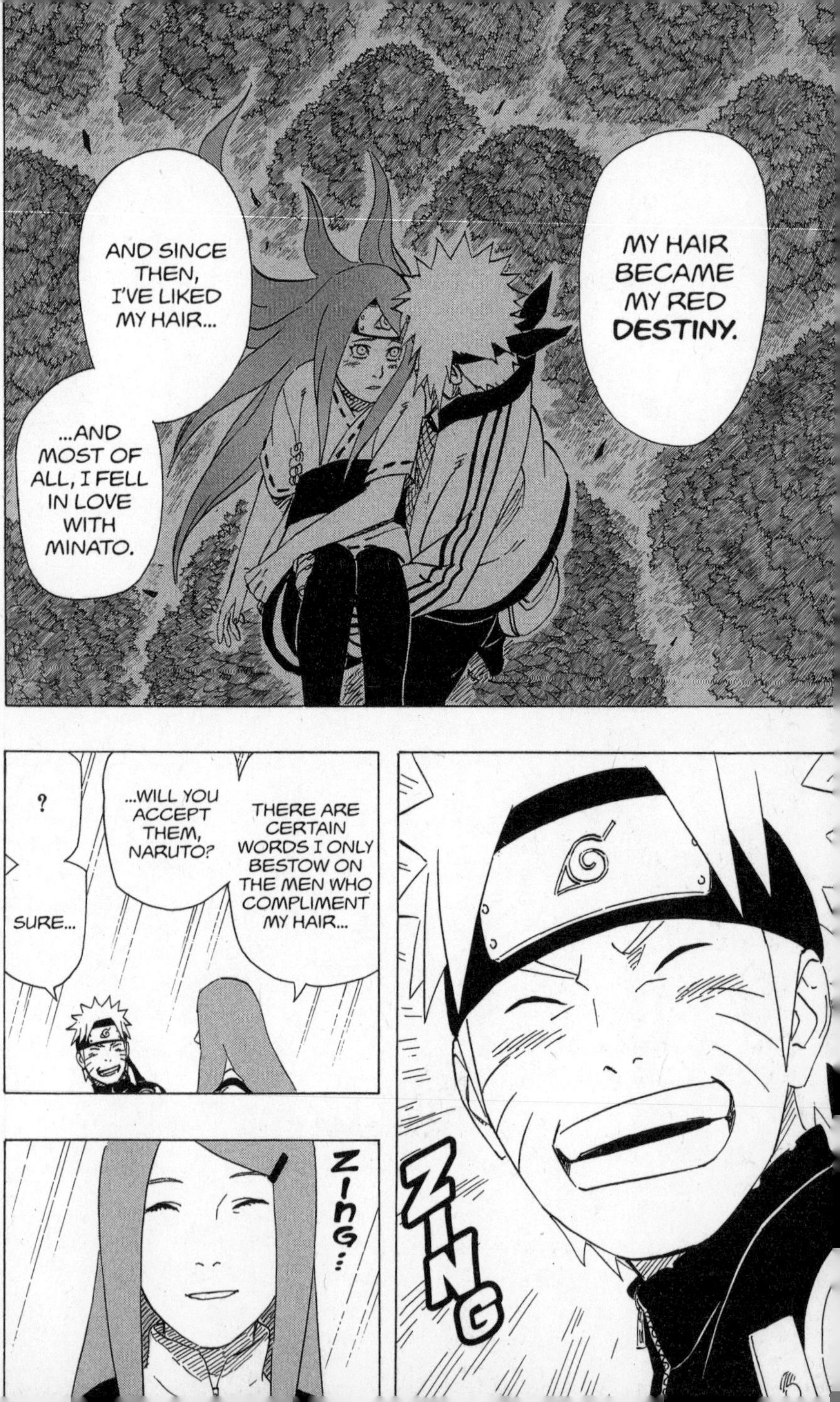
MY HAIR BECAME MY RED DESTINY.
AND SINCE THEN, I'VE LIKED MY HAIR...
...AND MOST OF ALL, I FELL IN LOVE WITH MINATO.
ZING
THERE ARE CERTAIN WORDS I ONLY BESTOW ON THE MEN WHO COMPLIMENT MY HAIR...
...WILL YOU ACCEPT THEM, NARUTO?
?
SURE...
ZING...

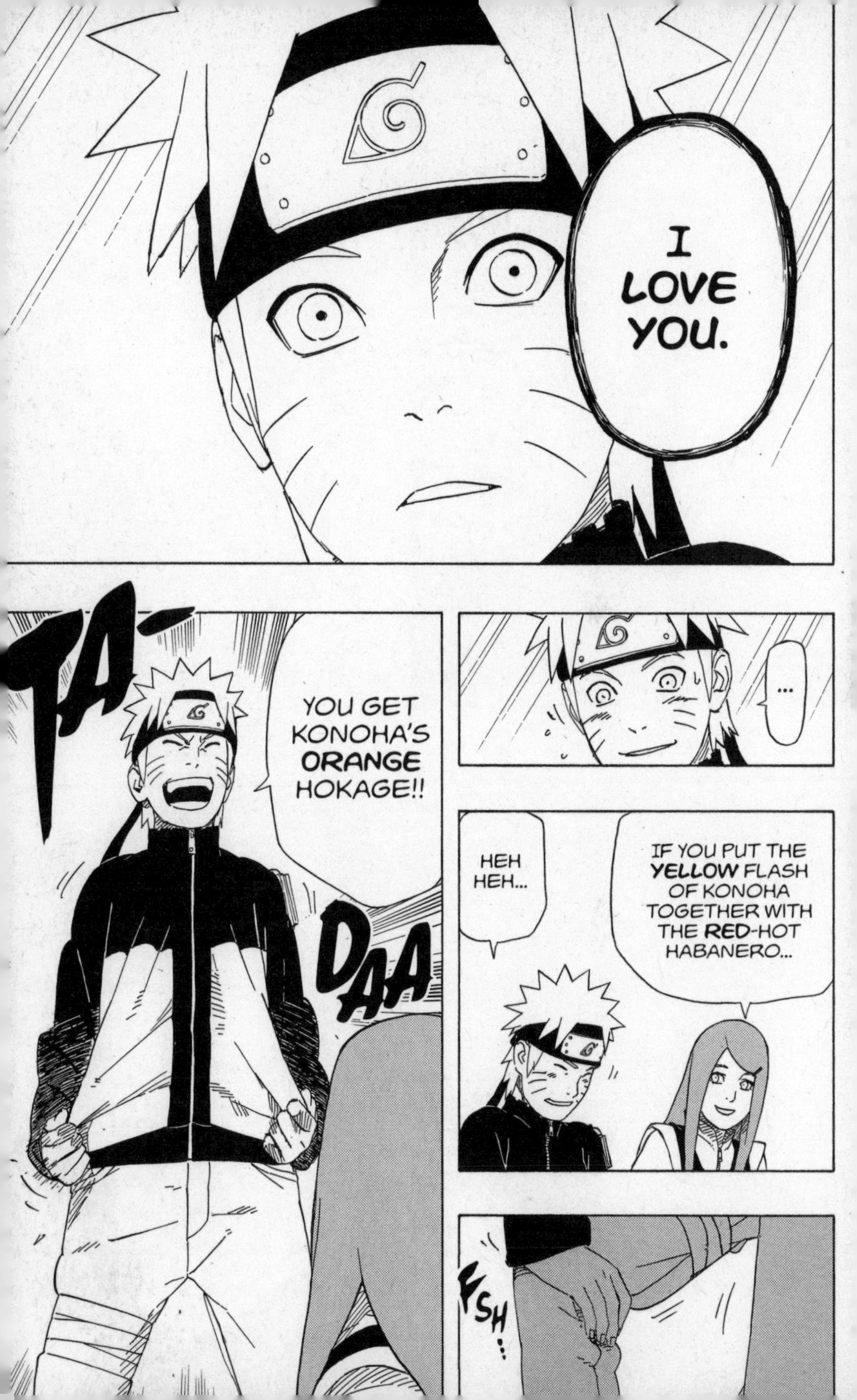
I LOVE YOU.
...
IF YOU PUT THE YELLOW FLASH OF KONOHA TOGETHER WITH THE RED-HOT HABANERO...
HEH HEH...
FSH..
TA-DAA
YOU GET KONOHA'S ORANGE HOKAGE!!

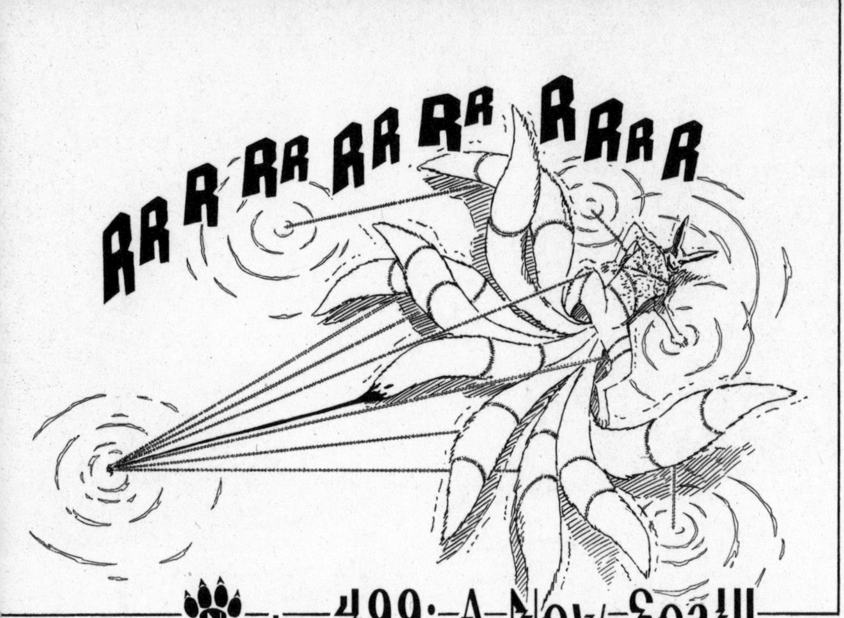
RRRRRRRRRRRRRRRRR

Number 499: A New Seal!!

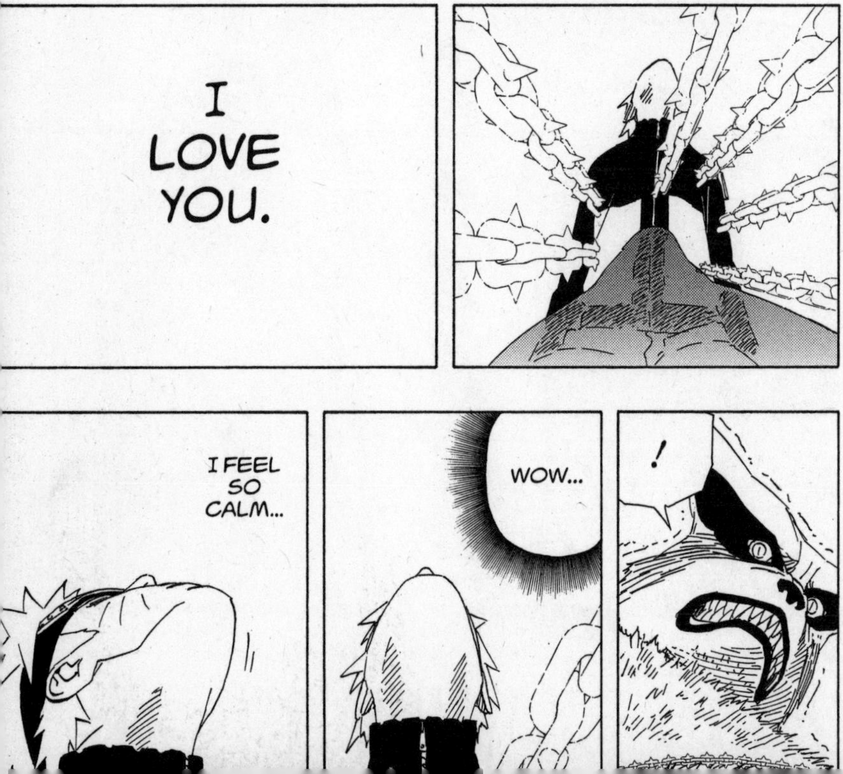
I LOVE YOU.
!
WOW...
I FEEL SO CALM...

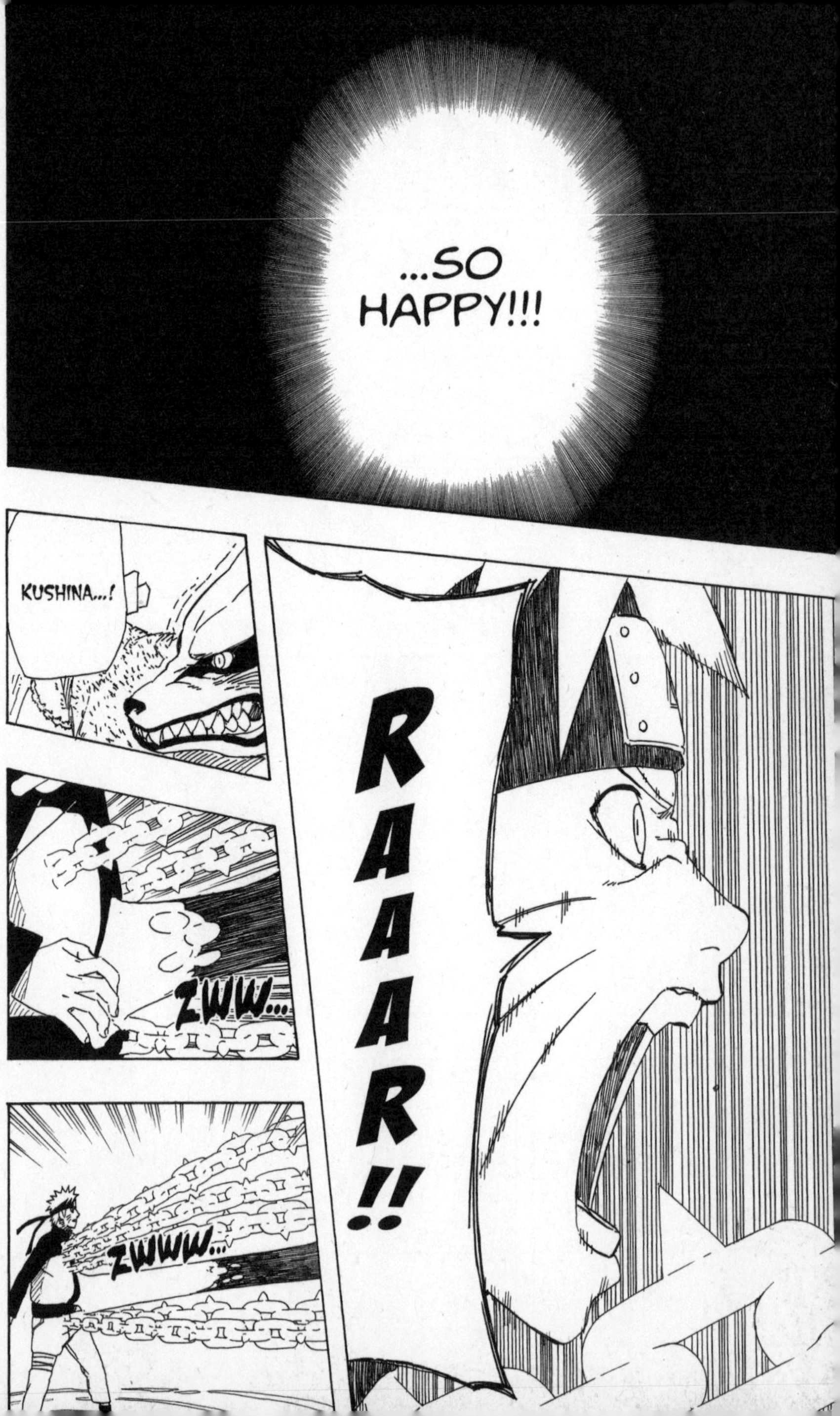
...SO HAPPY!!!
RAAAAR!!
KUSHINA...!
ZWW...
ZWWW...

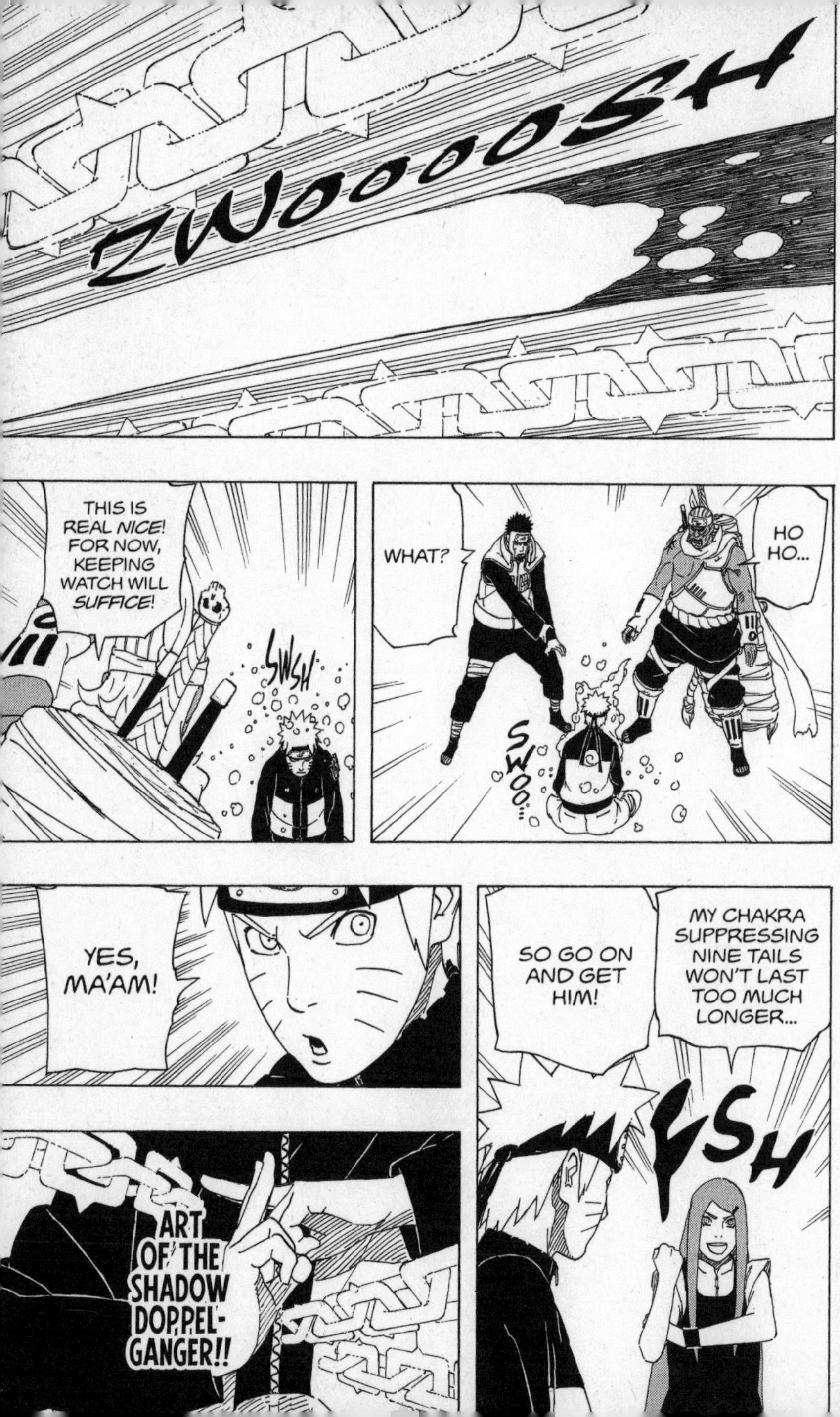
ZWOOOOOSH
HO HO...
WHAT?
SWOO...
THIS IS REAL NICE! FOR NOW, KEEPING WATCH WILL SUFFICE!
SWSH
MY CHAKRA SUPPRESSING NINE TAILS WON'T LAST TOO MUCH LONGER...
SO GO ON AND GET HIM!
YSH
YES, MA'AM!
ART OF THE SHADOW DOPPEL-GANGER!!

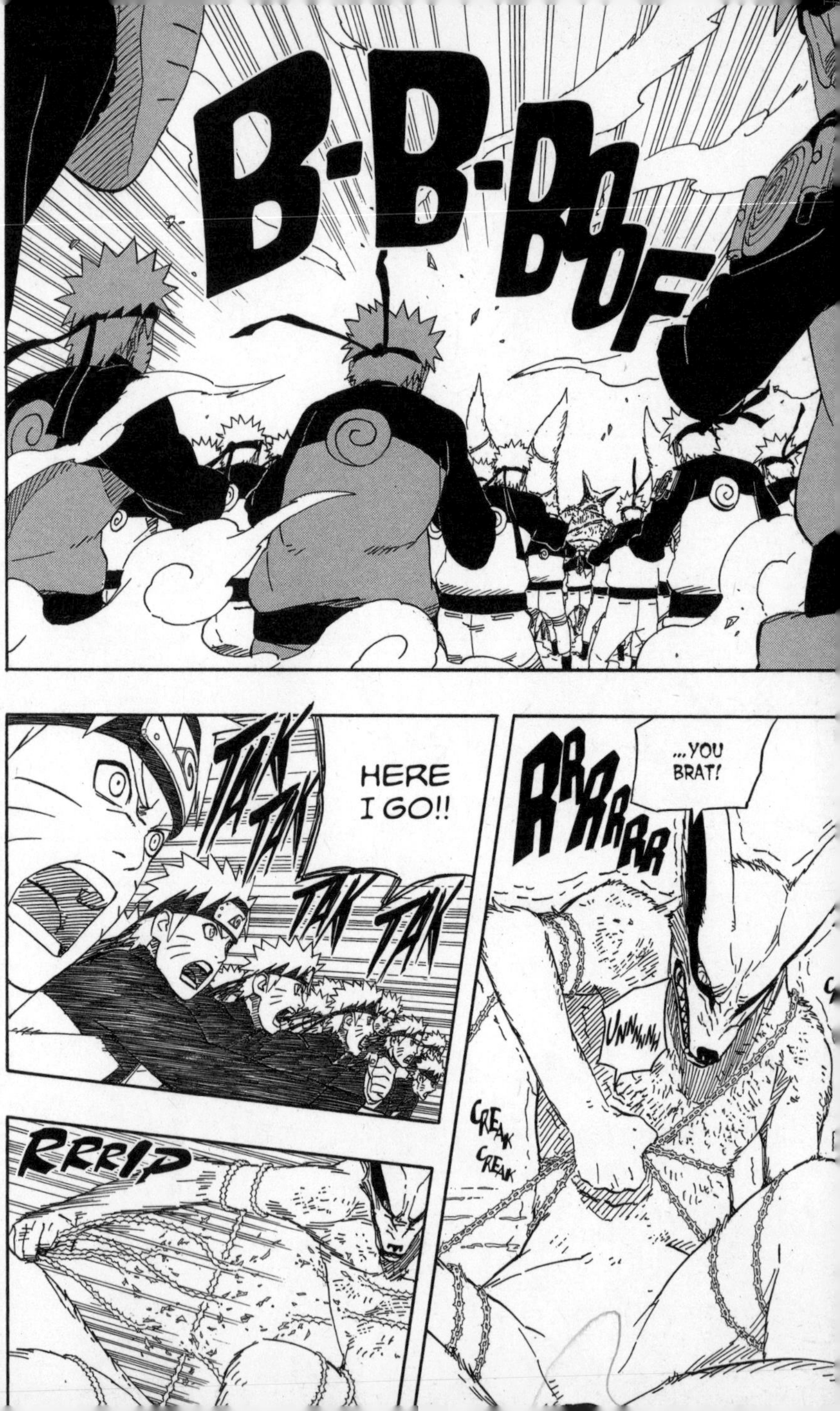
...YOU BRAT!
RRRRRRR
UNNNNH
CREAK
CREAK
HERE I GO!!
TAK TAK TAK TAK TAK
RRRIP

READ THIS WAY

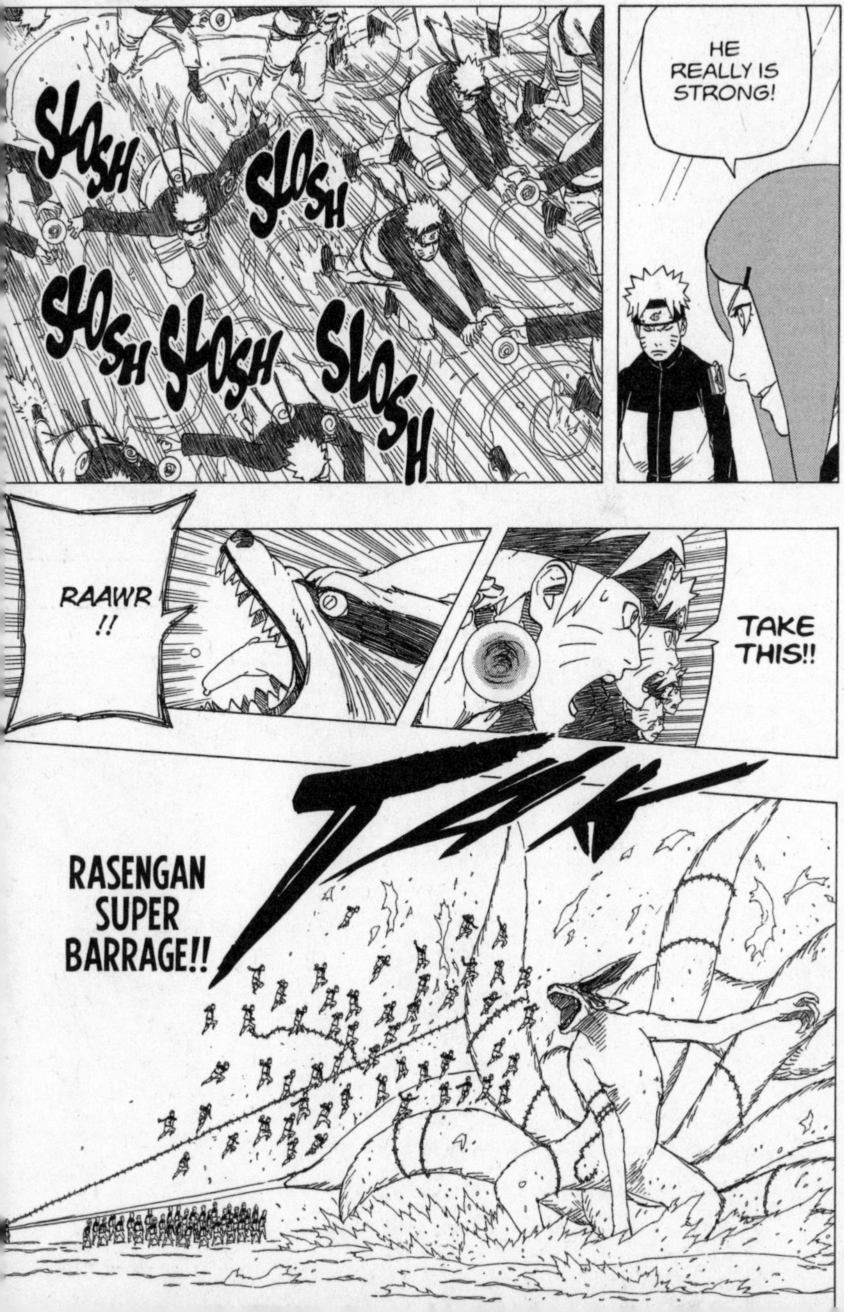
HE REALLY IS STRONG!
SLOSH
SLOSH
SLOSH
SLOSH
SLOSH
TAKE THIS!!
RAAWR !!
TAK
RASENGAN SUPER BARRAGE!!

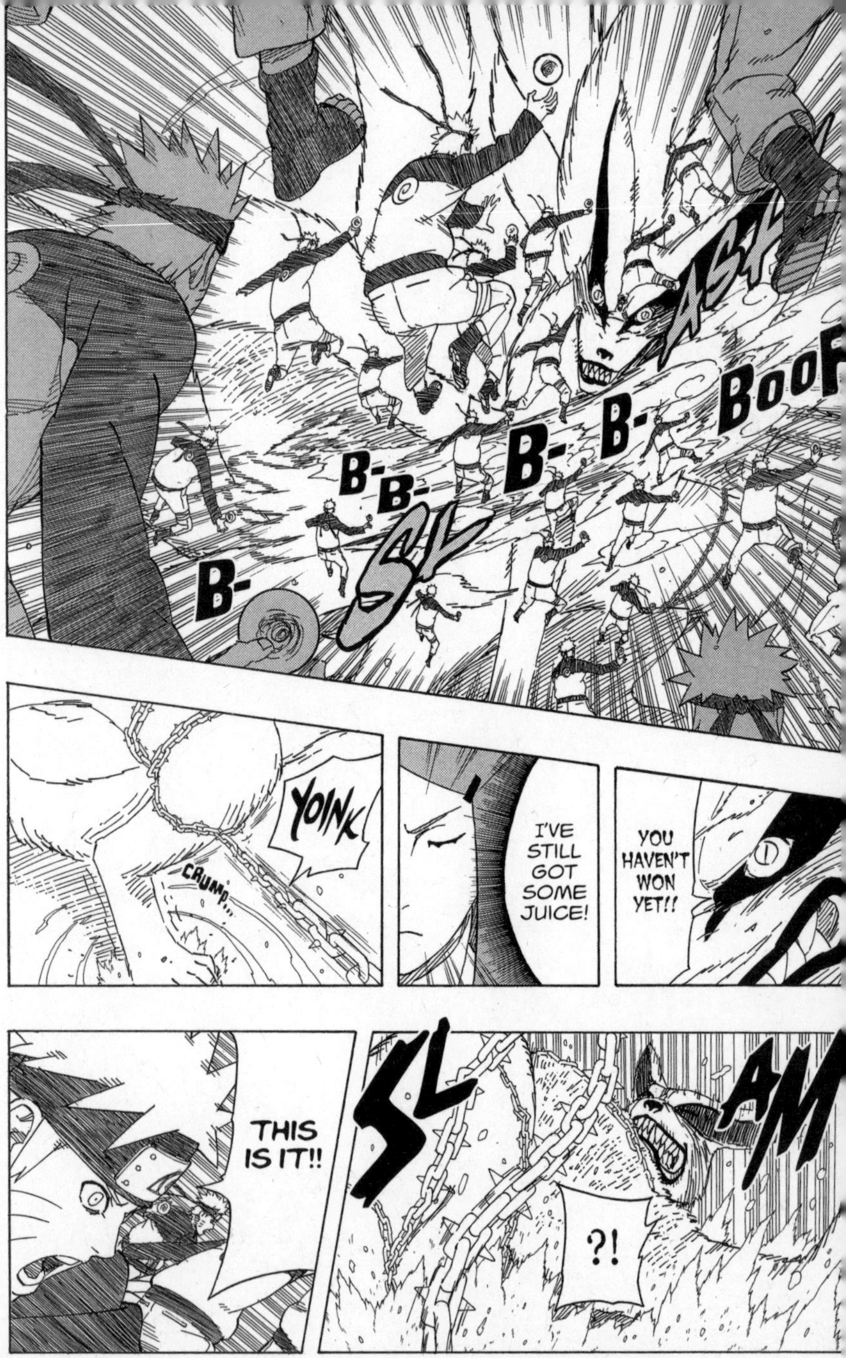
ASH
BOOF
B-
B-
B-
B-
B-
SY
YOU HAVEN'T WON YET!!
I'VE STILL GOT SOME JUICE!
YOINK
CRUMP...
SL
AM
?!
THIS IS IT!!

THAT'S...

SAGE MODE!!

SSSH

SSSH...

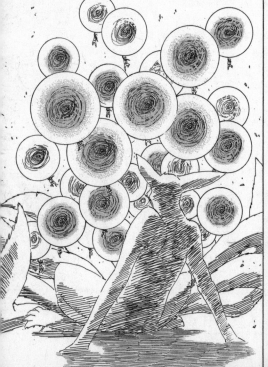

ZWOOO

OOO

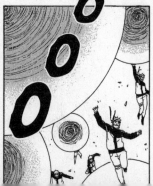

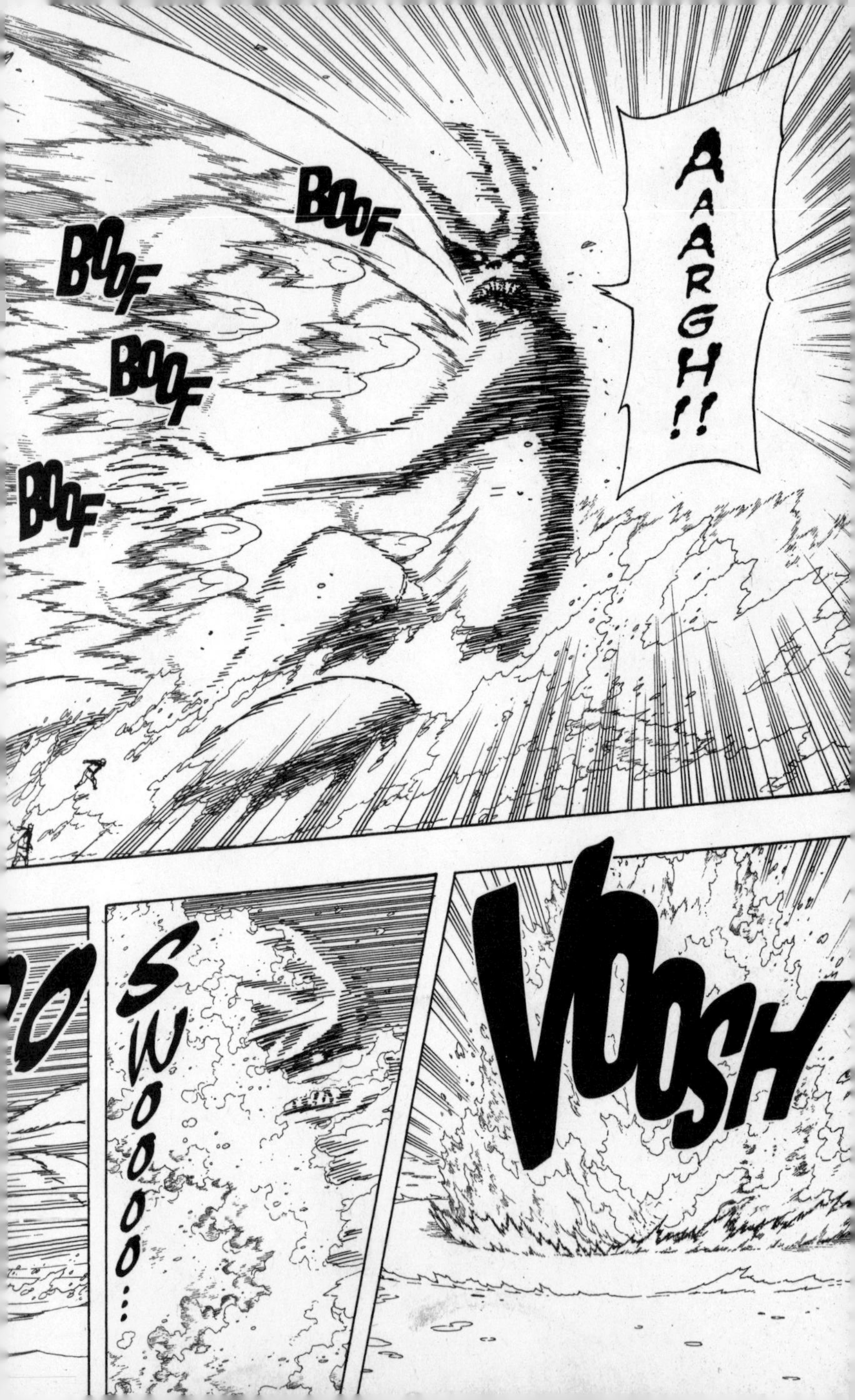
AAARGH!!
BOOF
BOOF
BOOF
BOOF
VOOSH
SWOOOO...

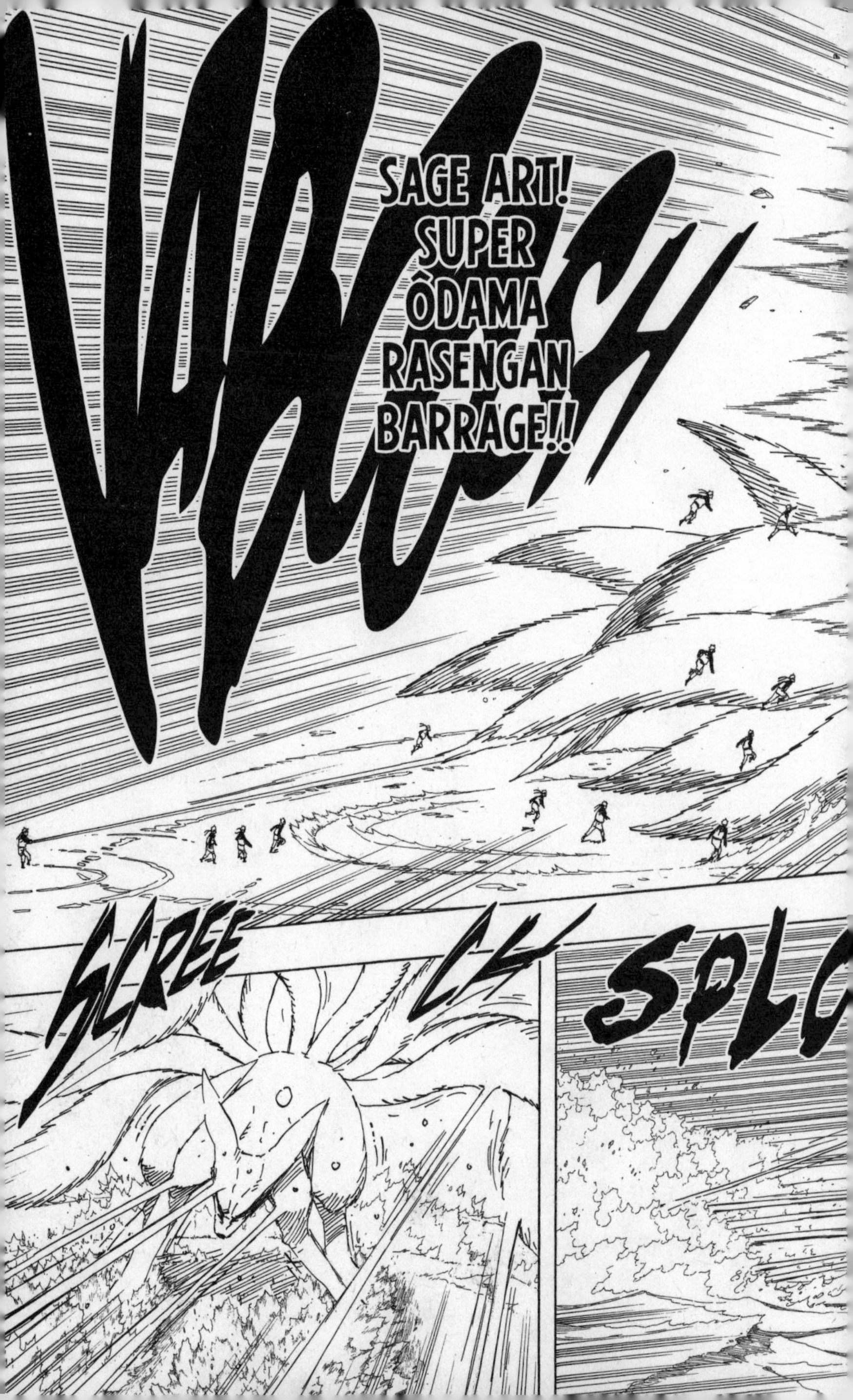
SAGE ART! SUPER ÔDAMA RASENGAN BARRAGE!!
SCREECH

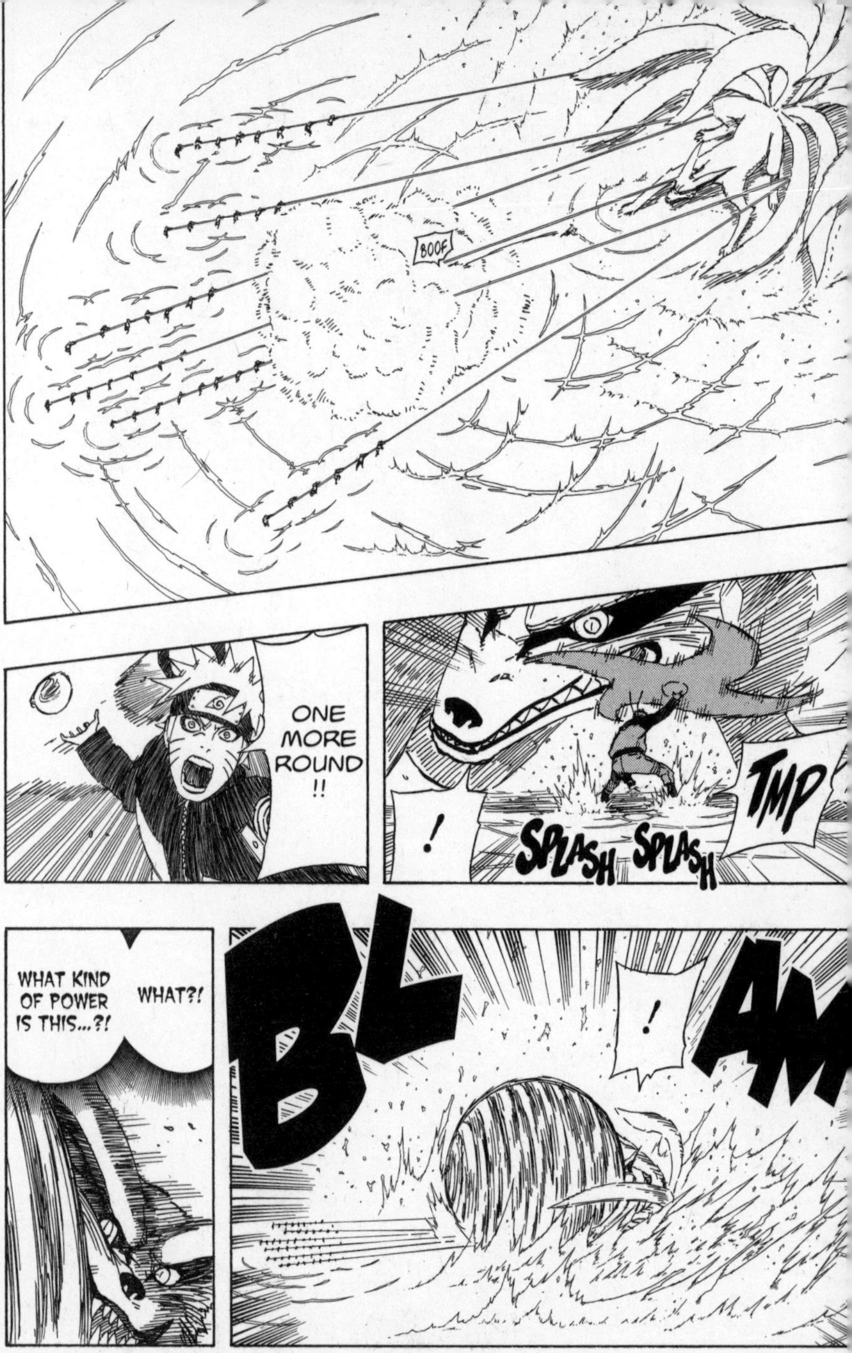
BOOF
TMP
!
SPLASH SPLASH
ONE MORE ROUND !!
!
BLAM
WHAT?!
WHAT KIND OF POWER IS THIS...?!

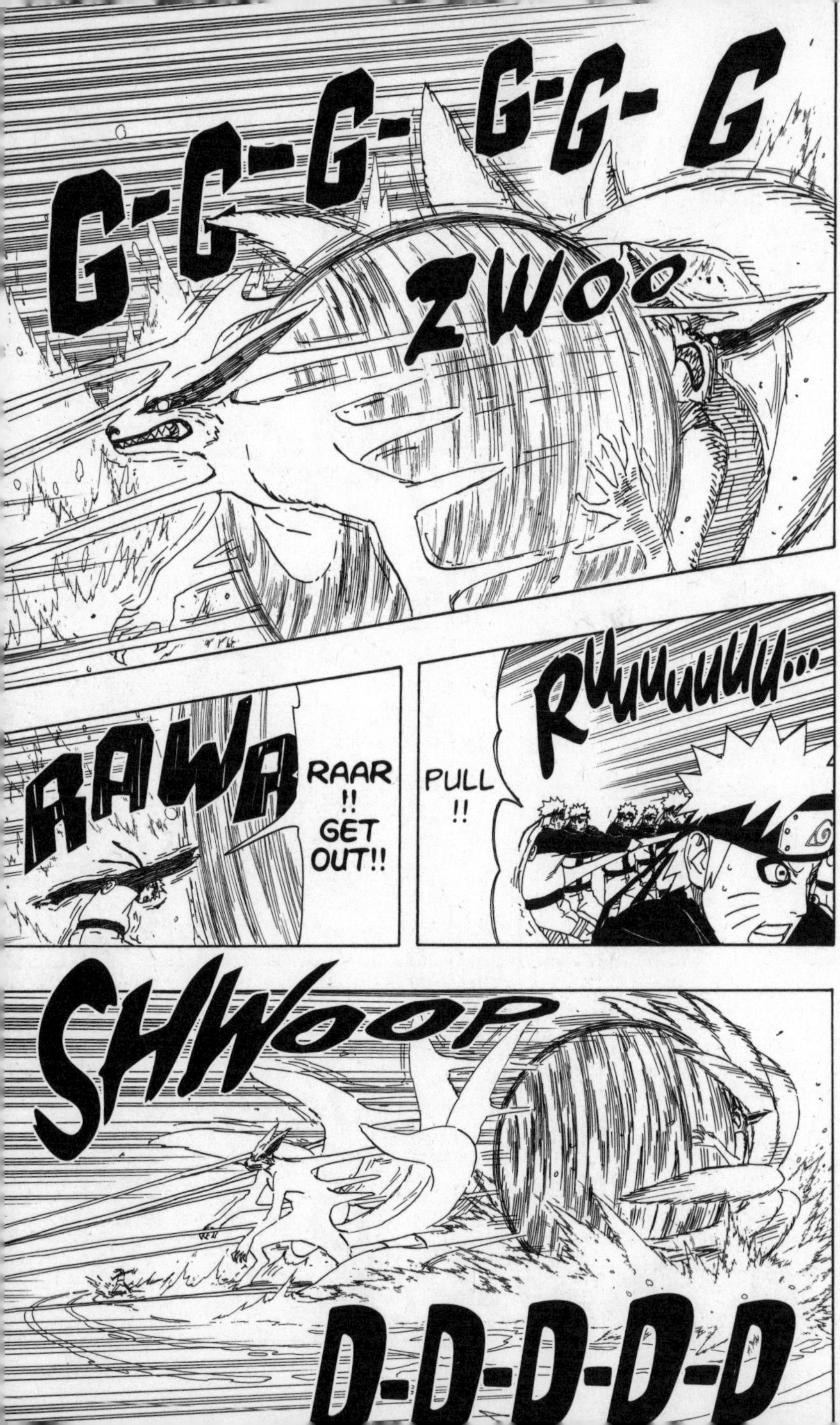
G-G-G-G-G-G
ZWOO
RUUUUUU...
PULL !!
RAWR
RAAR !! GET OUT!!
SHWOOP
D-D-D-D-D

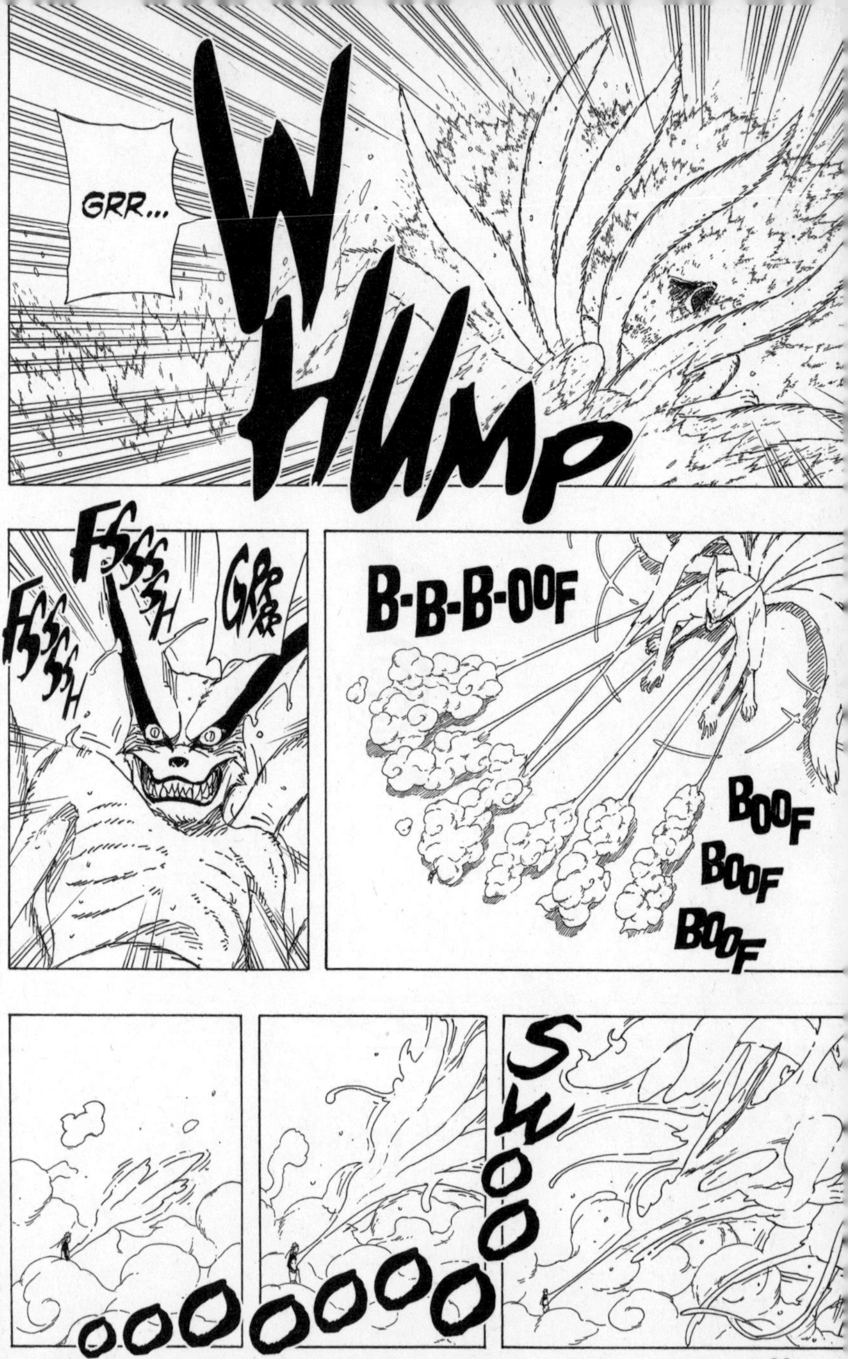
GRR...
WHUMP
B-B-B-OOF
BOOF
BOOF
BOOF
FSSSSH
FSSSSH
GRRR
SWOOOOOOOOOOOO

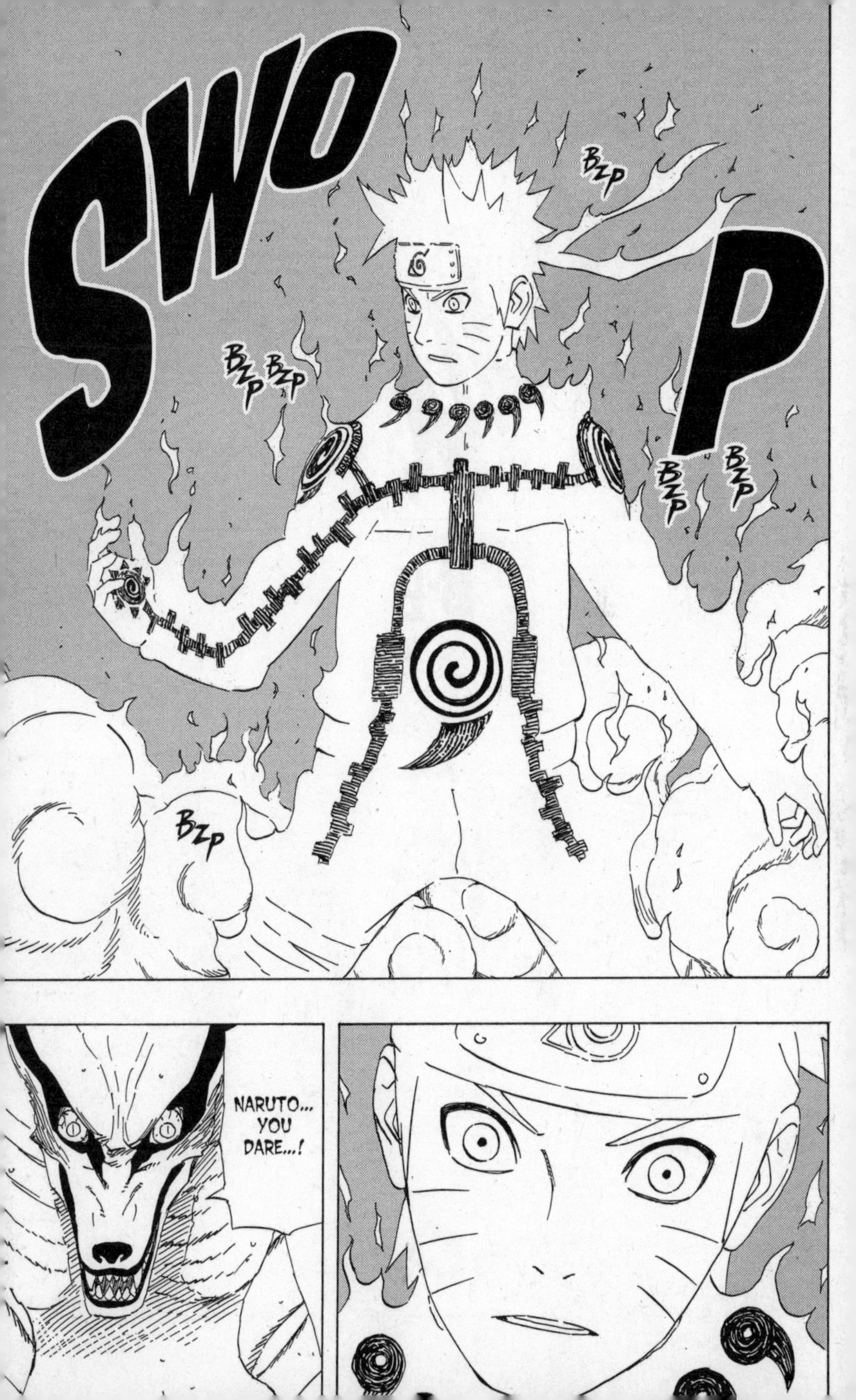
SWOP
BZP
BZP BZP
BZP BZP
BZP
NARUTO... YOU DARE...!

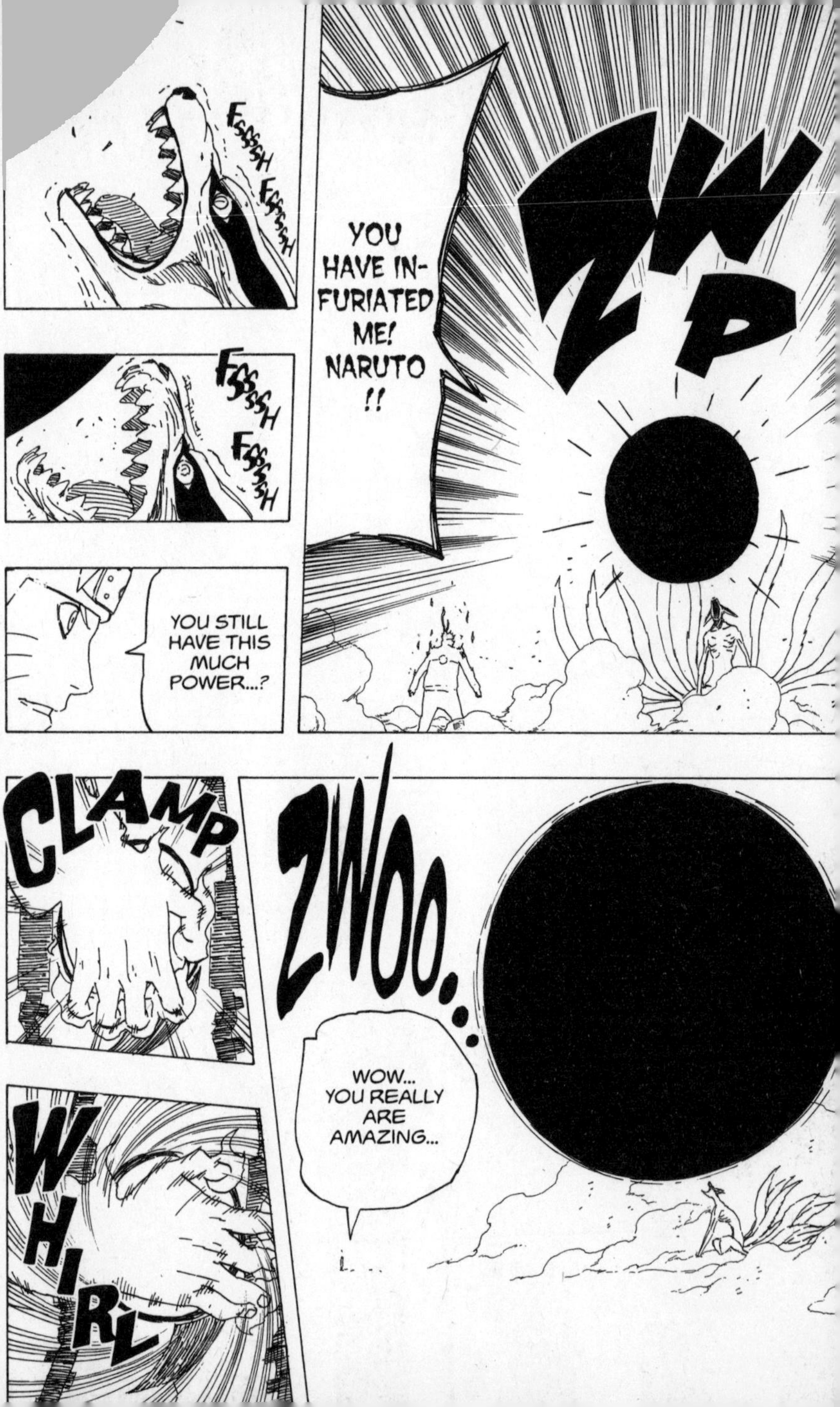
ZWIP
YOU HAVE IN-FURIATED ME! NARUTO !!
FSSSSH FSSSSH
FSSSSH FSSSSH
YOU STILL HAVE THIS MUCH POWER...?
ZWOO...
WOW... YOU REALLY ARE AMAZING...
CLAMP
WHIRL

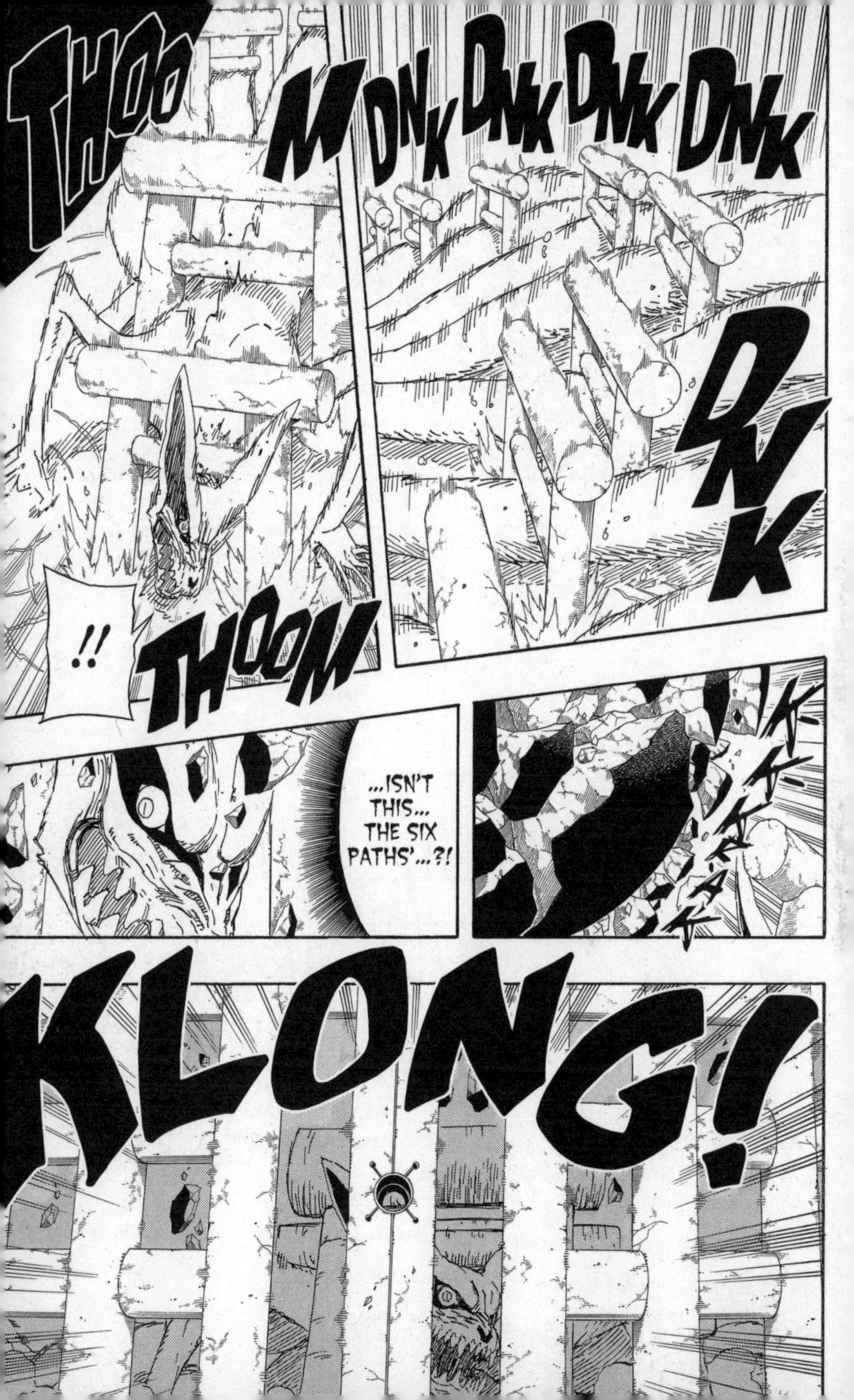
DNK DNK DNK DNK
DNK
THOOM
THOOM
!!
KA-KA-KA-KA-KA-K
...ISN'T THIS... THE SIX PATHS'...?!
KLONG!

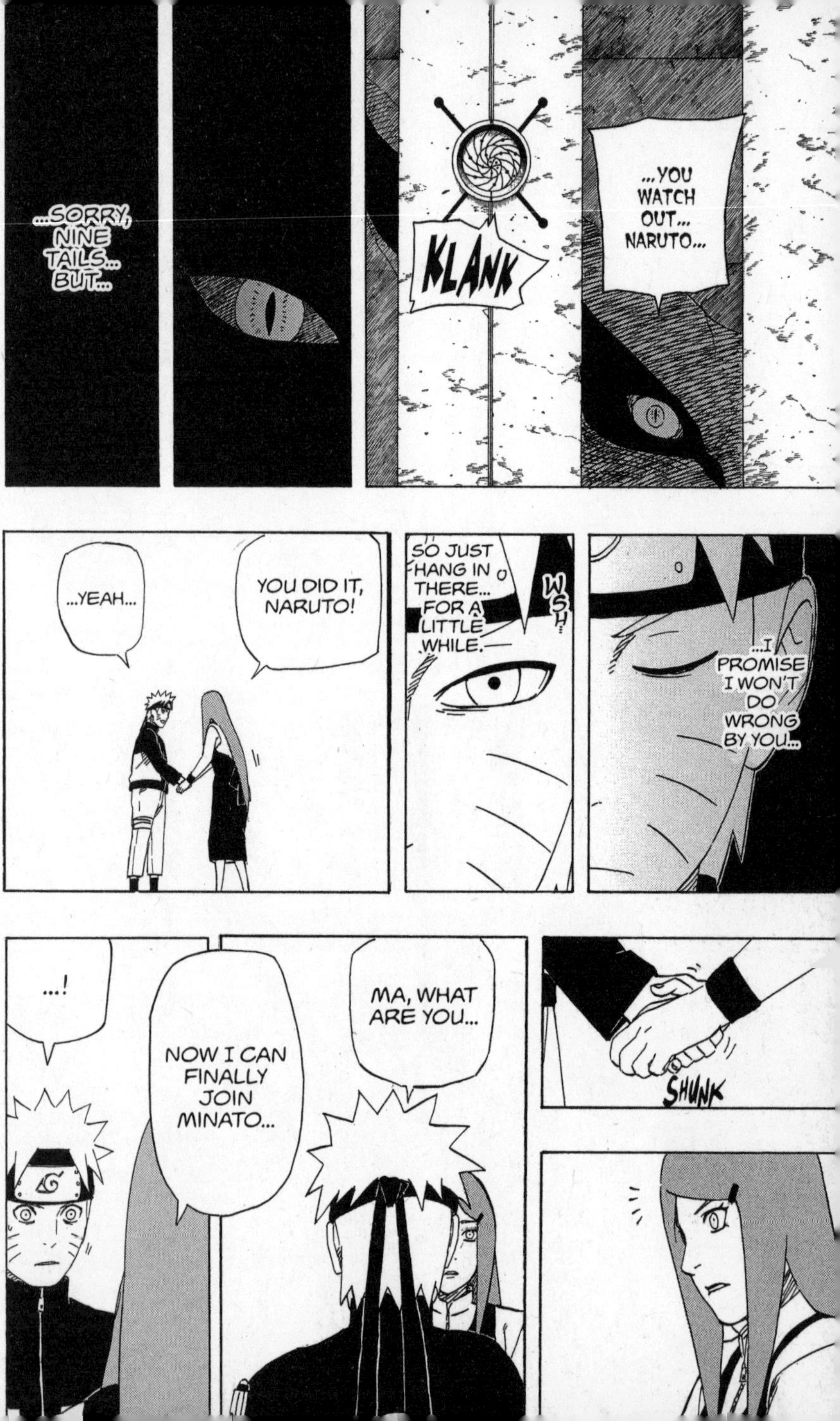
...YOU WATCH OUT... NARUTO...
KLANK
...SORRY, NINE TAILS... BUT...
...I PROMISE I WON'T DO WRONG BY YOU...
SO JUST HANG IN THERE... FOR A LITTLE WHILE.
WSH...
YOU DID IT, NARUTO!
...YEAH...
SHUNK
MA, WHAT ARE YOU...
NOW I CAN FINALLY JOIN MINATO...
...!

READ THIS WAY

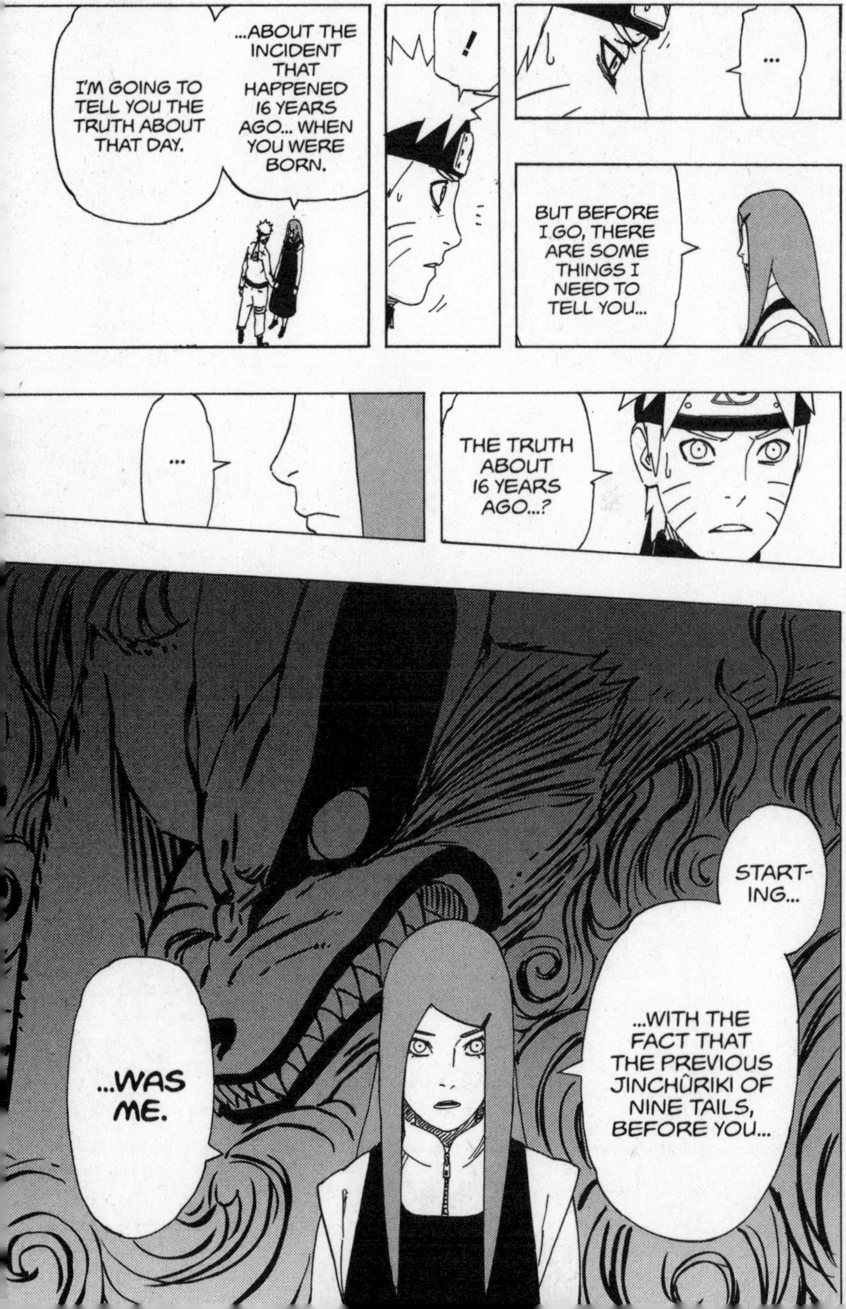
...
BUT BEFORE I GO, THERE ARE SOME THINGS I NEED TO TELL YOU...
!
I'M GOING TO TELL YOU THE TRUTH ABOUT THAT DAY.
...ABOUT THE INCIDENT THAT HAPPENED 16 YEARS AGO... WHEN YOU WERE BORN.
THE TRUTH ABOUT 16 YEARS AGO...?
...
START-ING...
...WITH THE FACT THAT THE PREVIOUS JINCHÛRIKI OF NINE TAILS, BEFORE YOU...
...WAS ME.

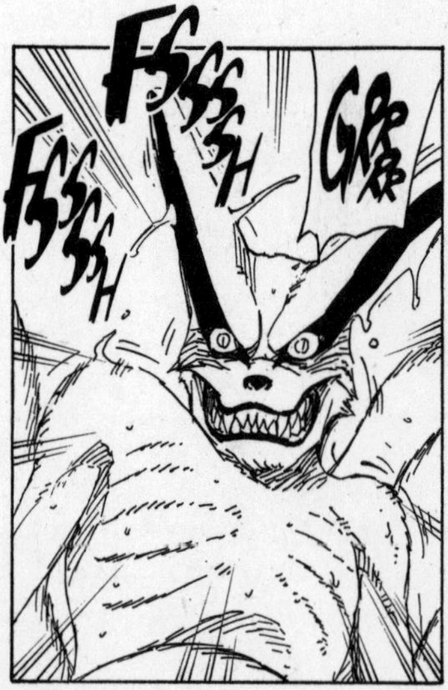
GRRR
FSSSSH
FSSSSH.

Number 500: The Birth of Naruto

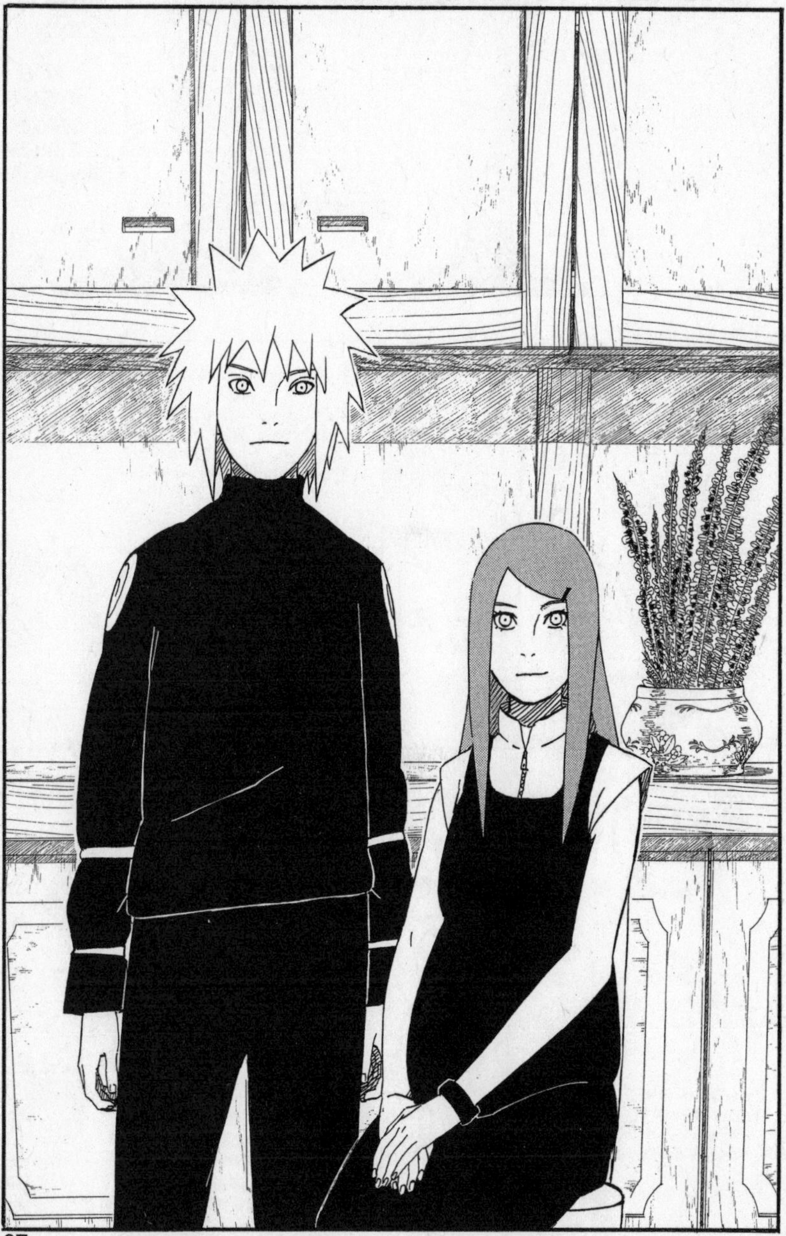

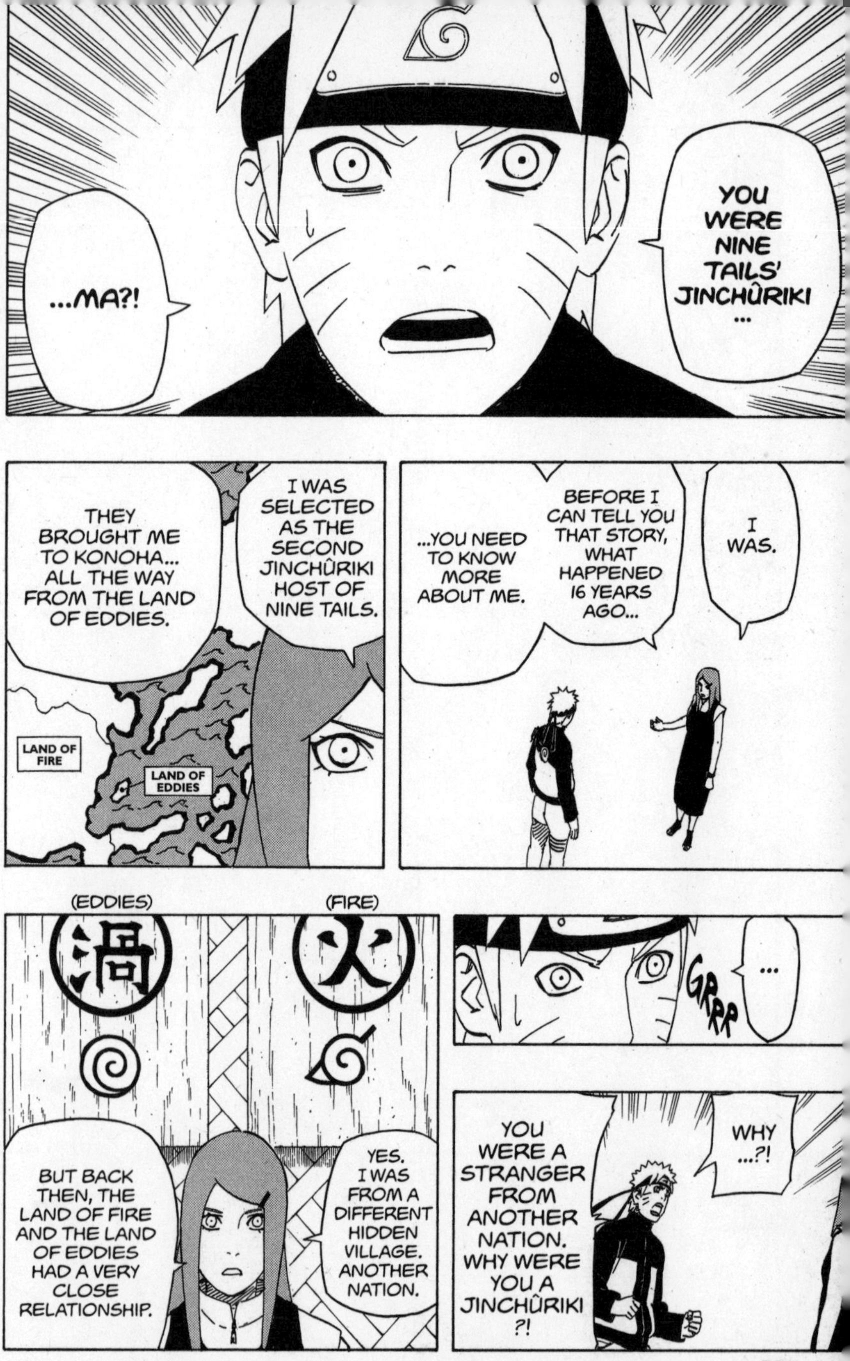
YOU WERE NINE TAILS' JINCHÛRIKI ...
...MA?!
I WAS.
BEFORE I CAN TELL YOU THAT STORY, WHAT HAPPENED 16 YEARS AGO...
...YOU NEED TO KNOW MORE ABOUT ME.
I WAS SELECTED AS THE SECOND JINCHÛRIKI HOST OF NINE TAILS.
THEY BROUGHT ME TO KONOHA... ALL THE WAY FROM THE LAND OF EDDIES.
LAND OF FIRE
LAND OF EDDIES
...
GRRR
WHY ...?!
YOU WERE A STRANGER FROM ANOTHER NATION. WHY WERE YOU A JINCHÛRIKI ?!
(FIRE)
火
(EDDIES)
渦
YES. I WAS FROM A DIFFERENT HIDDEN VILLAGE. ANOTHER NATION.
BUT BACK THEN, THE LAND OF FIRE AND THE LAND OF EDDIES HAD A VERY CLOSE RELATIONSHIP.

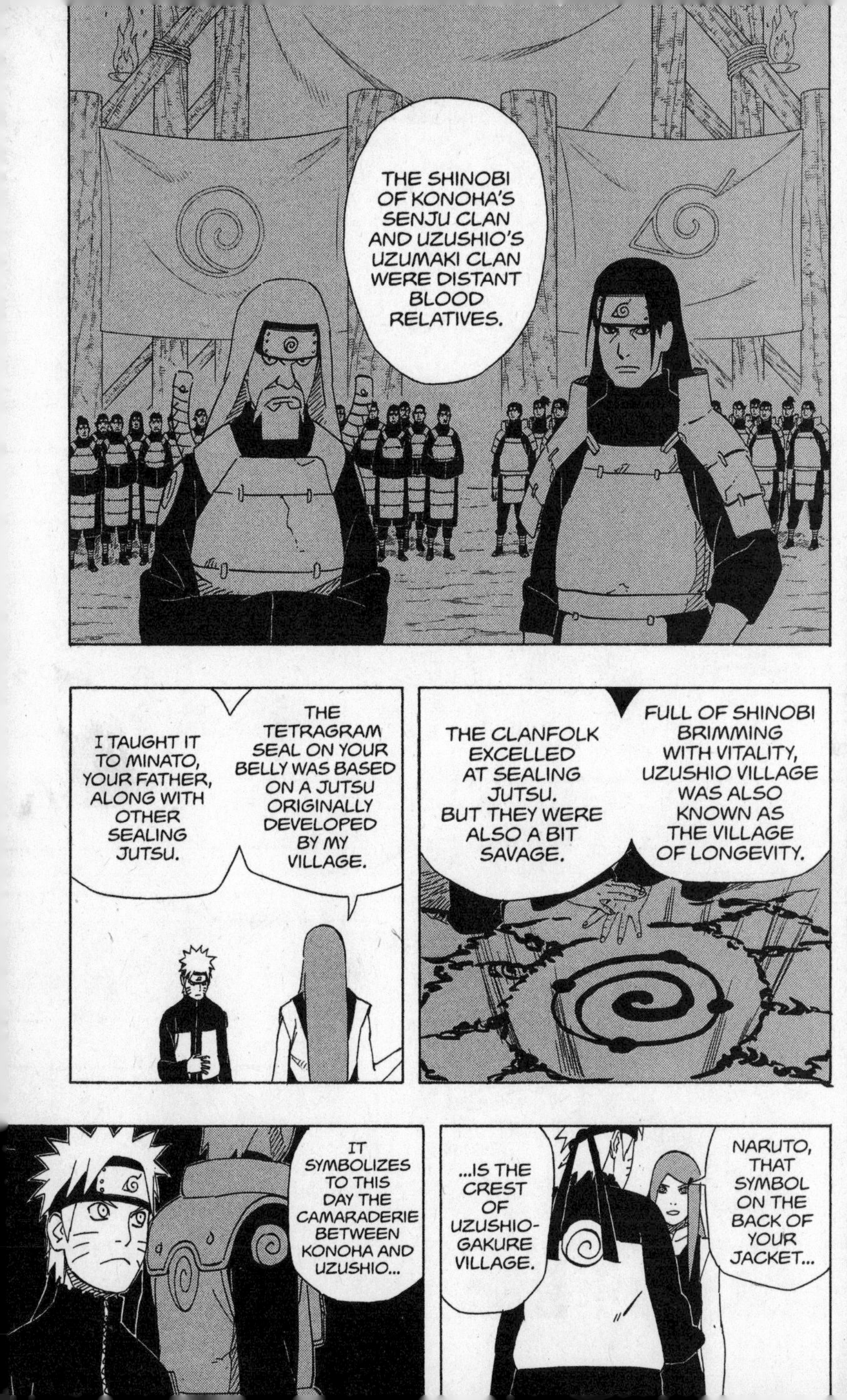
THE SHINOBI OF KONOHA'S SENJU CLAN AND UZUSHIO'S UZUMAKI CLAN WERE DISTANT BLOOD RELATIVES.
FULL OF SHINOBI BRIMMING WITH VITALITY, UZUSHIO VILLAGE WAS ALSO KNOWN AS THE VILLAGE OF LONGEVITY.
THE CLANFOLK EXCELLED AT SEALING JUTSU. BUT THEY WERE ALSO A BIT SAVAGE.
THE TETRAGRAM SEAL ON YOUR BELLY WAS BASED ON A JUTSU ORIGINALLY DEVELOPED BY MY VILLAGE.
I TAUGHT IT TO MINATO, YOUR FATHER, ALONG WITH OTHER SEALING JUTSU.
NARUTO, THAT SYMBOL ON THE BACK OF YOUR JACKET...
...IS THE CREST OF UZUSHIO-GAKURE VILLAGE.
IT SYMBOLIZES TO THIS DAY THE CAMARADERIE BETWEEN KONOHA AND UZUSHIO...

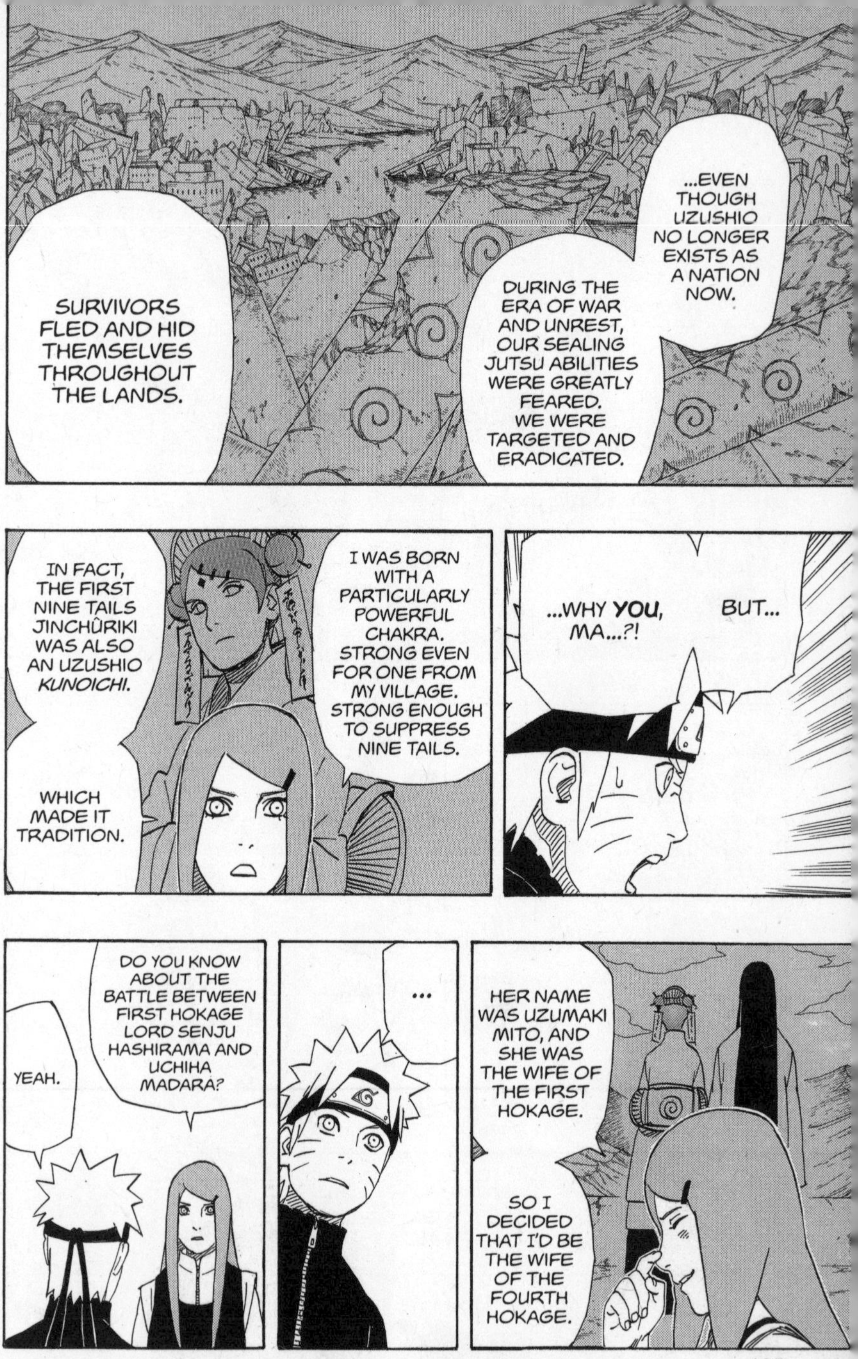
...EVEN THOUGH UZUSHIO NO LONGER EXISTS AS A NATION NOW.
DURING THE ERA OF WAR AND UNREST, OUR SEALING JUTSU ABILITIES WERE GREATLY FEARED. WE WERE TARGETED AND ERADICATED.
SURVIVORS FLED AND HID THEMSELVES THROUGHOUT THE LANDS.
BUT...
...WHY **YOU**, MA...?!
I WAS BORN WITH A PARTICULARLY POWERFUL CHAKRA. STRONG EVEN FOR ONE FROM MY VILLAGE. STRONG ENOUGH TO SUPPRESS NINE TAILS.
IN FACT, THE FIRST NINE TAILS JINCHÛRIKI WAS ALSO AN UZUSHIO *KUNOICHI*.
WHICH MADE IT TRADITION.
HER NAME WAS UZUMAKI MITO, AND SHE WAS THE WIFE OF THE FIRST HOKAGE.
SO I DECIDED THAT I'D BE THE WIFE OF THE FOURTH HOKAGE.
...
DO YOU KNOW ABOUT THE BATTLE BETWEEN FIRST HOKAGE LORD SENJU HASHIRAMA AND UCHIHA MADARA?
YEAH.

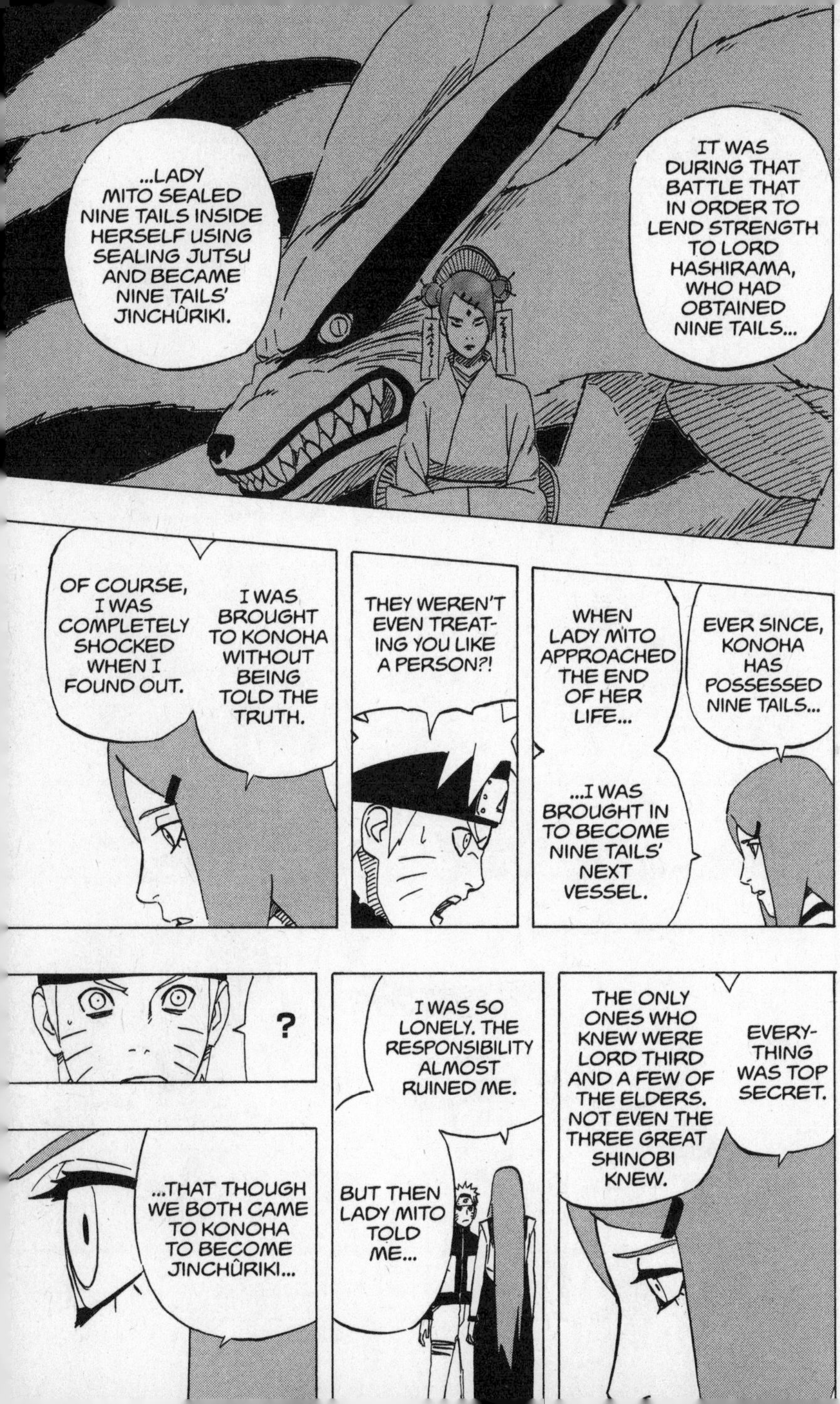
IT WAS DURING THAT BATTLE THAT IN ORDER TO LEND STRENGTH TO LORD HASHIRAMA, WHO HAD OBTAINED NINE TAILS...
...LADY MITO SEALED NINE TAILS INSIDE HERSELF USING SEALING JUTSU AND BECAME NINE TAILS' JINCHÛRIKI.
EVER SINCE, KONOHA HAS POSSESSED NINE TAILS...
WHEN LADY MITO APPROACHED THE END OF HER LIFE...
...I WAS BROUGHT IN TO BECOME NINE TAILS' NEXT VESSEL.
THEY WEREN'T EVEN TREAT-ING YOU LIKE A PERSON?!
I WAS BROUGHT TO KONOHA WITHOUT BEING TOLD THE TRUTH.
OF COURSE, I WAS COMPLETELY SHOCKED WHEN I FOUND OUT.
EVERY-THING WAS TOP SECRET.
THE ONLY ONES WHO KNEW WERE LORD THIRD AND A FEW OF THE ELDERS. NOT EVEN THE THREE GREAT SHINOBI KNEW.
I WAS SO LONELY. THE RESPONSIBILITY ALMOST RUINED ME.
BUT THEN LADY MITO TOLD ME...
?
...THAT THOUGH WE BOTH CAME TO KONOHA TO BECOME JINCHÛRIKI...

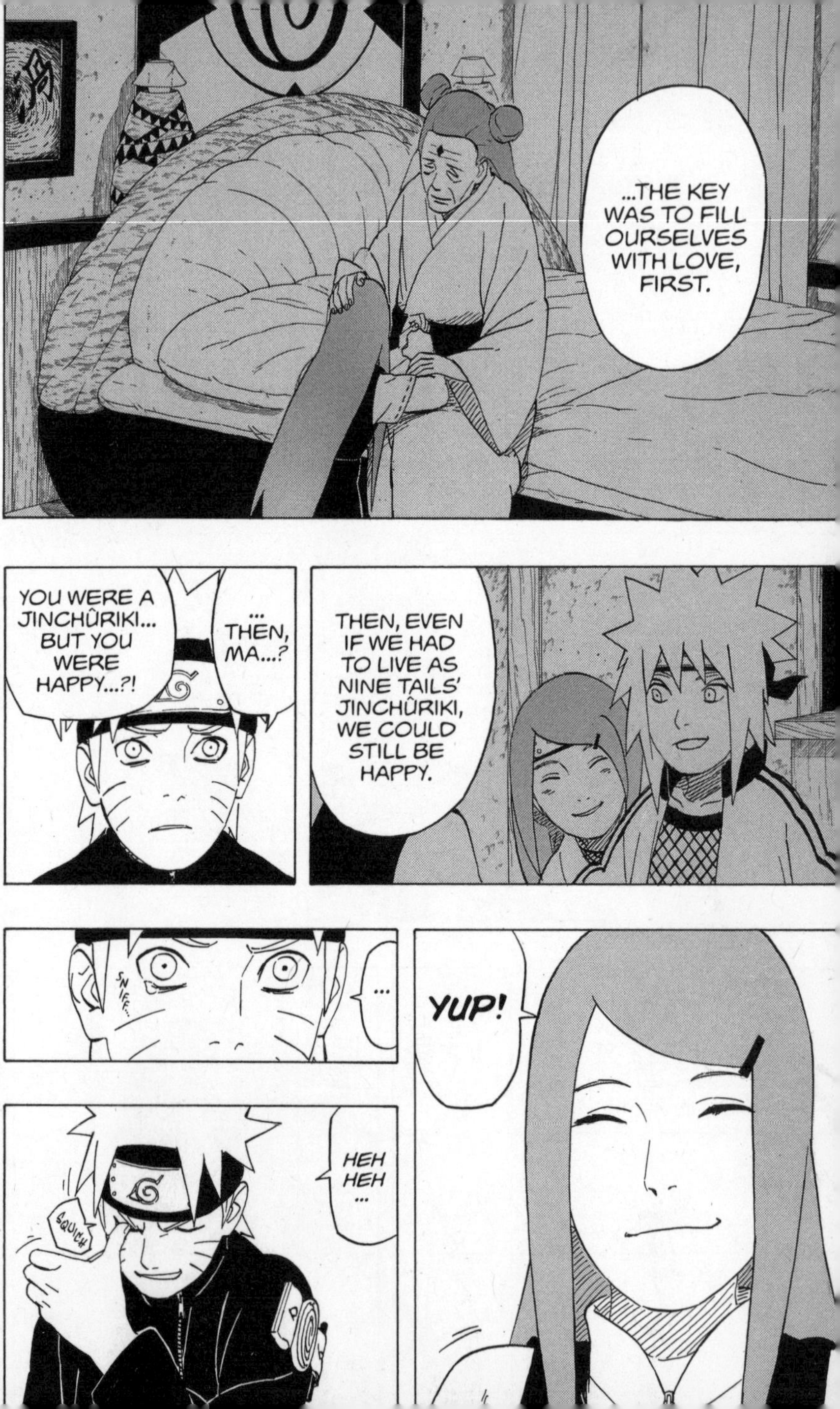
...THE KEY WAS TO FILL OURSELVES WITH LOVE, FIRST.
THEN, EVEN IF WE HAD TO LIVE AS NINE TAILS' JINCHÛRIKI, WE COULD STILL BE HAPPY.
... THEN, MA...?
YOU WERE A JINCHÛRIKI... BUT YOU WERE HAPPY...?!
YUP!
...
SNIFF...
HEH HEH ...
SQUICH

READ THIS WAY

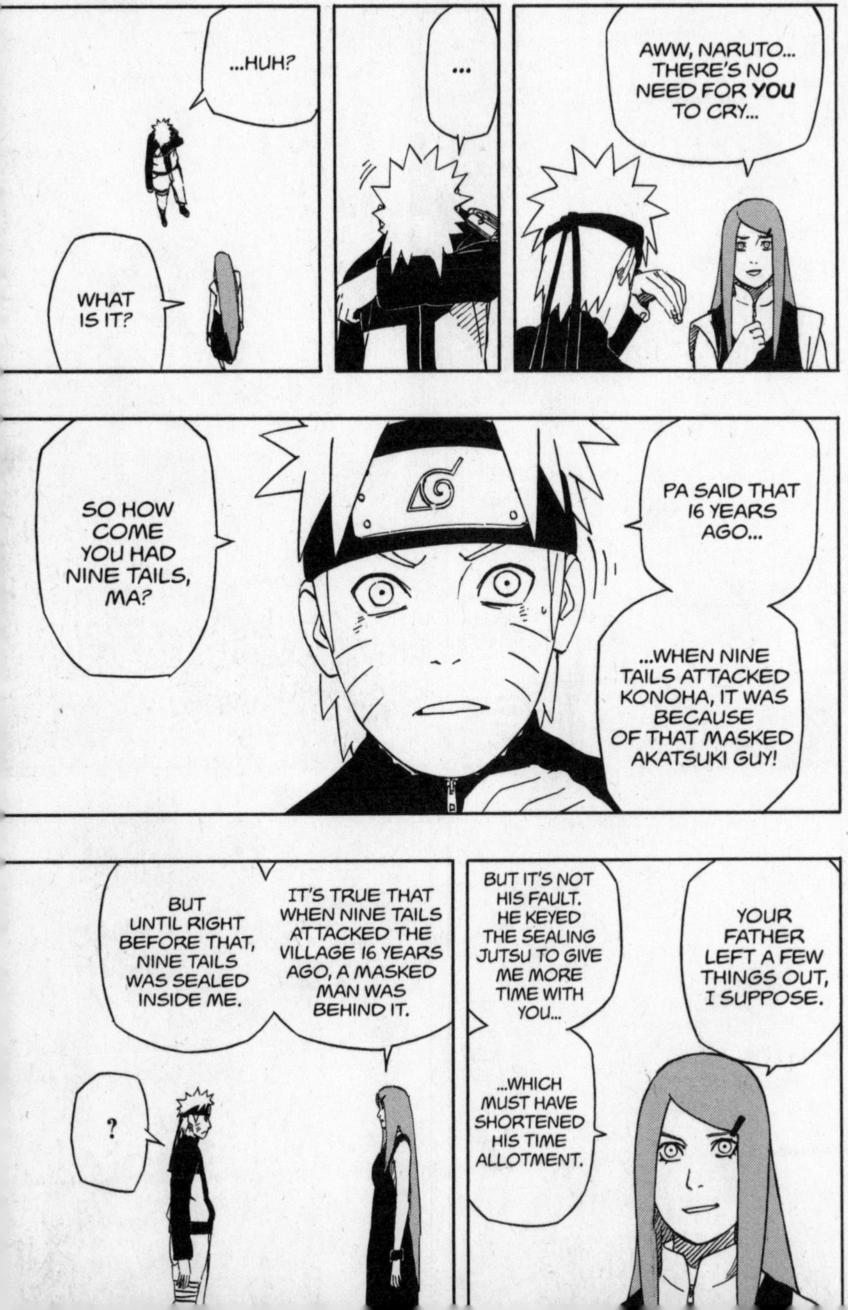
AWW, NARUTO... THERE'S NO NEED FOR **YOU** TO CRY...
...
...HUH?
WHAT IS IT?
PA SAID THAT 16 YEARS AGO...
...WHEN NINE TAILS ATTACKED KONOHA, IT WAS BECAUSE OF THAT MASKED AKATSUKI GUY!
SO HOW COME YOU HAD NINE TAILS, MA?
YOUR FATHER LEFT A FEW THINGS OUT, I SUPPOSE.
BUT IT'S NOT HIS FAULT. HE KEYED THE SEALING JUTSU TO GIVE ME MORE TIME WITH YOU...
...WHICH MUST HAVE SHORTENED HIS TIME ALLOTMENT.
IT'S TRUE THAT WHEN NINE TAILS ATTACKED THE VILLAGE 16 YEARS AGO, A MASKED MAN WAS BEHIND IT.
BUT UNTIL RIGHT BEFORE THAT, NINE TAILS WAS SEALED INSIDE ME.
?

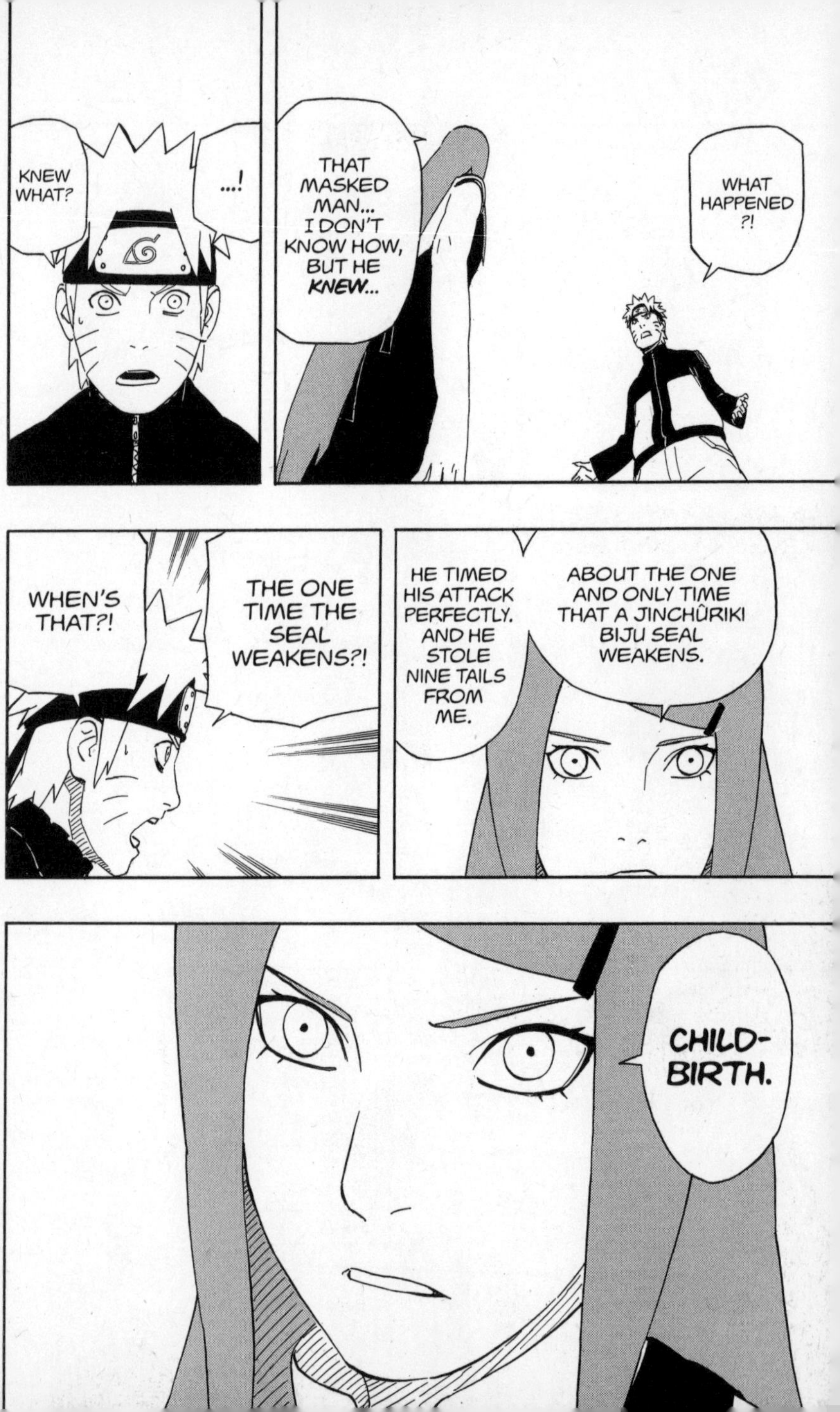
WHAT HAPPENED ?!
THAT MASKED MAN... I DON'T KNOW HOW, BUT HE *KNEW*...
...!
KNEW WHAT?
ABOUT THE ONE AND ONLY TIME THAT A JINCHÛRIKI BIJU SEAL WEAKENS.
HE TIMED HIS ATTACK PERFECTLY. AND HE STOLE NINE TAILS FROM ME.
THE ONE TIME THE SEAL WEAKENS?!
WHEN'S THAT?!
CHILD-BIRTH.

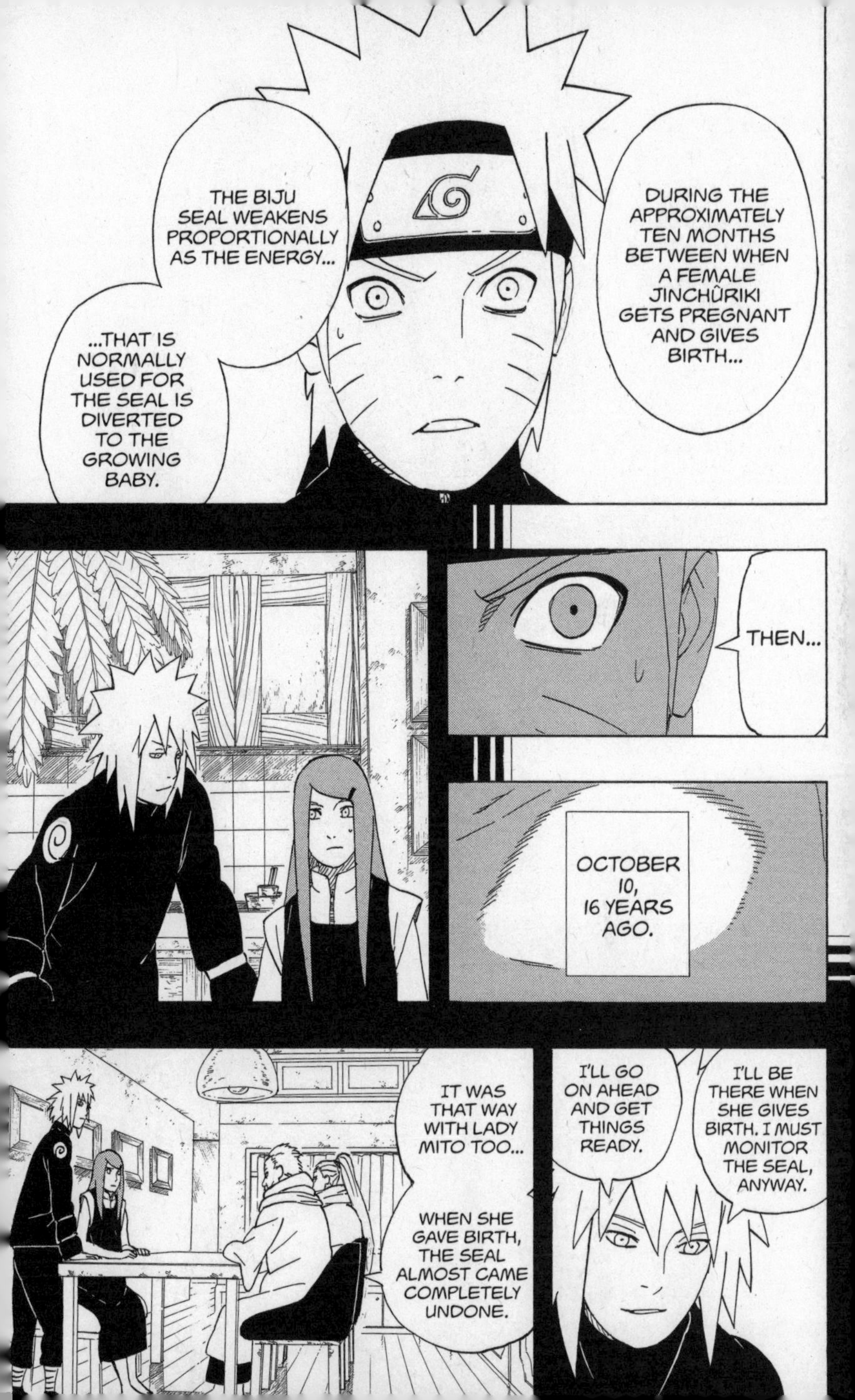
DURING THE APPROXIMATELY TEN MONTHS BETWEEN WHEN A FEMALE JINCHÛRIKI GETS PREGNANT AND GIVES BIRTH...
THE BIJU SEAL WEAKENS PROPORTIONALLY AS THE ENERGY...
...THAT IS NORMALLY USED FOR THE SEAL IS DIVERTED TO THE GROWING BABY.
THEN...
OCTOBER 10, 16 YEARS AGO.
I'LL BE THERE WHEN SHE GIVES BIRTH. I MUST MONITOR THE SEAL, ANYWAY.
I'LL GO ON AHEAD AND GET THINGS READY.
IT WAS THAT WAY WITH LADY MITO TOO...
WHEN SHE GAVE BIRTH, THE SEAL ALMOST CAME COMPLETELY UNDONE.

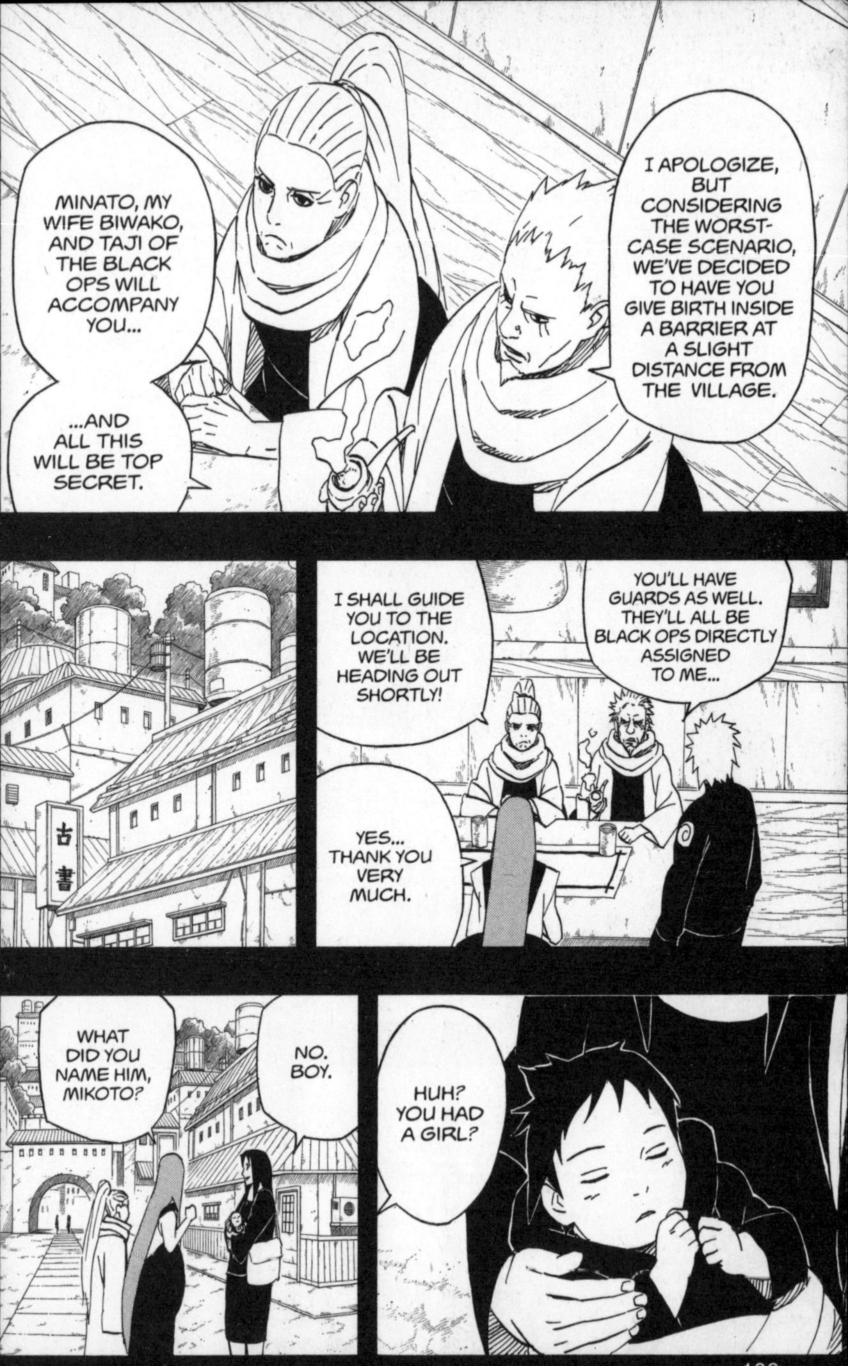
I APOLOGIZE, BUT CONSIDERING THE WORST-CASE SCENARIO, WE'VE DECIDED TO HAVE YOU GIVE BIRTH INSIDE A BARRIER AT A SLIGHT DISTANCE FROM THE VILLAGE.
MINATO, MY WIFE BIWAKO, AND TAJI OF THE BLACK OPS WILL ACCOMPANY YOU...
...AND ALL THIS WILL BE TOP SECRET.
YOU'LL HAVE GUARDS AS WELL. THEY'LL ALL BE BLACK OPS DIRECTLY ASSIGNED TO ME...
I SHALL GUIDE YOU TO THE LOCATION. WE'LL BE HEADING OUT SHORTLY!
YES... THANK YOU VERY MUCH.
古書
HUH? YOU HAD A GIRL?
NO. BOY.
WHAT DID YOU NAME HIM, MIKOTO?

READ THIS WAY

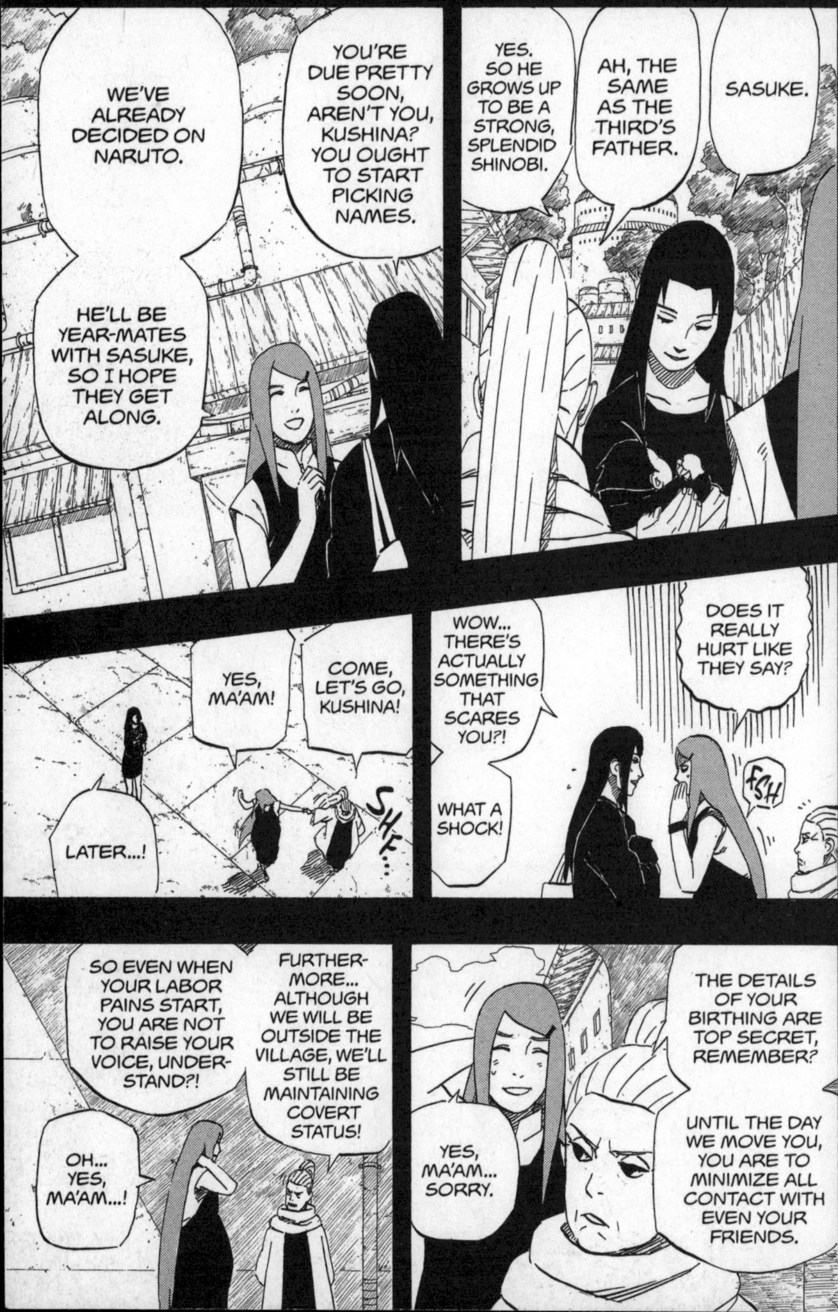
SASUKE.
AH, THE SAME AS THE THIRD'S FATHER.
YES. SO HE GROWS UP TO BE A STRONG, SPLENDID SHINOBI.
YOU'RE DUE PRETTY SOON, AREN'T YOU, KUSHINA? YOU OUGHT TO START PICKING NAMES.
WE'VE ALREADY DECIDED ON NARUTO.
HE'LL BE YEAR-MATES WITH SASUKE, SO I HOPE THEY GET ALONG.
DOES IT REALLY HURT LIKE THEY SAY?
FSH
WOW... THERE'S ACTUALLY SOMETHING THAT SCARES YOU?!
WHAT A SHOCK!
COME, LET'S GO, KUSHINA!
SHF...
YES, MA'AM!
LATER...!
THE DETAILS OF YOUR BIRTHING ARE TOP SECRET, REMEMBER?
UNTIL THE DAY WE MOVE YOU, YOU ARE TO MINIMIZE ALL CONTACT WITH EVEN YOUR FRIENDS.
YES, MA'AM... SORRY.
FURTHER-MORE... ALTHOUGH WE WILL BE OUTSIDE THE VILLAGE, WE'LL STILL BE MAINTAINING COVERT STATUS!
SO EVEN WHEN YOUR LABOR PAINS START, YOU ARE NOT TO RAISE YOUR VOICE, UNDER-STAND?!
OH... YES, MA'AM...!

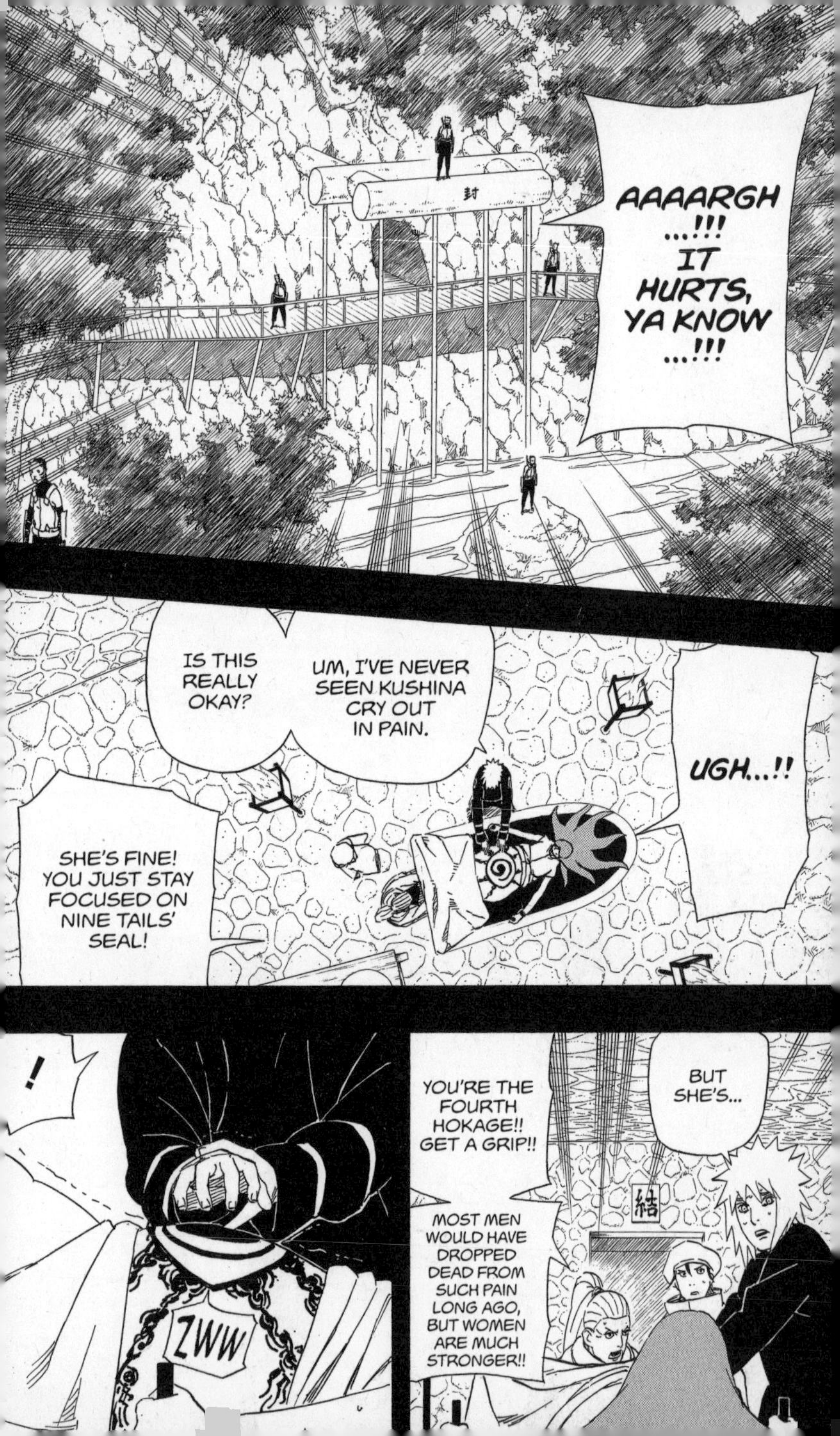
AAAARGH ...!!! IT HURTS, YA KNOW ...!!!
封
UGH...!!
UM, I'VE NEVER SEEN KUSHINA CRY OUT IN PAIN.
IS THIS REALLY OKAY?
SHE'S FINE! YOU JUST STAY FOCUSED ON NINE TAILS' SEAL!
BUT SHE'S...
YOU'RE THE FOURTH HOKAGE!! GET A GRIP!!
MOST MEN WOULD HAVE DROPPED DEAD FROM SUCH PAIN LONG AGO, BUT WOMEN ARE MUCH STRONGER!!
結
!
ZWW

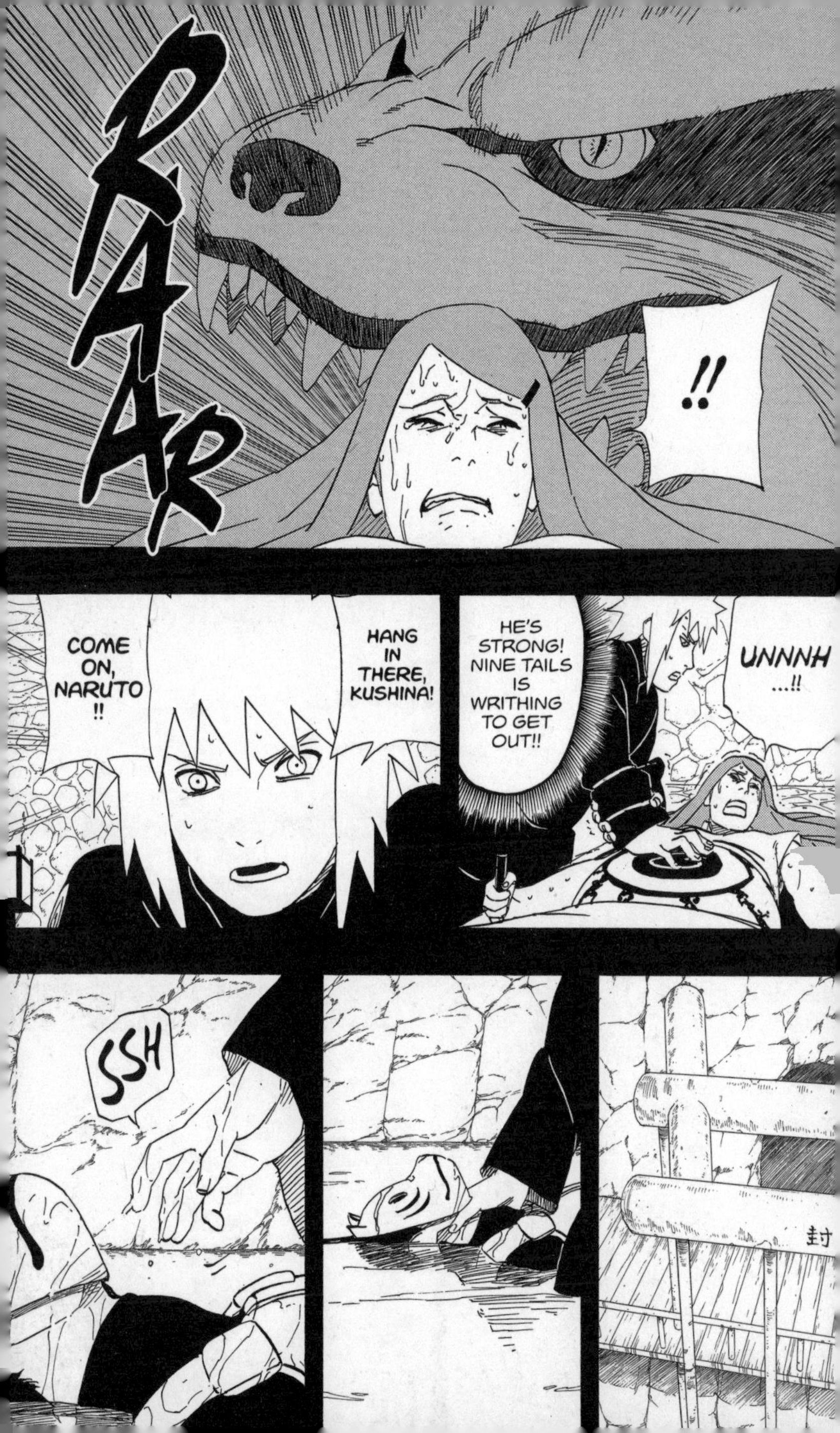
!!
RAAR
UNNNH...!!
HE'S STRONG! NINE TAILS IS WRITHING TO GET OUT!!
HANG IN THERE, KUSHINA!
COME ON, NARUTO!!
封
SSH

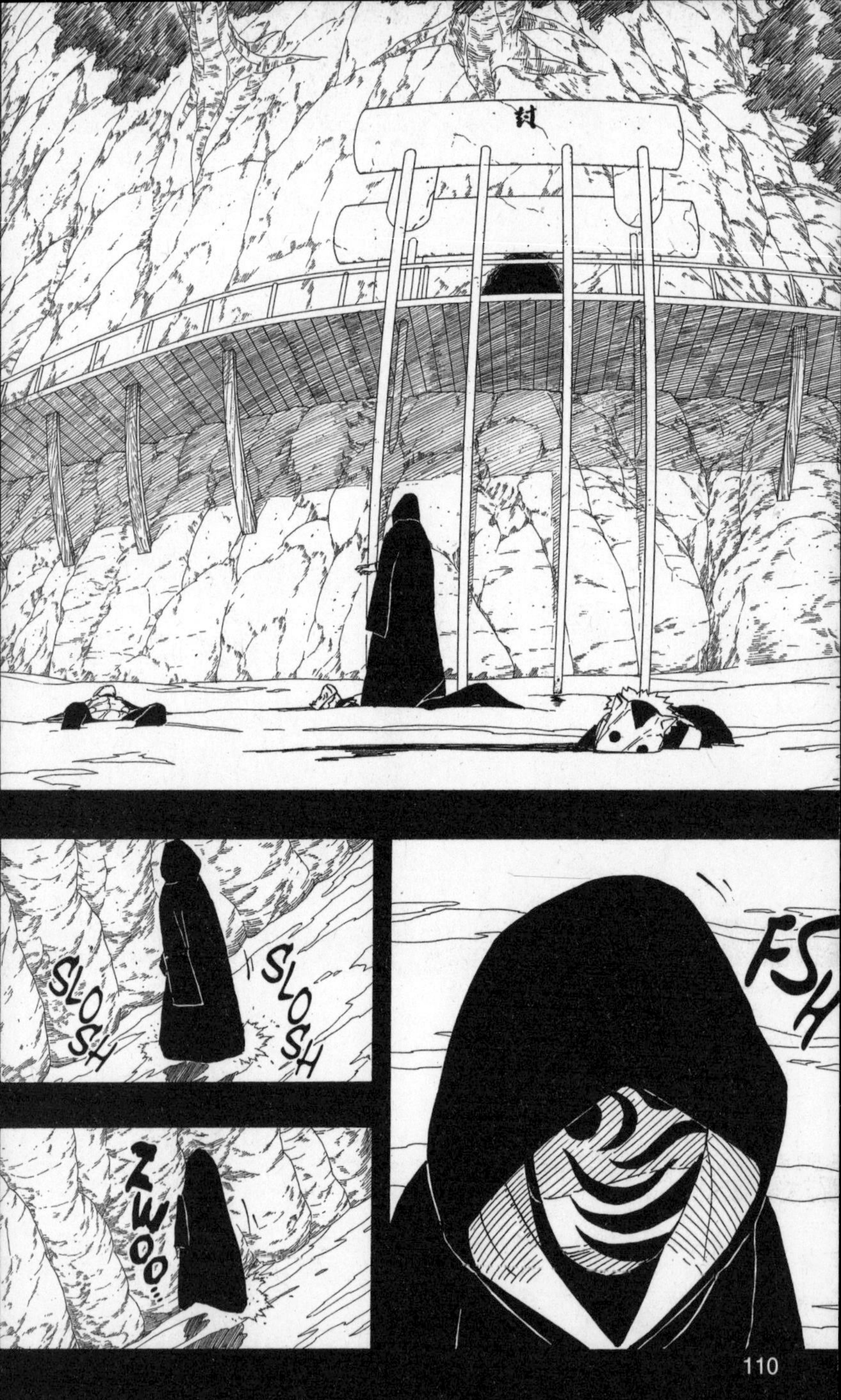
封
FSH
SLOSH
SLOSH
ZWOO...

READ THIS WAY

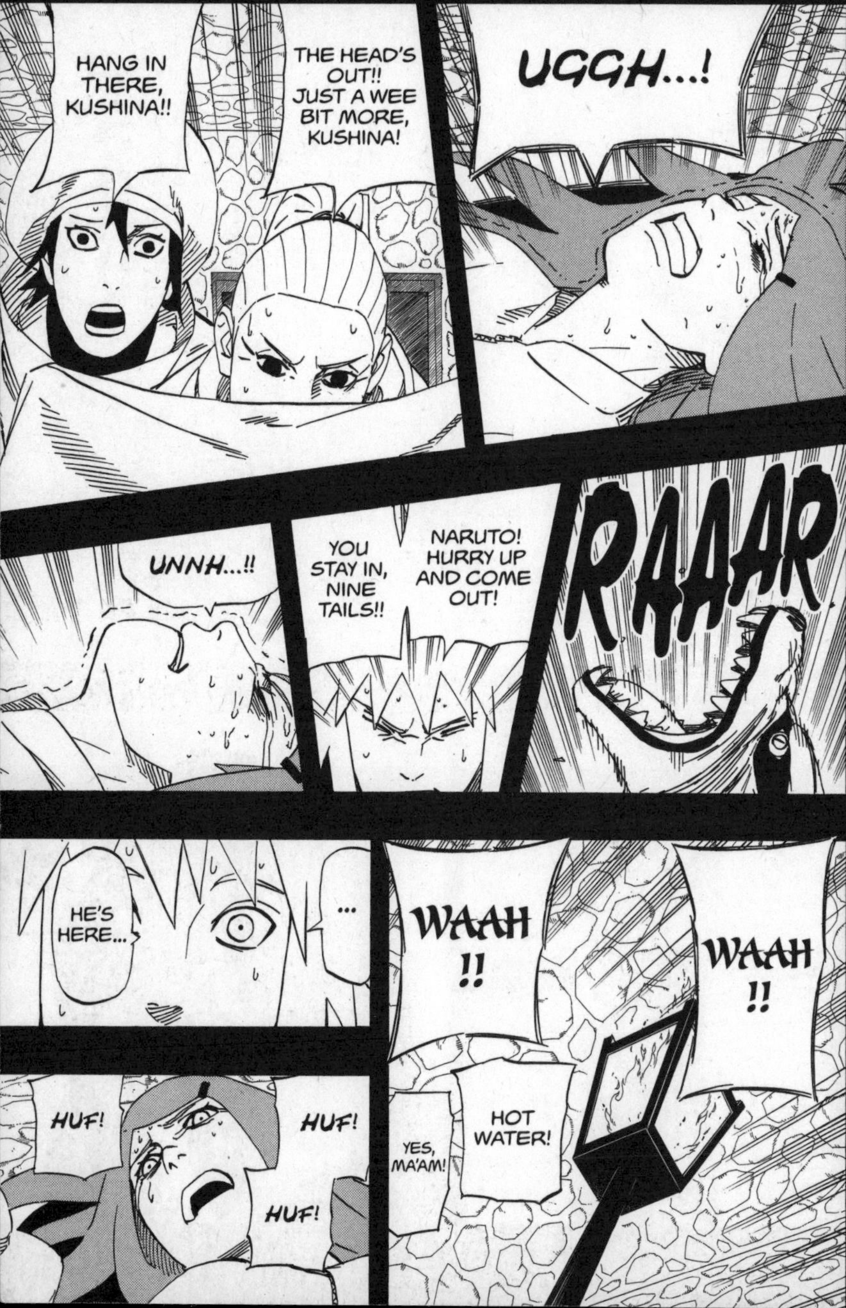
UGGH...!
THE HEAD'S OUT!! JUST A WEE BIT MORE, KUSHINA!
HANG IN THERE, KUSHINA!!
RAAAR
NARUTO! HURRY UP AND COME OUT!
YOU STAY IN, NINE TAILS!!
UNNH...!!
WAAH!!
WAAH!!
HOT WATER!
YES, MA'AM!
...
HE'S HERE...
HUF!
HUF!
HUF!

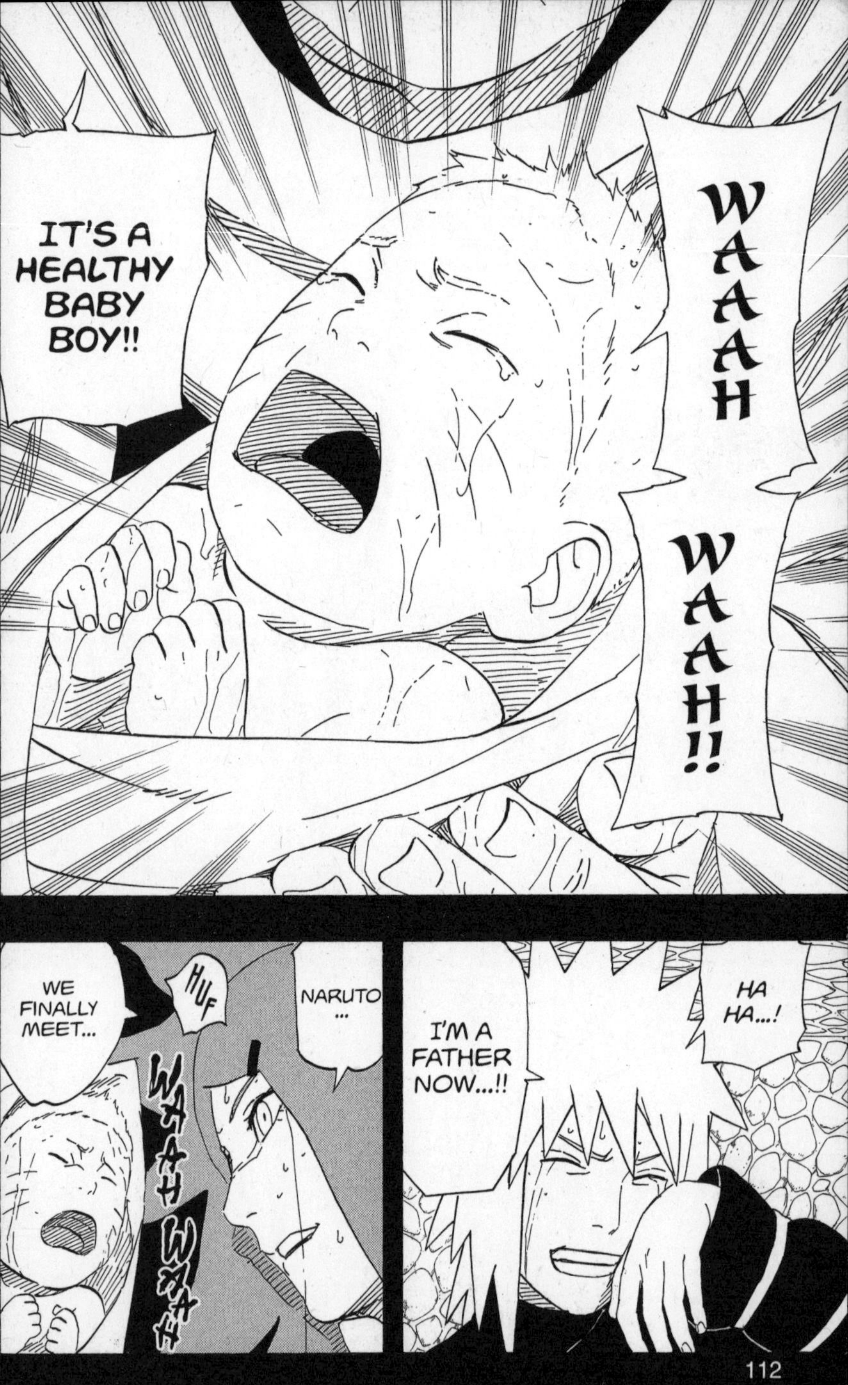
WAAAH WAAAH!!
IT'S A HEALTHY BABY BOY!!
HA HA...!
I'M A FATHER NOW...!!
NARUTO...
HUF
WE FINALLY MEET...
WAAH WAAH

READ THIS WAY

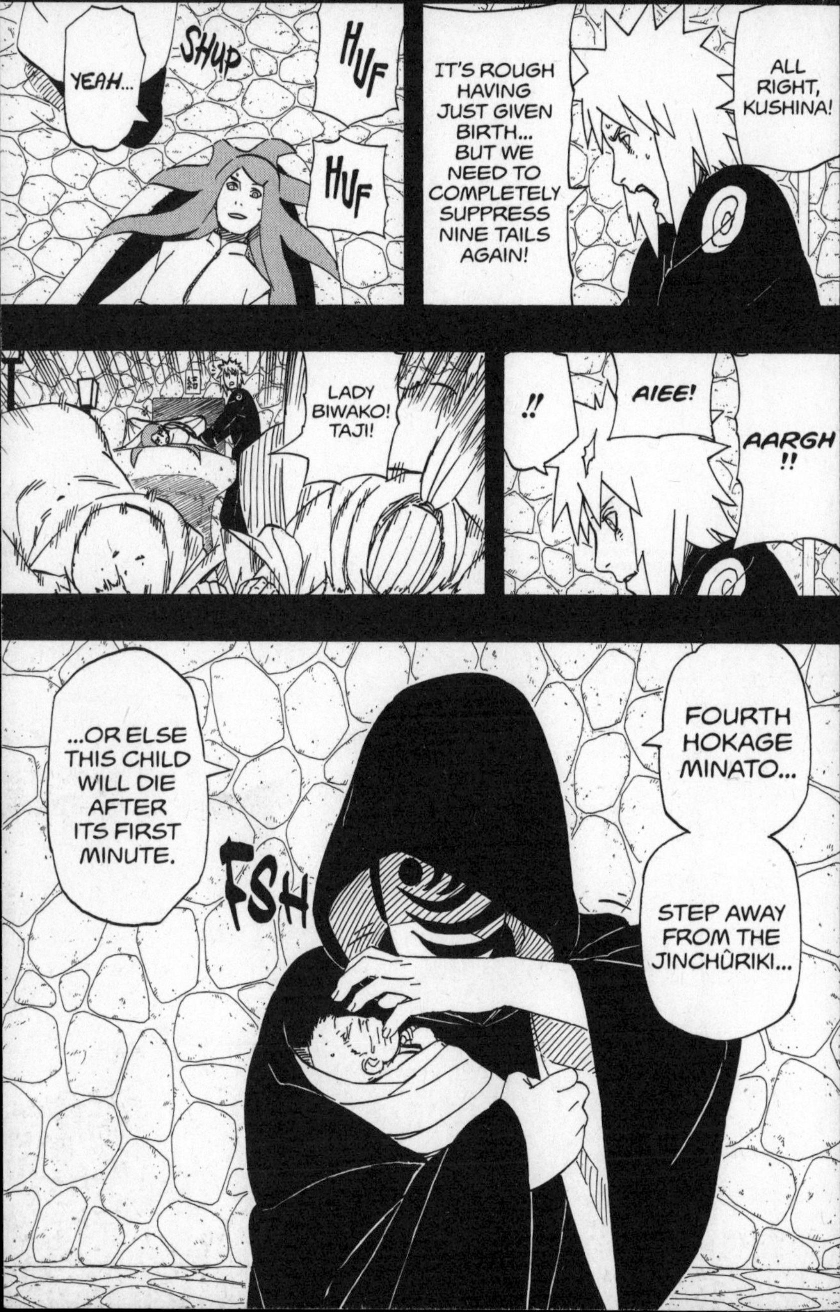
ALL RIGHT, KUSHINA!
IT'S ROUGH HAVING JUST GIVEN BIRTH... BUT WE NEED TO COMPLETELY SUPPRESS NINE TAILS AGAIN!
HUF
HUF
SHUP
YEAH...
AIEE!
AARGH !!
!!
LADY BIWAKO! TAJI!
FOURTH HOKAGE MINATO...
STEP AWAY FROM THE JINCHÛRIKI...
FSH
...OR ELSE THIS CHILD WILL DIE AFTER ITS FIRST MINUTE.

NARUTO

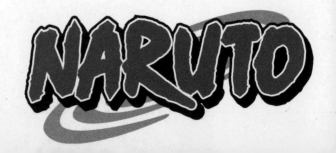

Number 501: Nine Tails Attacks!!

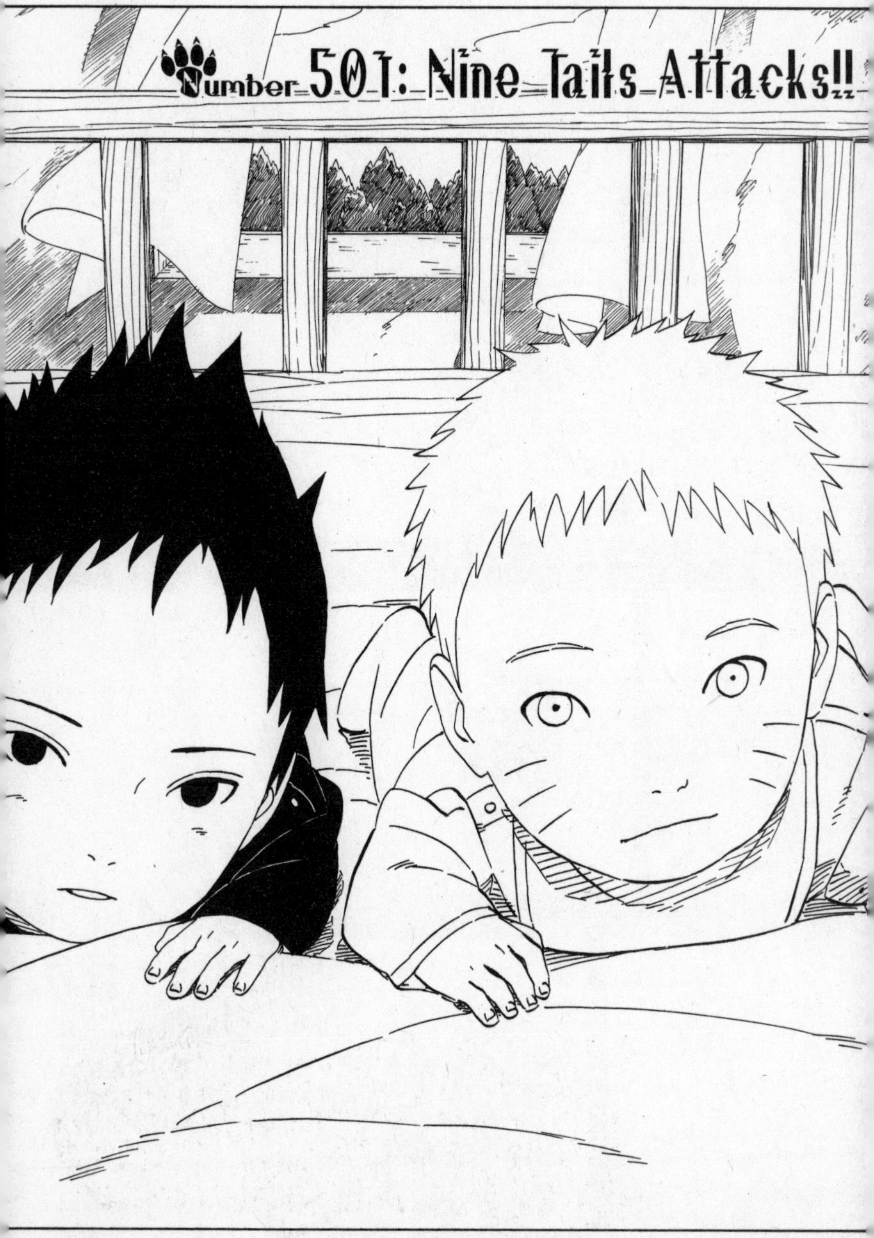

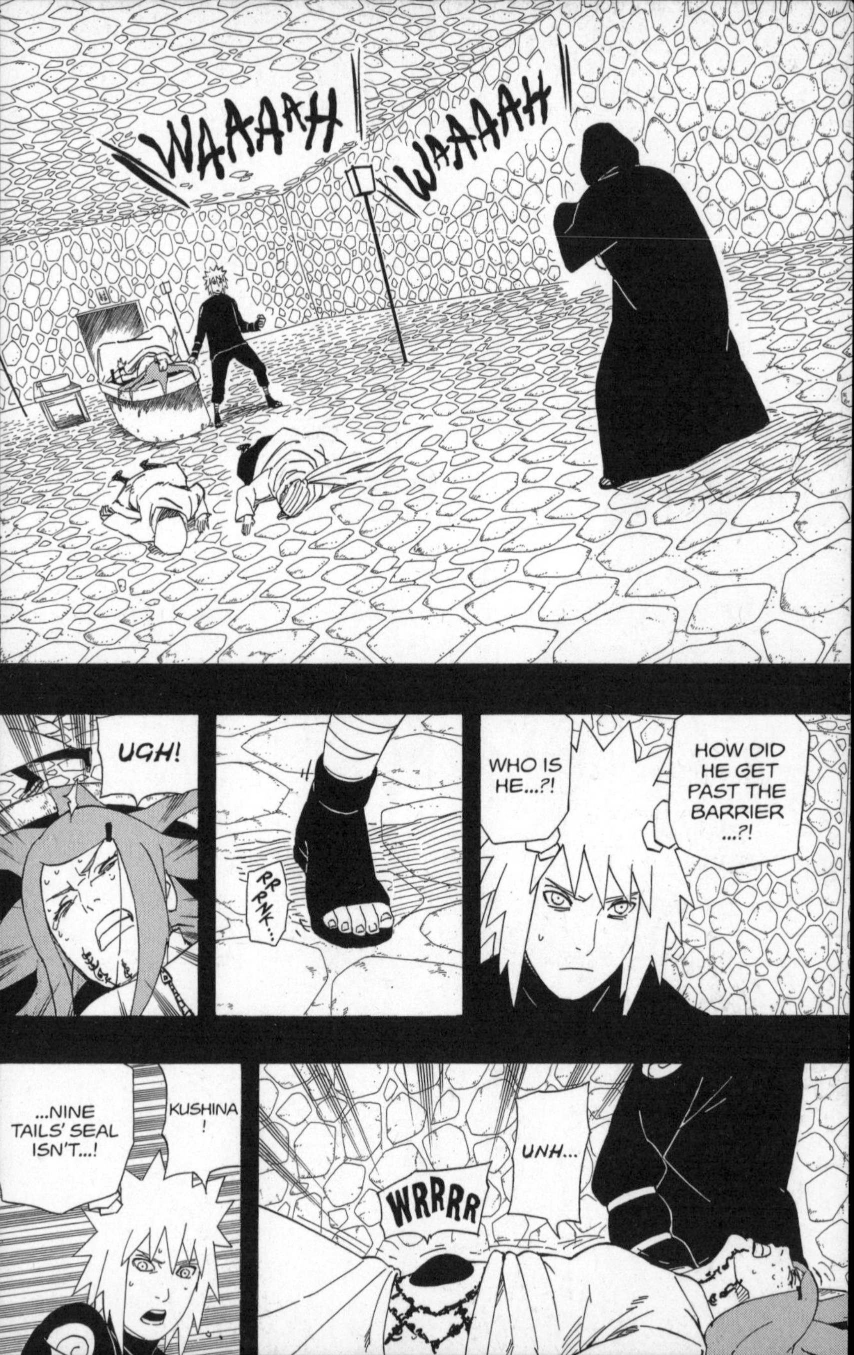
WAAAAH
WAAAAH
HOW DID HE GET PAST THE BARRIER ...?!
WHO IS HE...?!
RRRNK...
UGH!
UNH...
WRRRR
KUSHINA!
...NINE TAILS' SEAL ISN'T...!

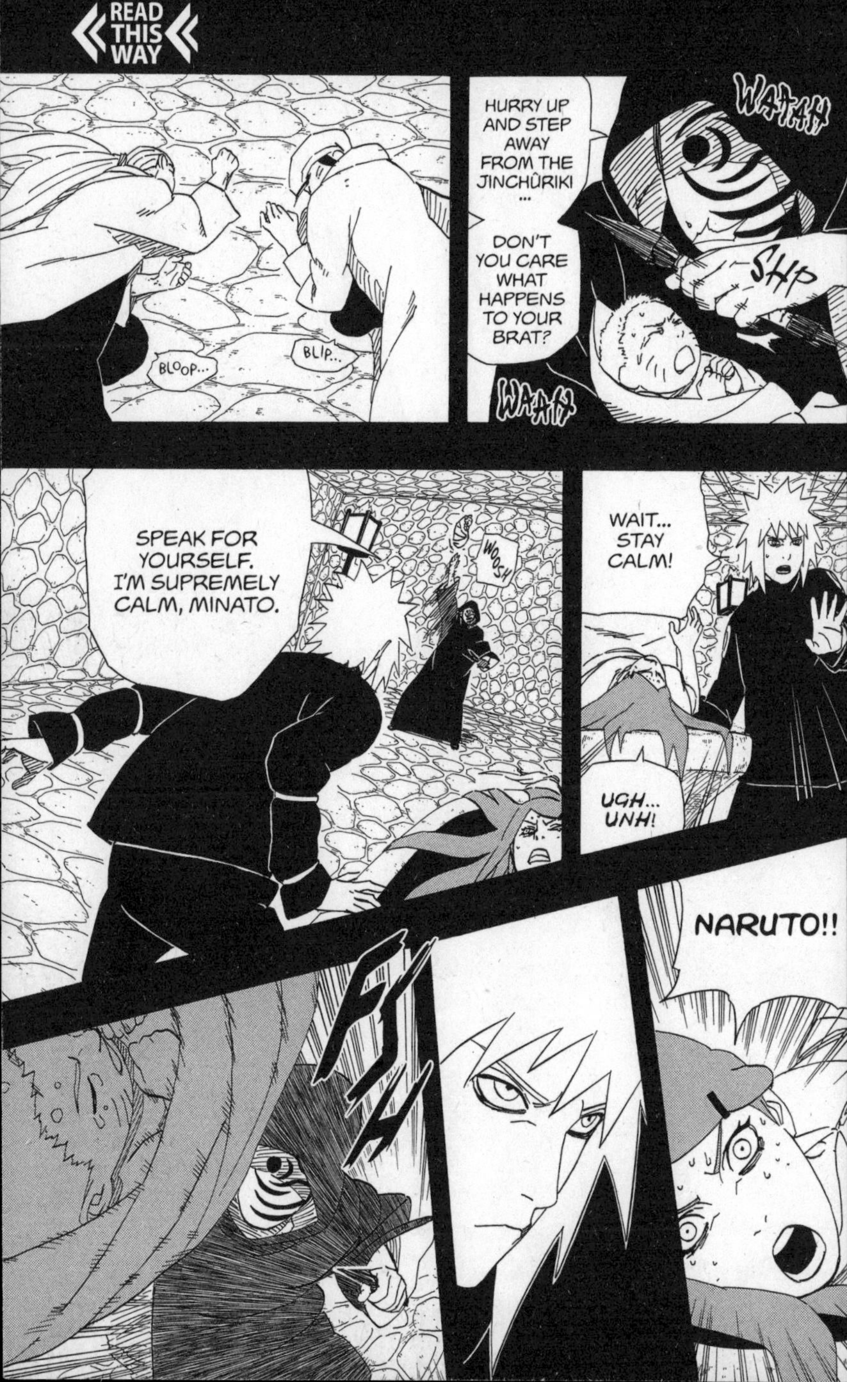
READ THIS WAY
WATAH
HURRY UP AND STEP AWAY FROM THE JINCHÛRIKI ...
DON'T YOU CARE WHAT HAPPENS TO YOUR BRAT?
SHP
WAAH
BLIP...
BLOOP...
WAIT... STAY CALM!
UGH... UNH!
SPEAK FOR YOURSELF. I'M SUPREMELY CALM, MINATO.
WOOSH
NARUTO!!

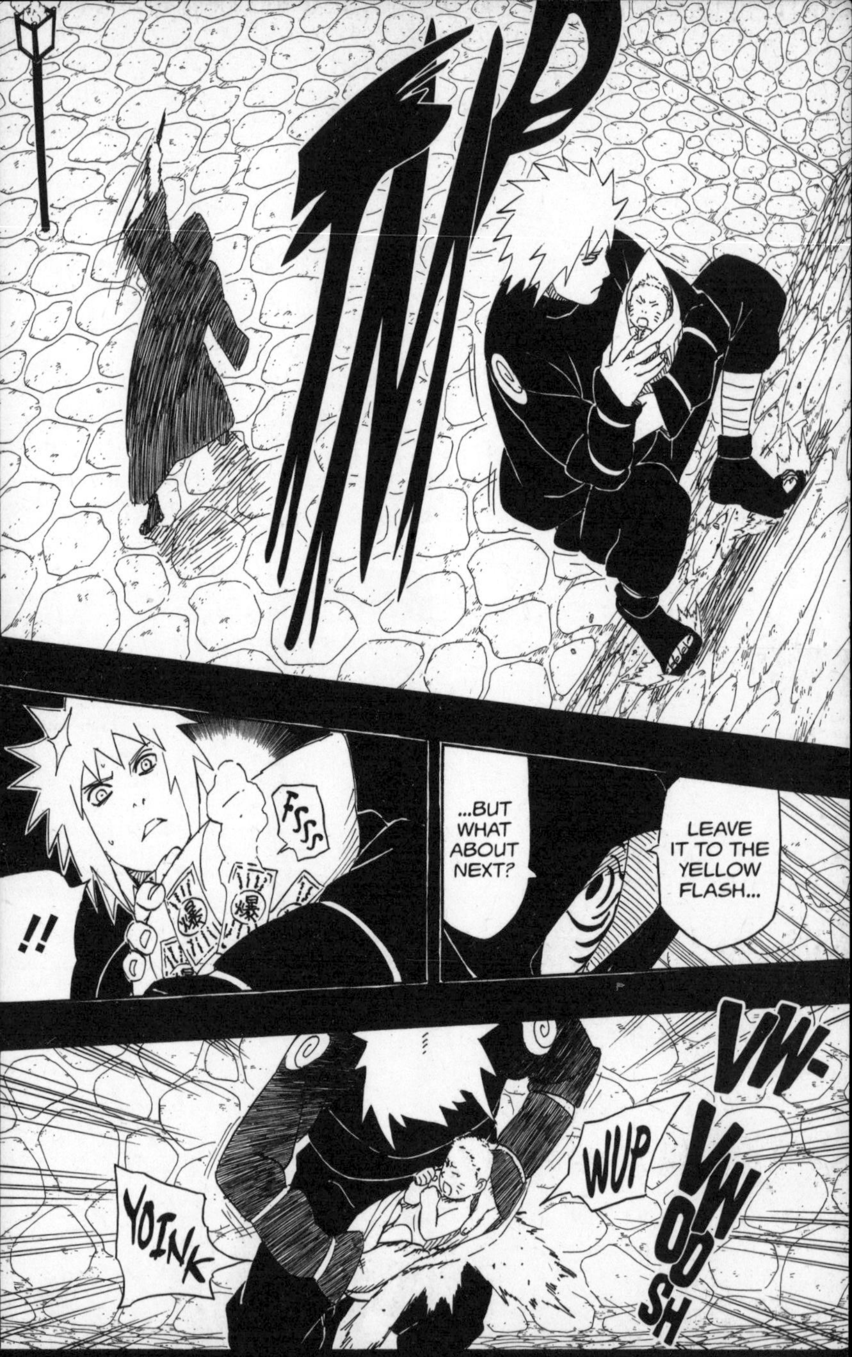
LEAVE IT TO THE YELLOW FLASH...
...BUT WHAT ABOUT NEXT?
FSSS
!!
VW-VWOOSH
WUP
YOINK

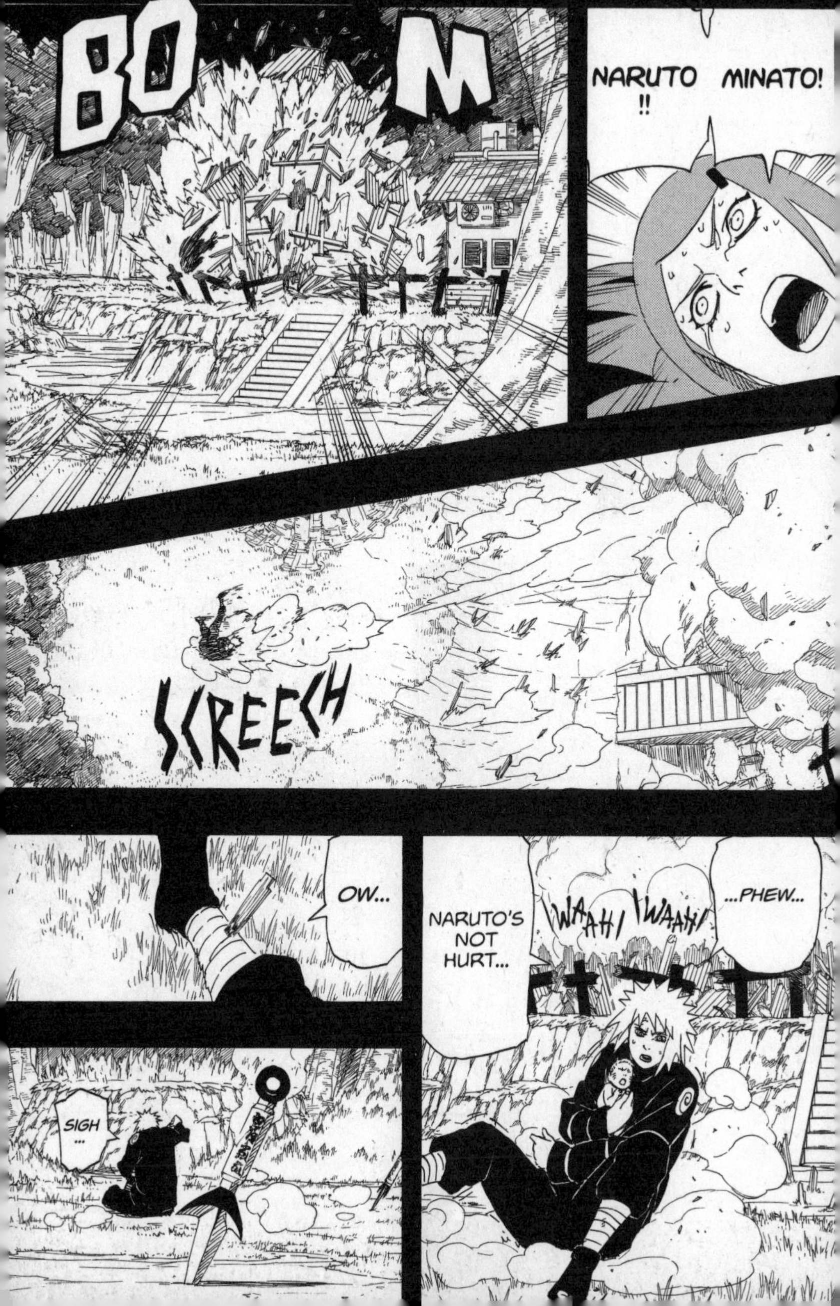
MINATO!
NARUTO!!
BOOM
SCREECH
...PHEW...
WAAH! WAAH!
NARUTO'S NOT HURT...
OW...
SIGH...

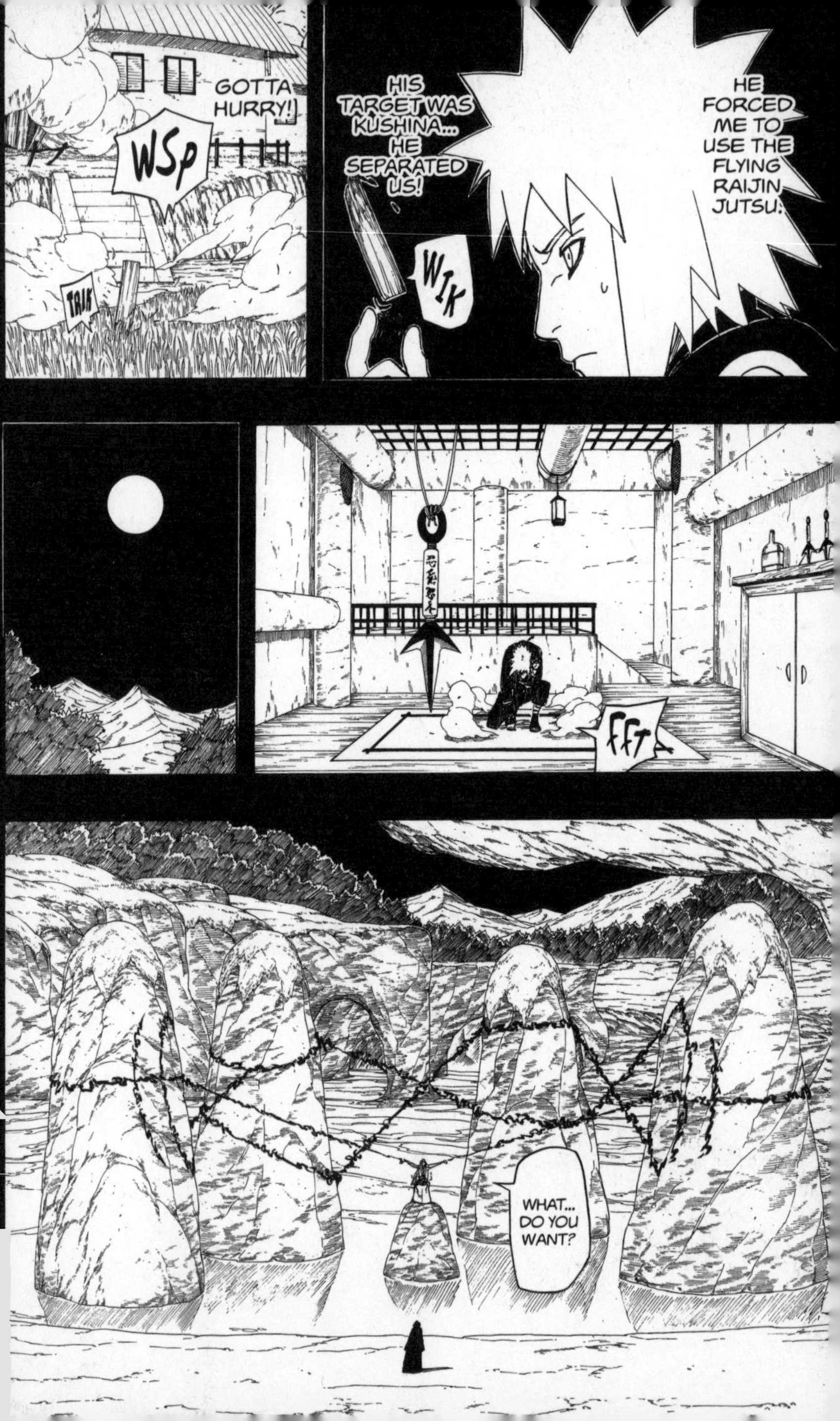
HE FORCED ME TO USE THE FLYING RAIJIN JUTSU!
HIS TARGET WAS KUSHINA... HE SEPARATED US!
WIK
GOTTA HURRY!
WSP
TRIK
FFT
WHAT... DO YOU WANT?

READ THIS WAY

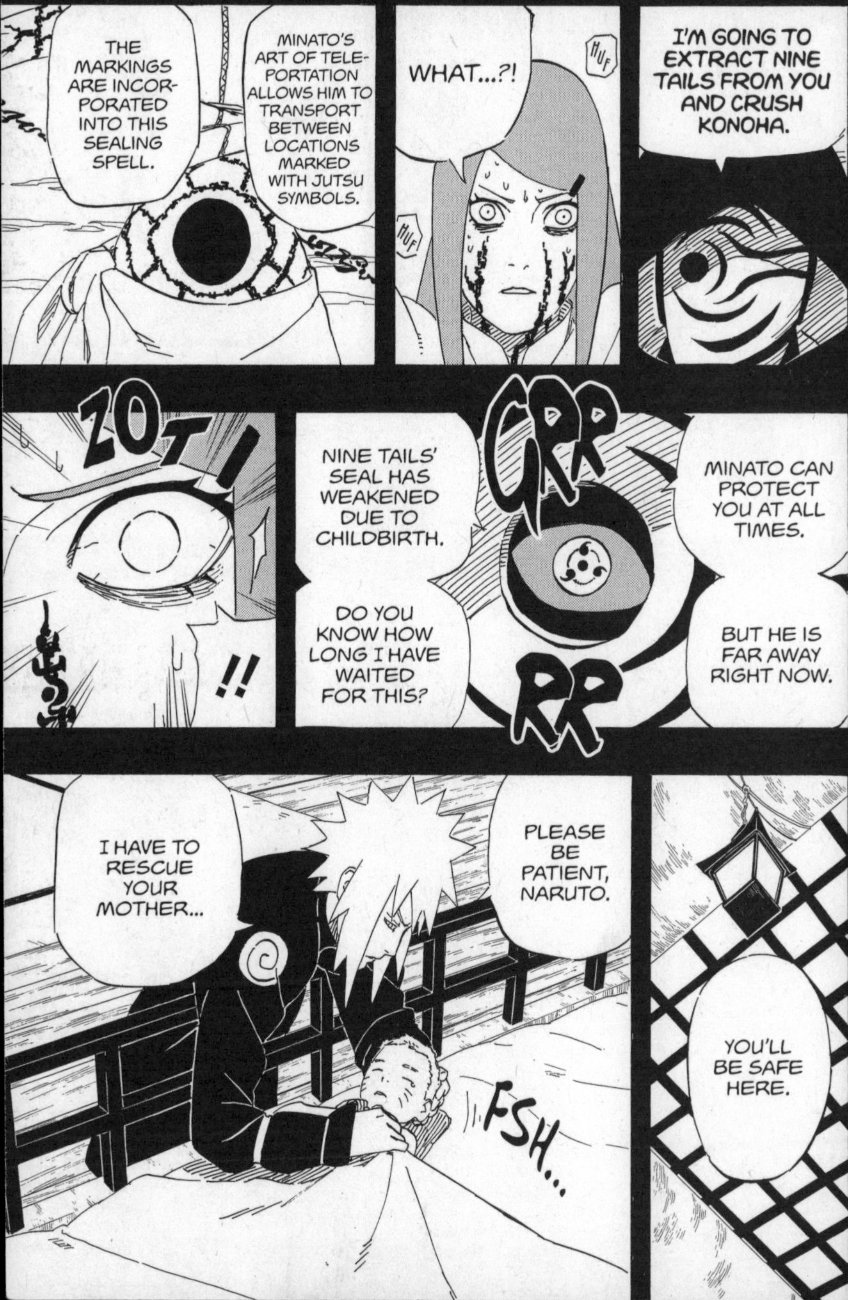
I'M GOING TO EXTRACT NINE TAILS FROM YOU AND CRUSH KONOHA.
HUF
WHAT...?!
HUF
MINATO'S ART OF TELE-PORTATION ALLOWS HIM TO TRANSPORT BETWEEN LOCATIONS MARKED WITH JUTSU SYMBOLS.
THE MARKINGS ARE INCOR-PORATED INTO THIS SEALING SPELL.
MINATO CAN PROTECT YOU AT ALL TIMES.
BUT HE IS FAR AWAY RIGHT NOW.
GRR
RR
NINE TAILS' SEAL HAS WEAKENED DUE TO CHILDBIRTH.
DO YOU KNOW HOW LONG I HAVE WAITED FOR THIS?
ZOT
!!
YOU'LL BE SAFE HERE.
PLEASE BE PATIENT, NARUTO.
I HAVE TO RESCUE YOUR MOTHER...
FSH...

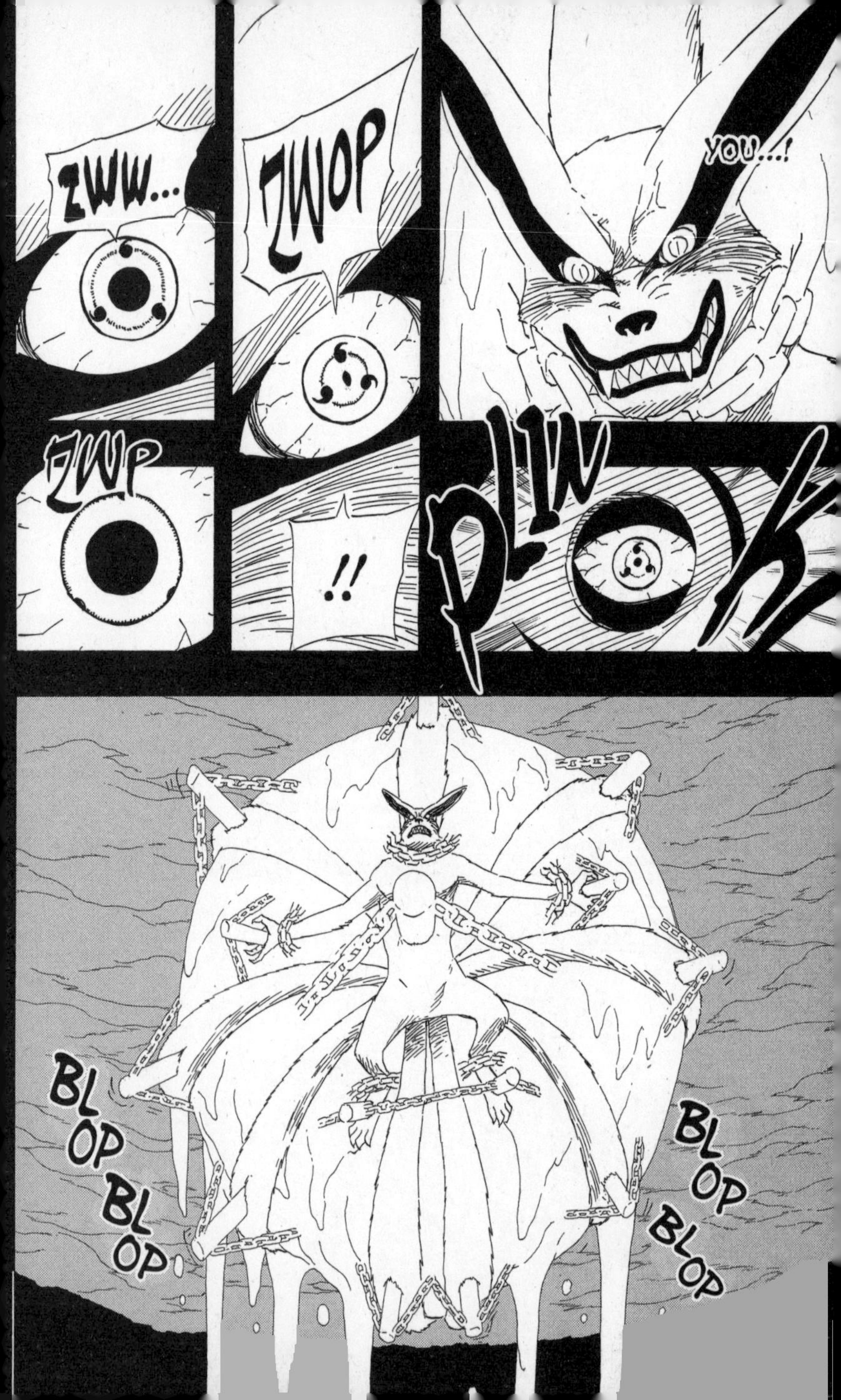
YOU...!
ZWOP
ZWW...
PLINK
!!
ZWP
BLOP BLOP
BLOP BLOP

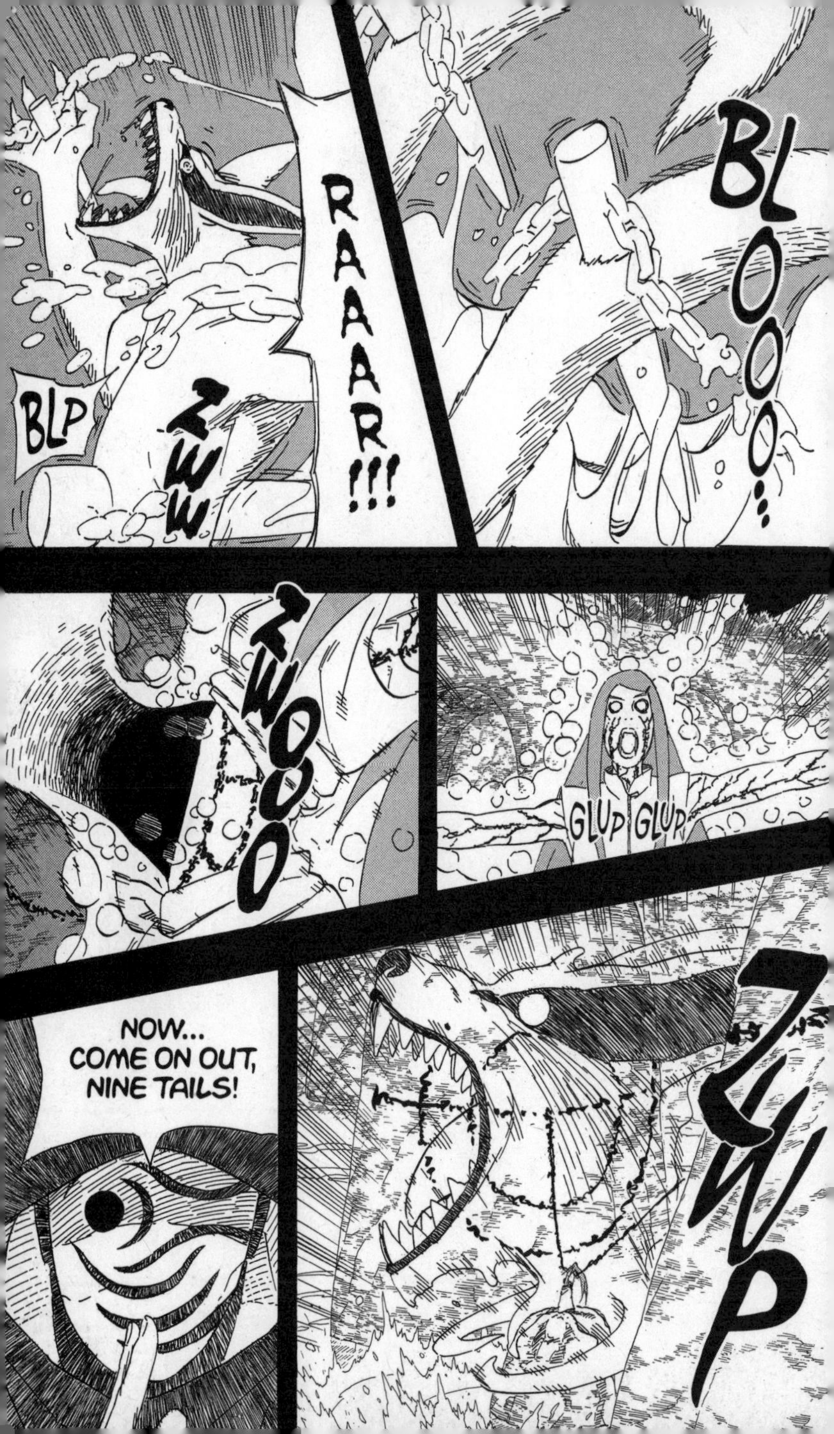
BLOOOO...
RAAAR!!!
ZWWW
BLP
GLUP GLUP
ZWOOO
ZWP
NOW... COME ON OUT, NINE TAILS!

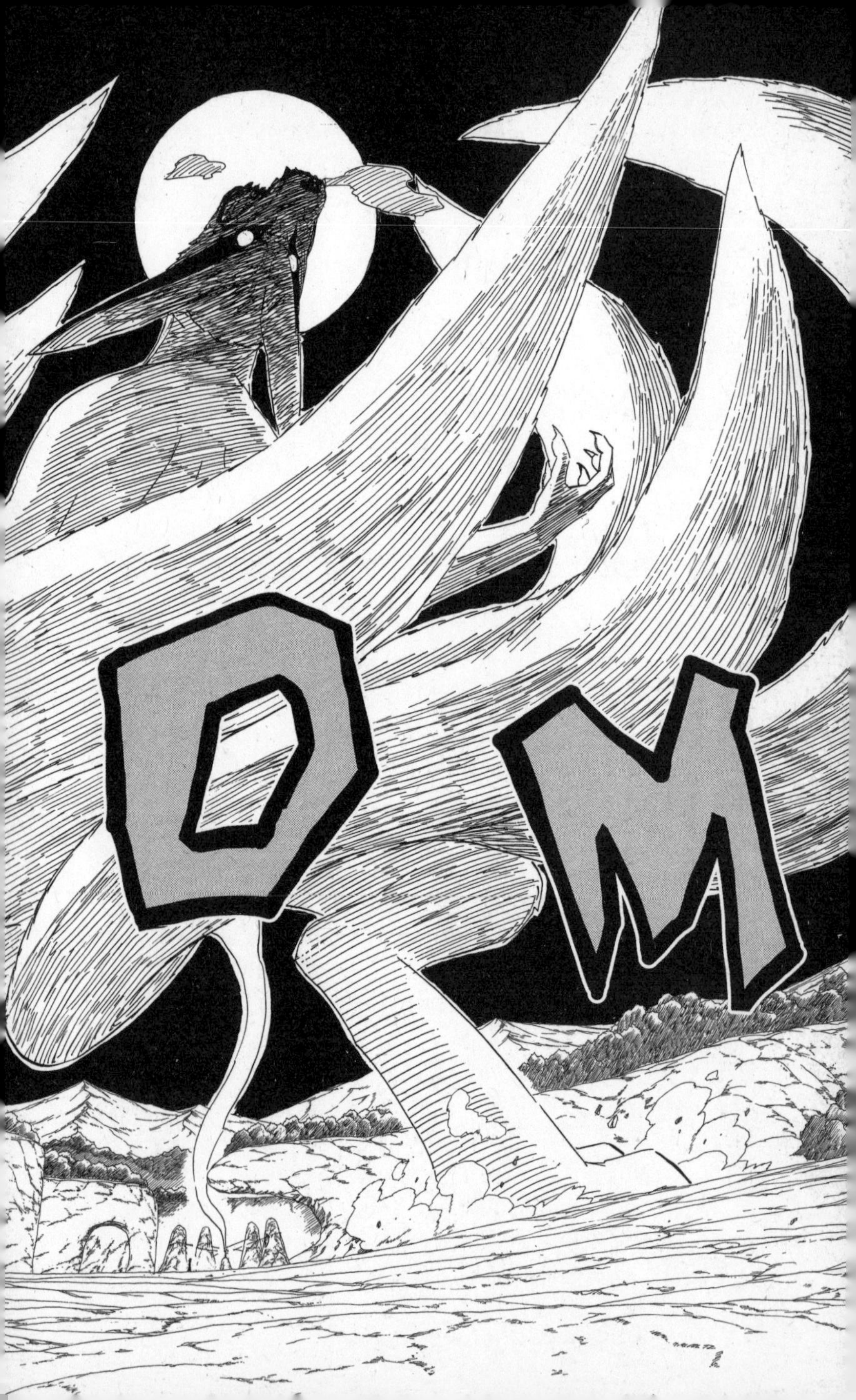
DOM

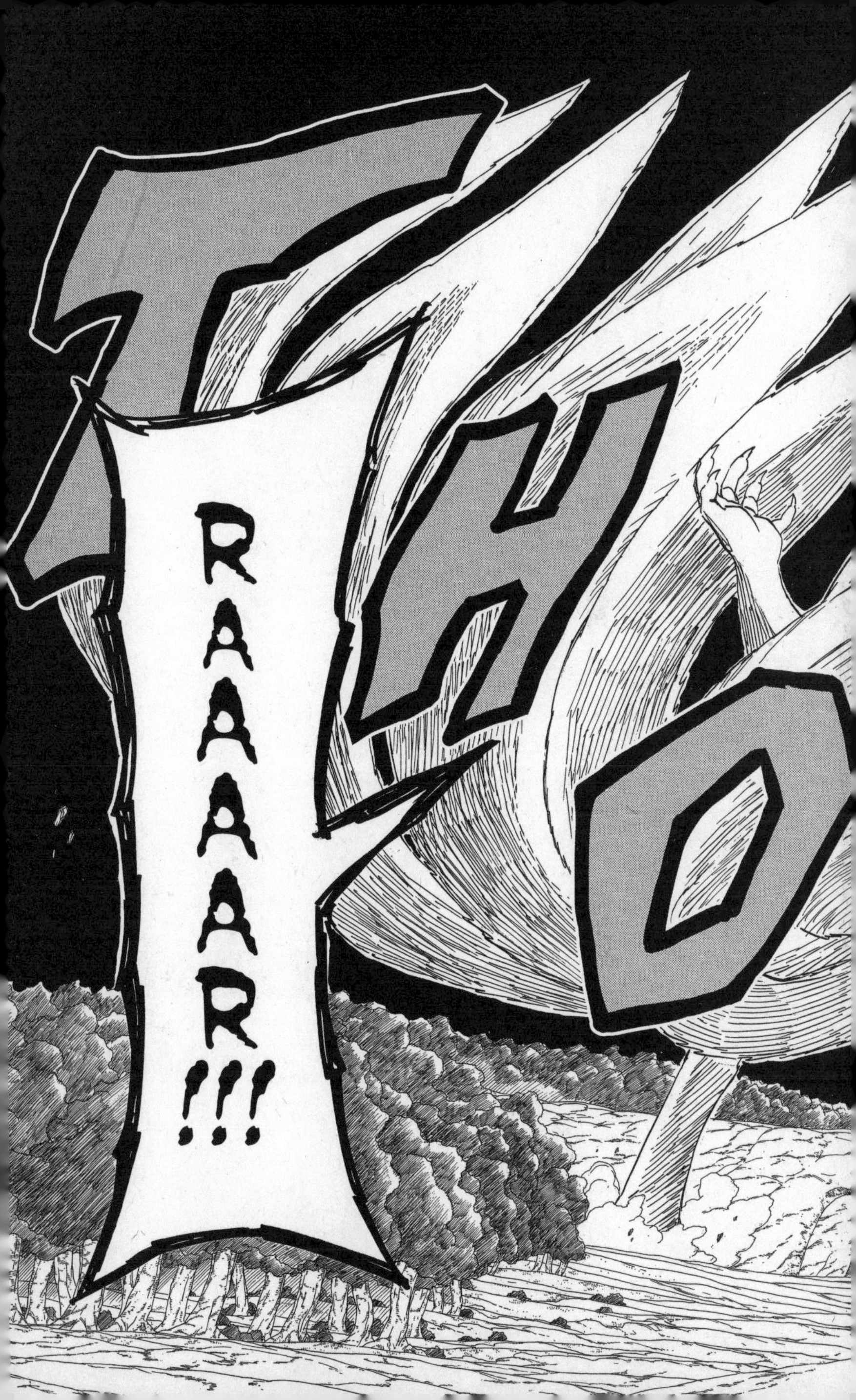
RAAAAR!!!

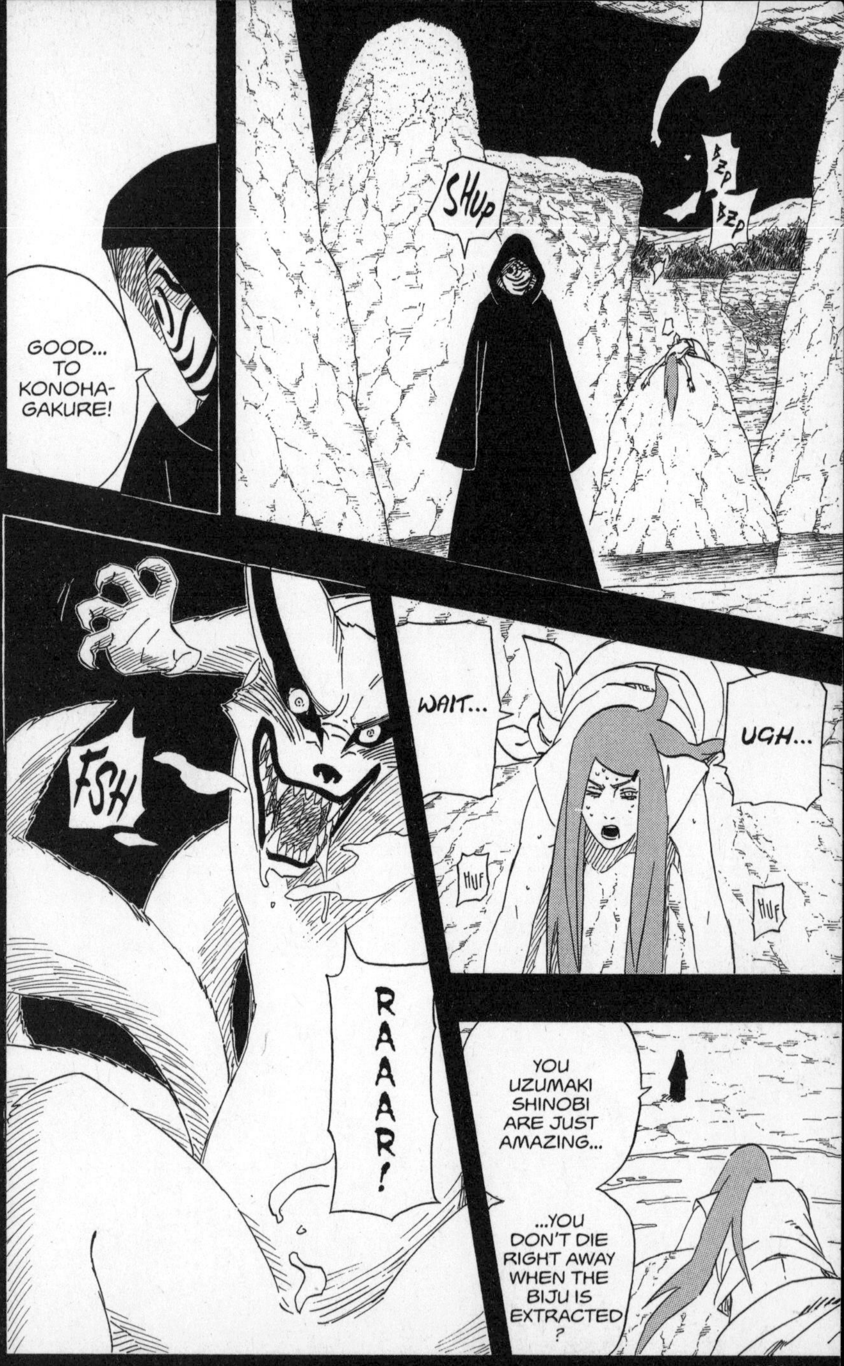
SHUP
BZP
BZP
GOOD... TO KONOHA-GAKURE!
UGH...
WAIT...
HUF
HUF
YOU UZUMAKI SHINOBI ARE JUST AMAZING...
...YOU DON'T DIE RIGHT AWAY WHEN THE BIJU IS EXTRACTED?
FSH
RAAAAR!

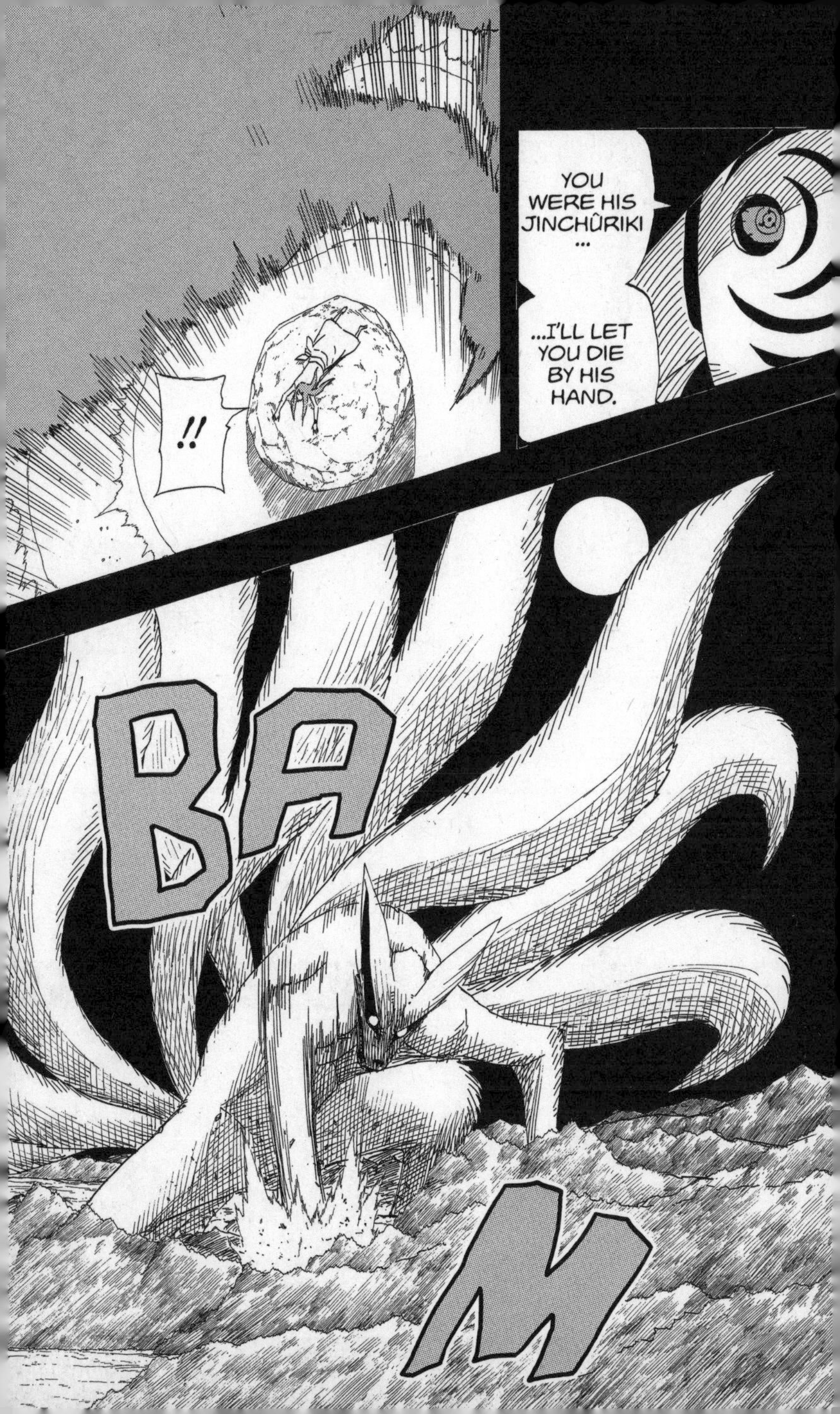
YOU WERE HIS JINCHÛRIKI ...
...I'LL LET YOU DIE BY HIS HAND.
!!
BA
M

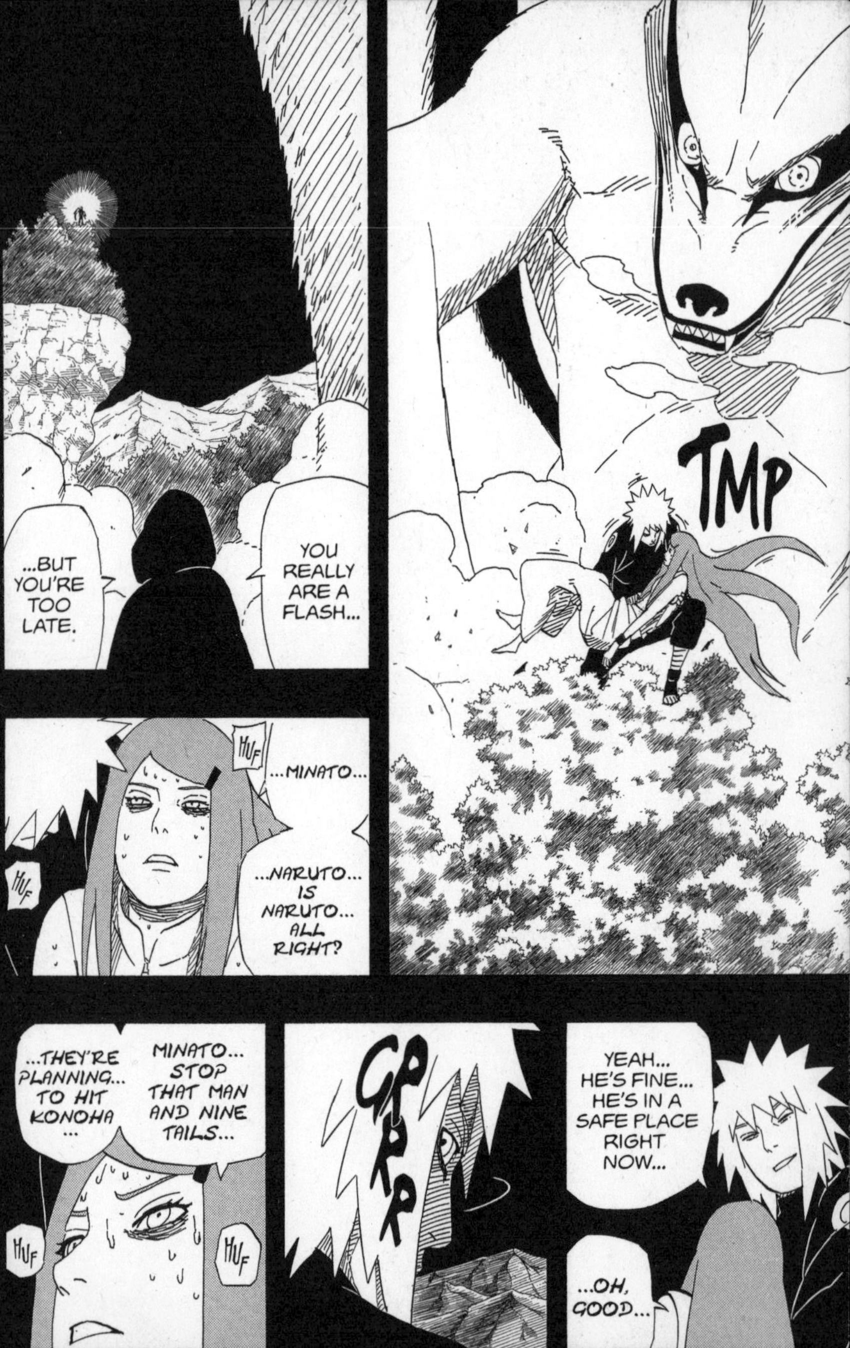
TMP
YOU REALLY ARE A FLASH...
...BUT YOU'RE TOO LATE.
HUF
...MINATO...
...NARUTO... IS NARUTO... ALL RIGHT?
HUF
YEAH... HE'S FINE... HE'S IN A SAFE PLACE RIGHT NOW...
...OH, GOOD...
GRRR
MINATO... STOP THAT MAN AND NINE TAILS...
...THEY'RE PLANNING... TO HIT KONOHA ...
HUF
HUF

READ THIS WAY

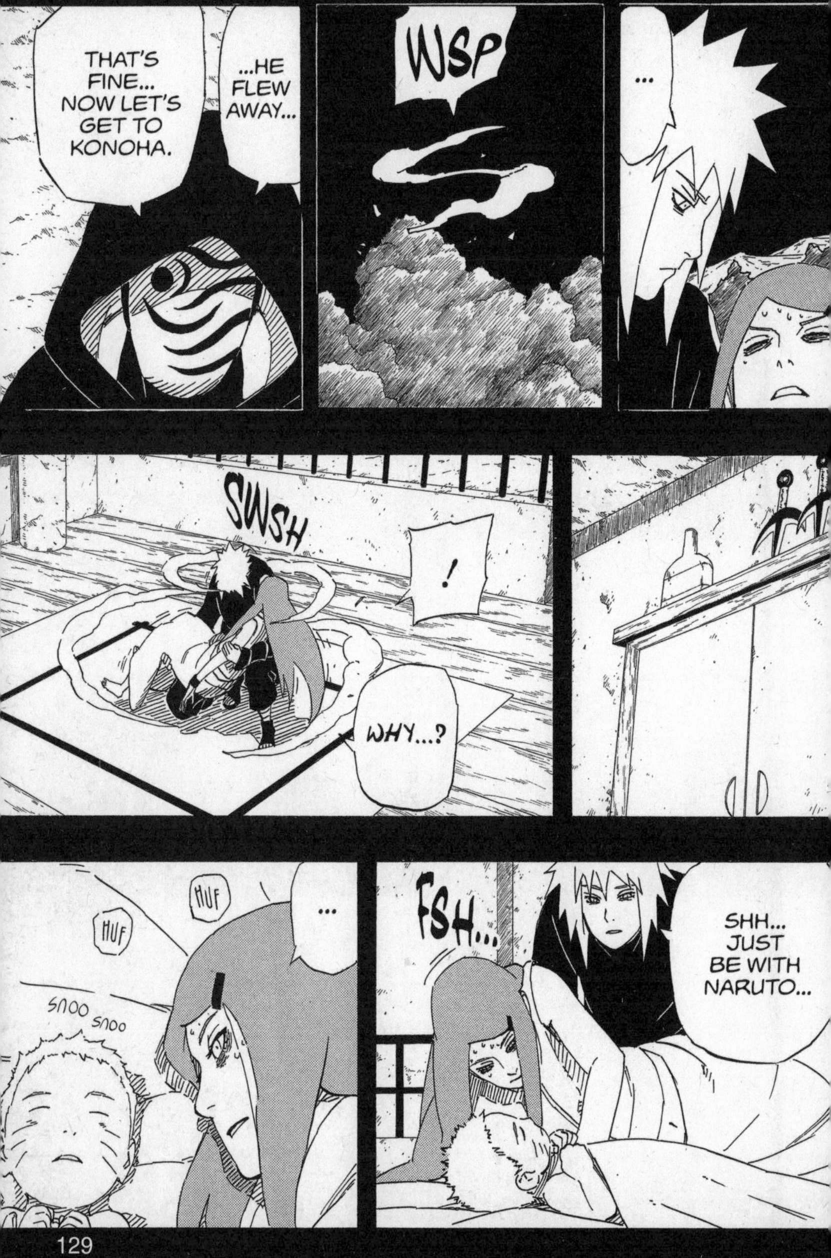
...
WSP
...HE FLEW AWAY...
THAT'S FINE... NOW LET'S GET TO KONOHA.
SWSH
!
WHY...?
FSH...
SHH... JUST BE WITH NARUTO...
...
HUF
HUF
SNOO SNOO

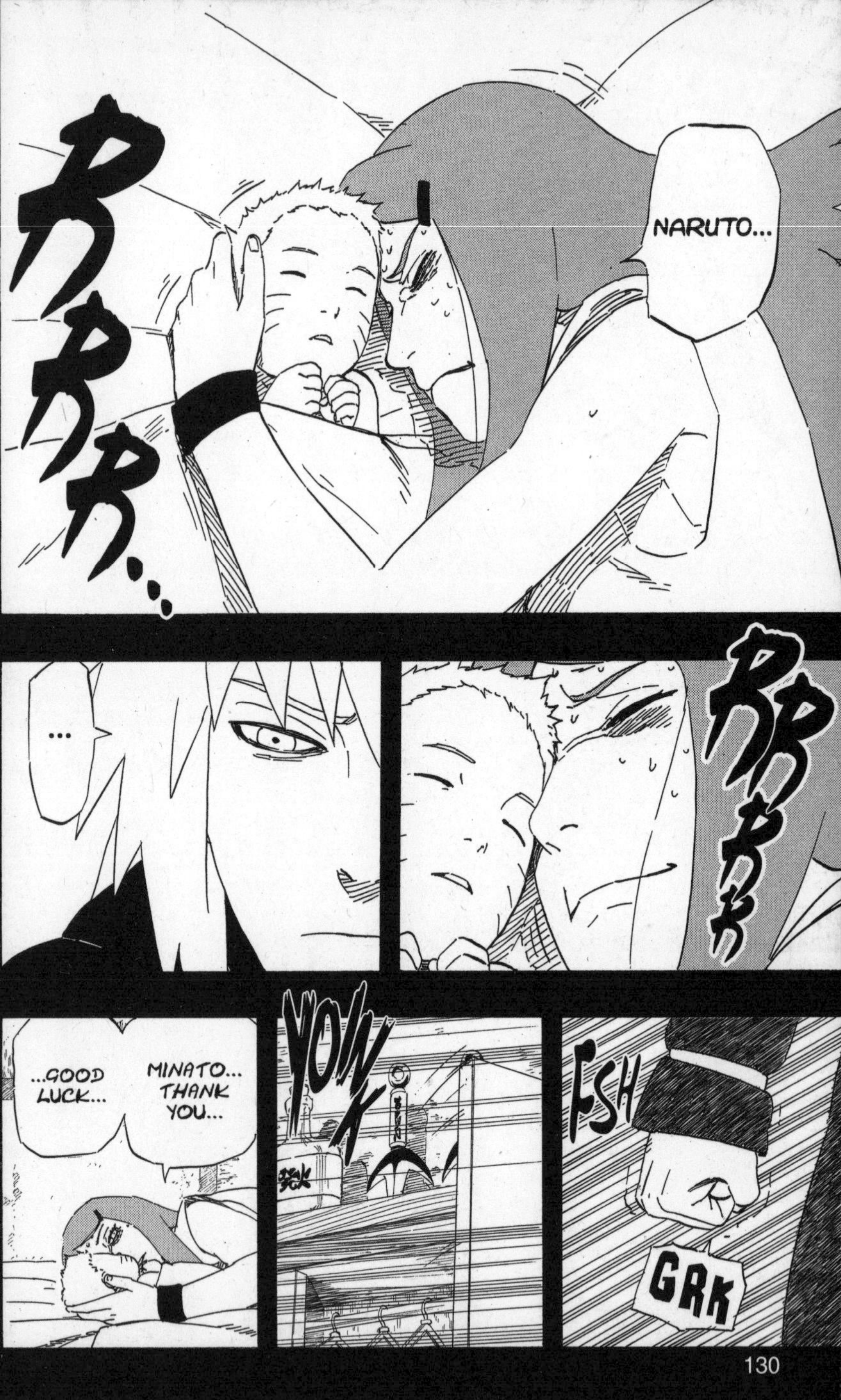
NARUTO...
...
FSH
GRK
MINATO... THANK YOU...
...GOOD LUCK...

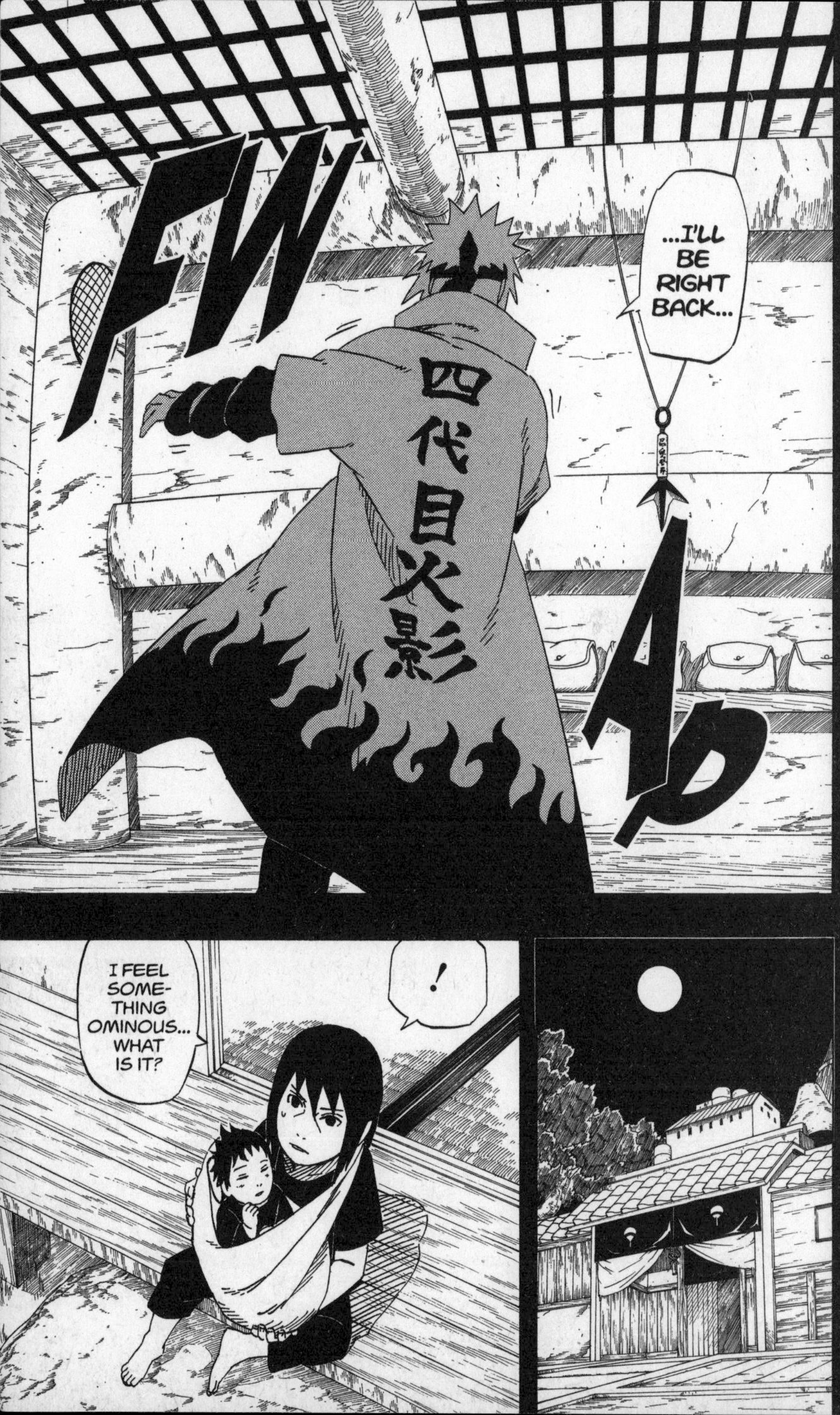
...I'LL BE RIGHT BACK...
FW
AP
四代目火影
!
I FEEL SOME-THING OMINOUS... WHAT IS IT?

NARUTO

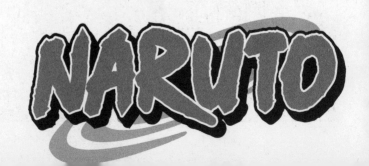

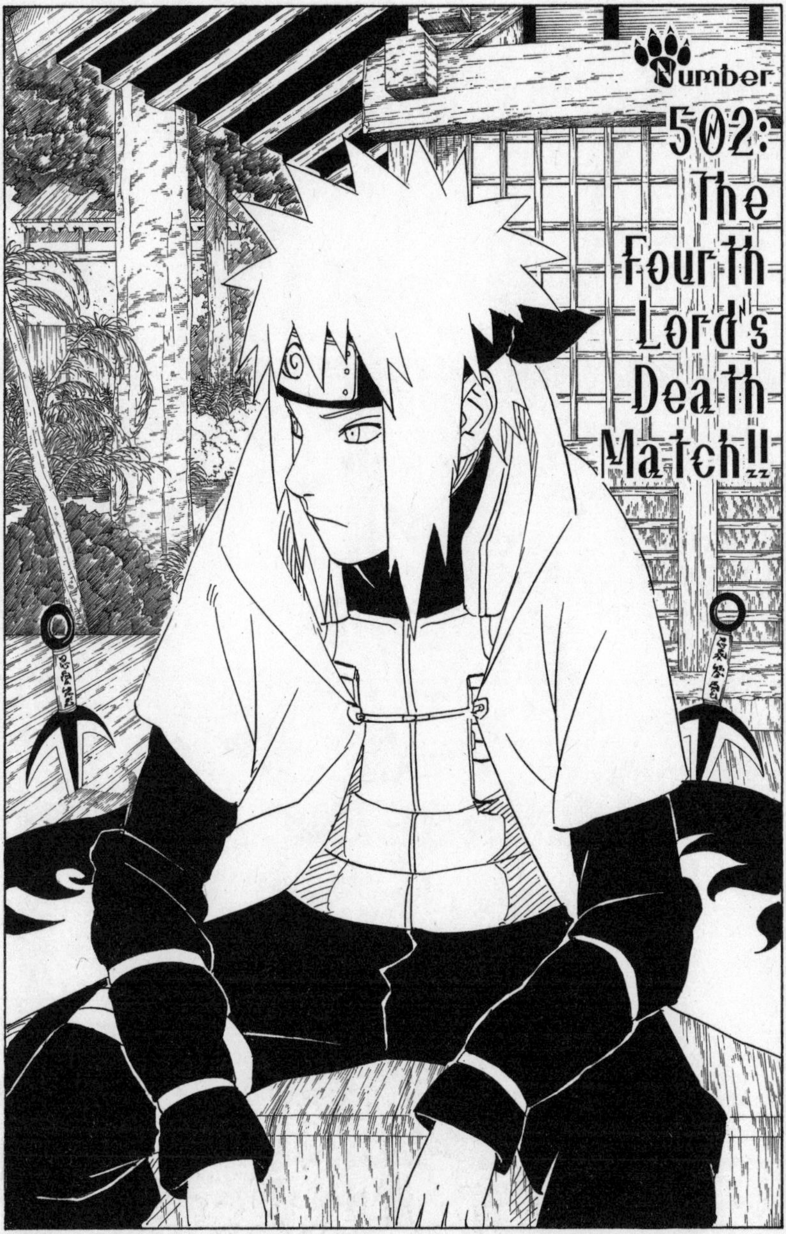
Number 502: The Fourth Lord's Death Match!!

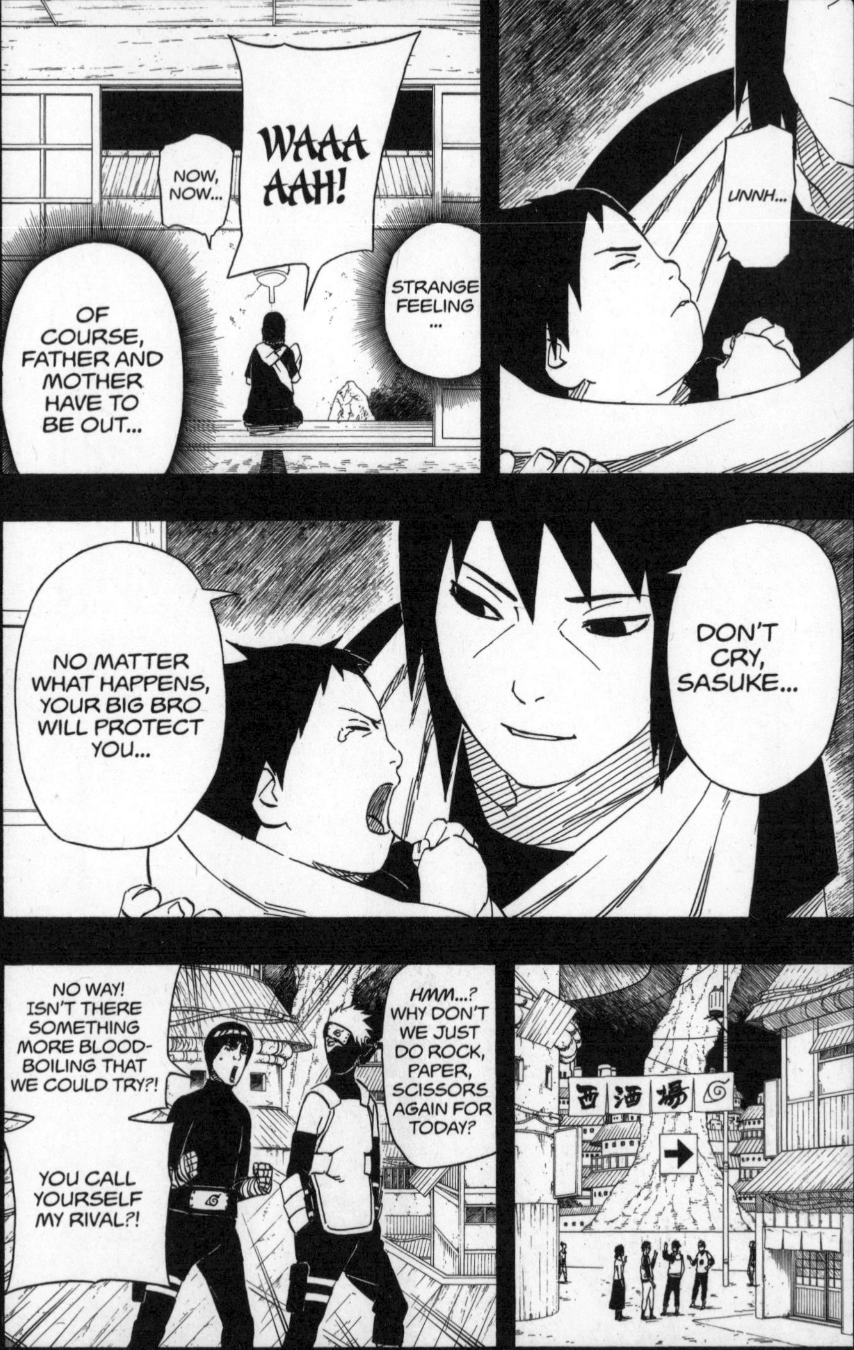
UNNH...
WAAAA AAH!
NOW, NOW...
STRANGE FEELING ...
OF COURSE, FATHER AND MOTHER HAVE TO BE OUT...
DON'T CRY, SASUKE...
NO MATTER WHAT HAPPENS, YOUR BIG BRO WILL PROTECT YOU...
西 酒 場
HMM...? WHY DON'T WE JUST DO ROCK, PAPER, SCISSORS AGAIN FOR TODAY?
NO WAY! ISN'T THERE SOMETHING MORE BLOOD-BOILING THAT WE COULD TRY?!
YOU CALL YOURSELF MY RIVAL?!

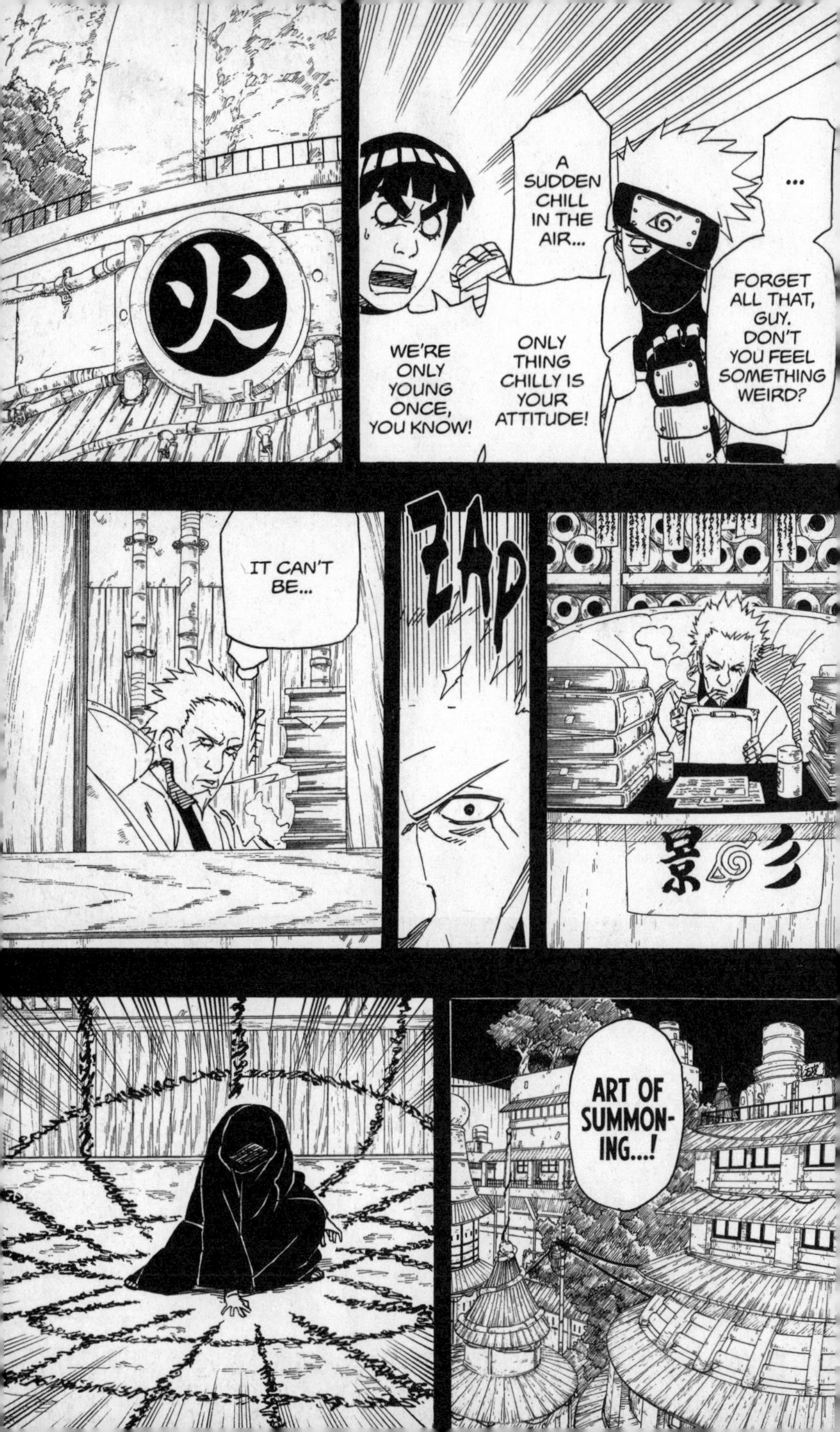
...
A SUDDEN CHILL IN THE AIR...
FORGET ALL THAT, GUY. DON'T YOU FEEL SOMETHING WEIRD?
ONLY THING CHILLY IS YOUR ATTITUDE!
WE'RE ONLY YOUNG ONCE, YOU KNOW!
ZAP
IT CAN'T BE...
ART OF SUMMONING...!

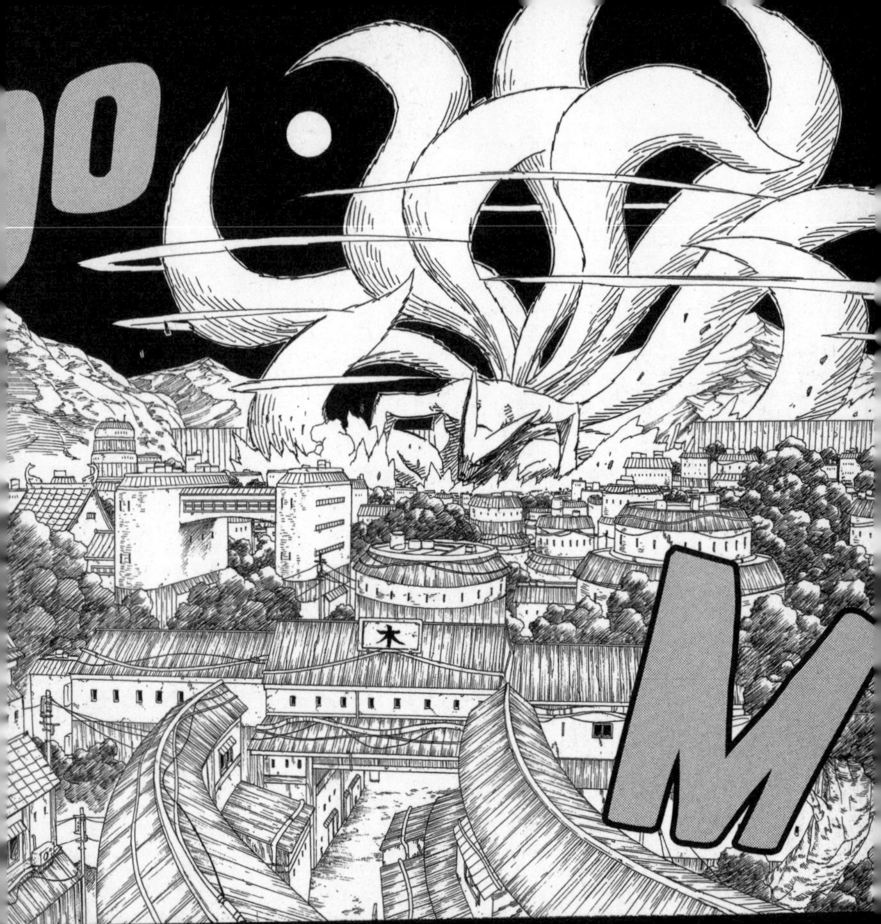

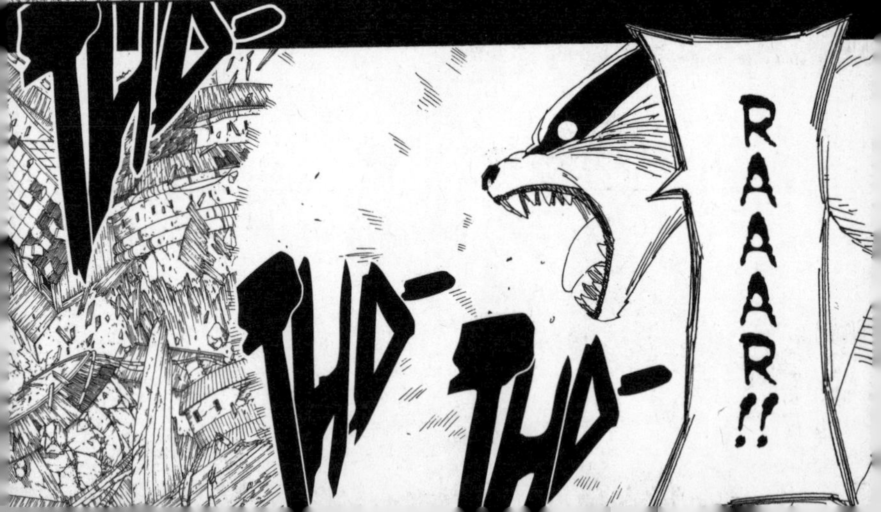
RAAAR!!
THD-
THD-
THD-

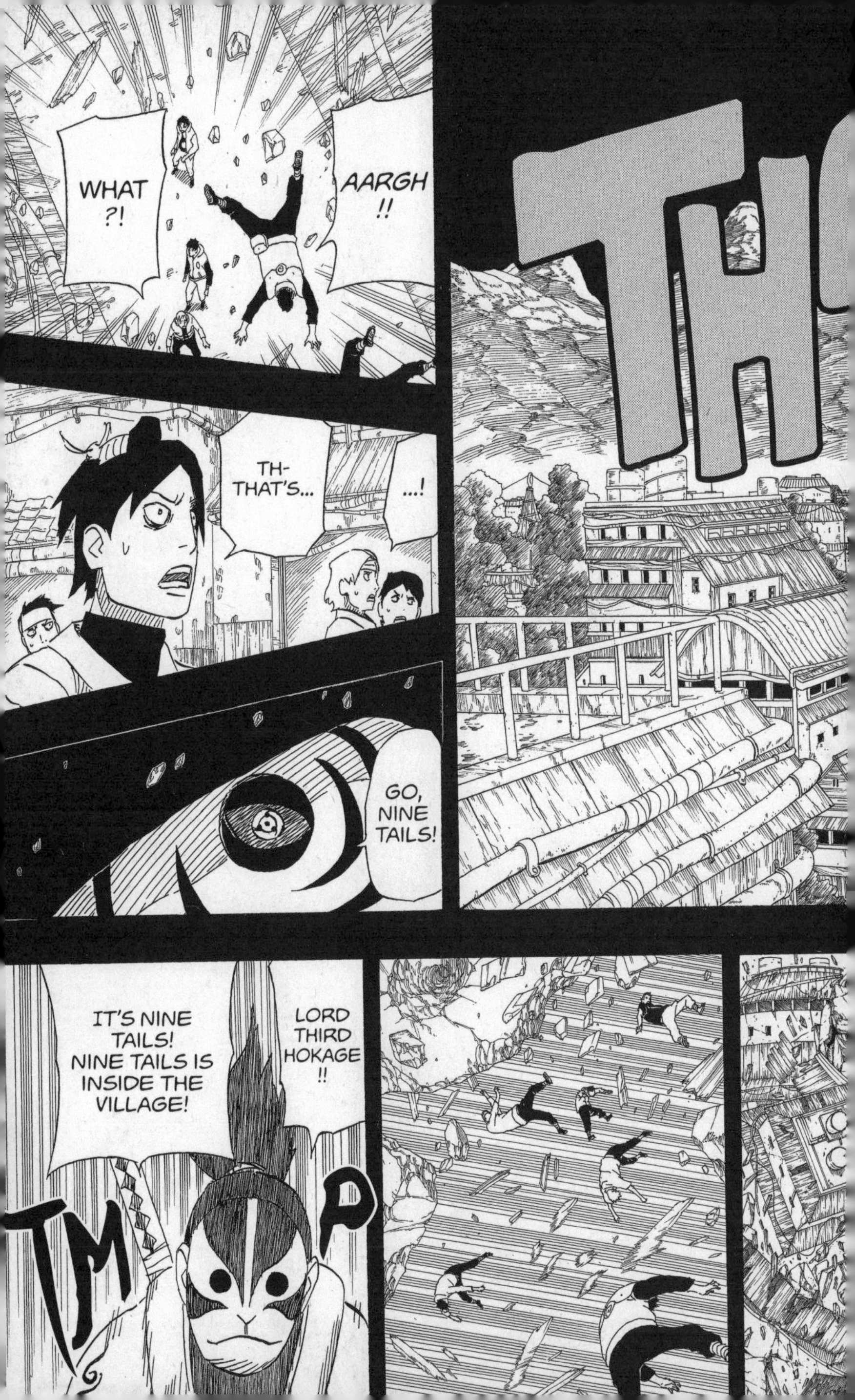
TH
AARGH!!
WHAT?!
TH- THAT'S...
...!
GO, NINE TAILS!
LORD THIRD HOKAGE!!
IT'S NINE TAILS! NINE TAILS IS INSIDE THE VILLAGE!
TMP

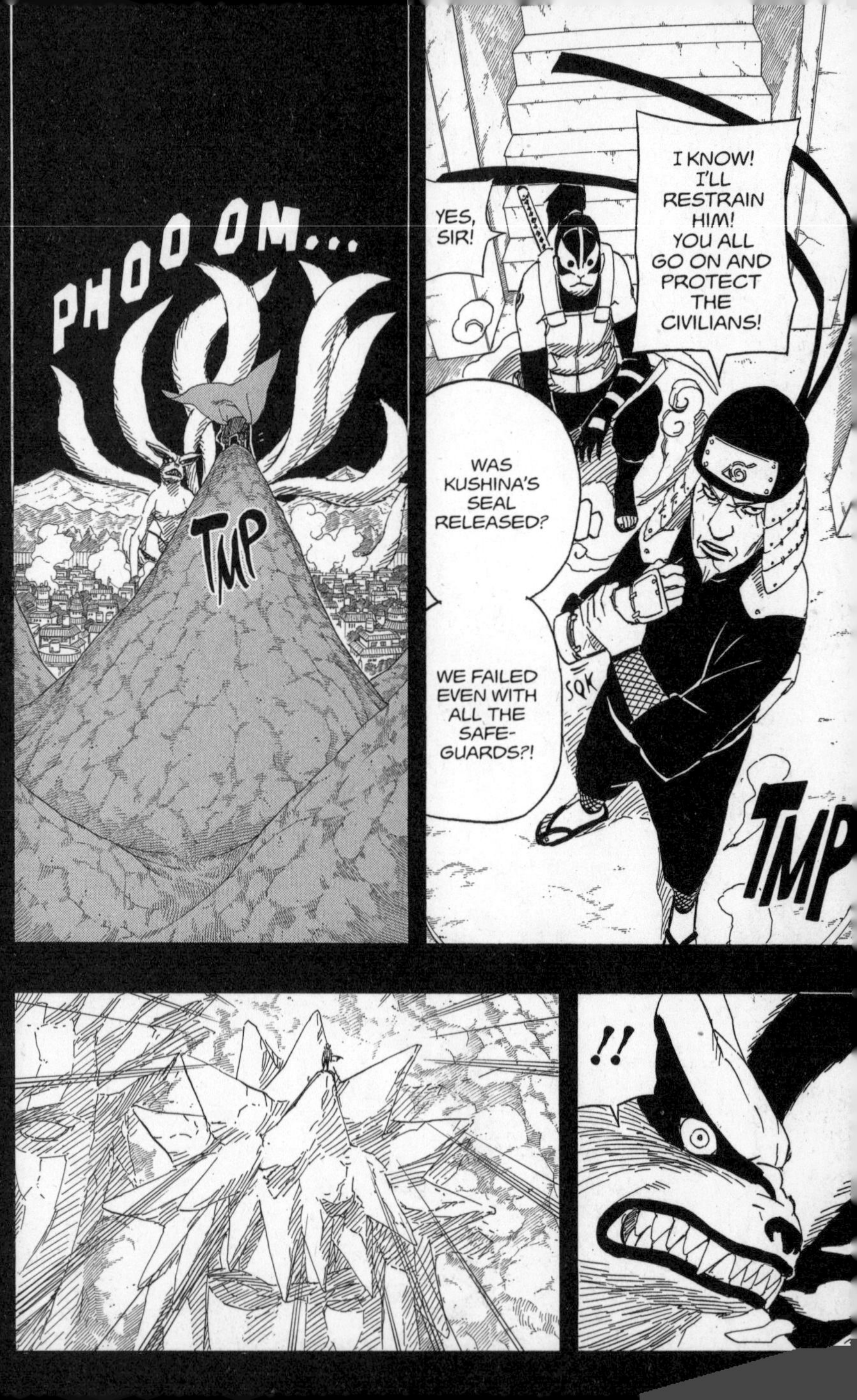
I KNOW! I'LL RESTRAIN HIM! YOU ALL GO ON AND PROTECT THE CIVILIANS!
YES, SIR!
WAS KUSHINA'S SEAL RELEASED?
WE FAILED EVEN WITH ALL THE SAFE-GUARDS?!
SQK
TMP
PHOO OM...
TMP
!!

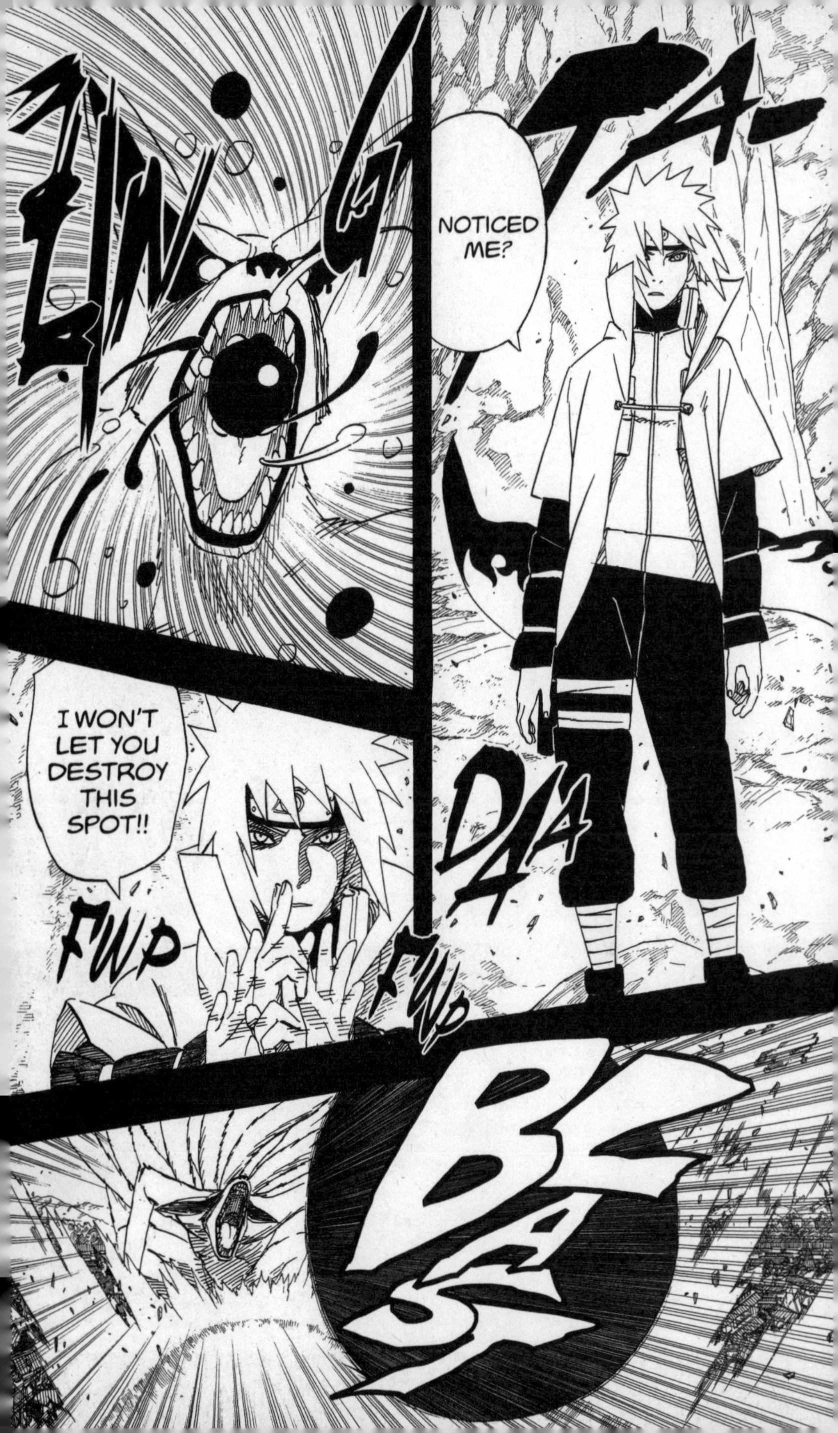
GATA
NOTICED ME?
DA DA
ZWING
I WON'T LET YOU DESTROY THIS SPOT!!
FWP
FWP
BASH

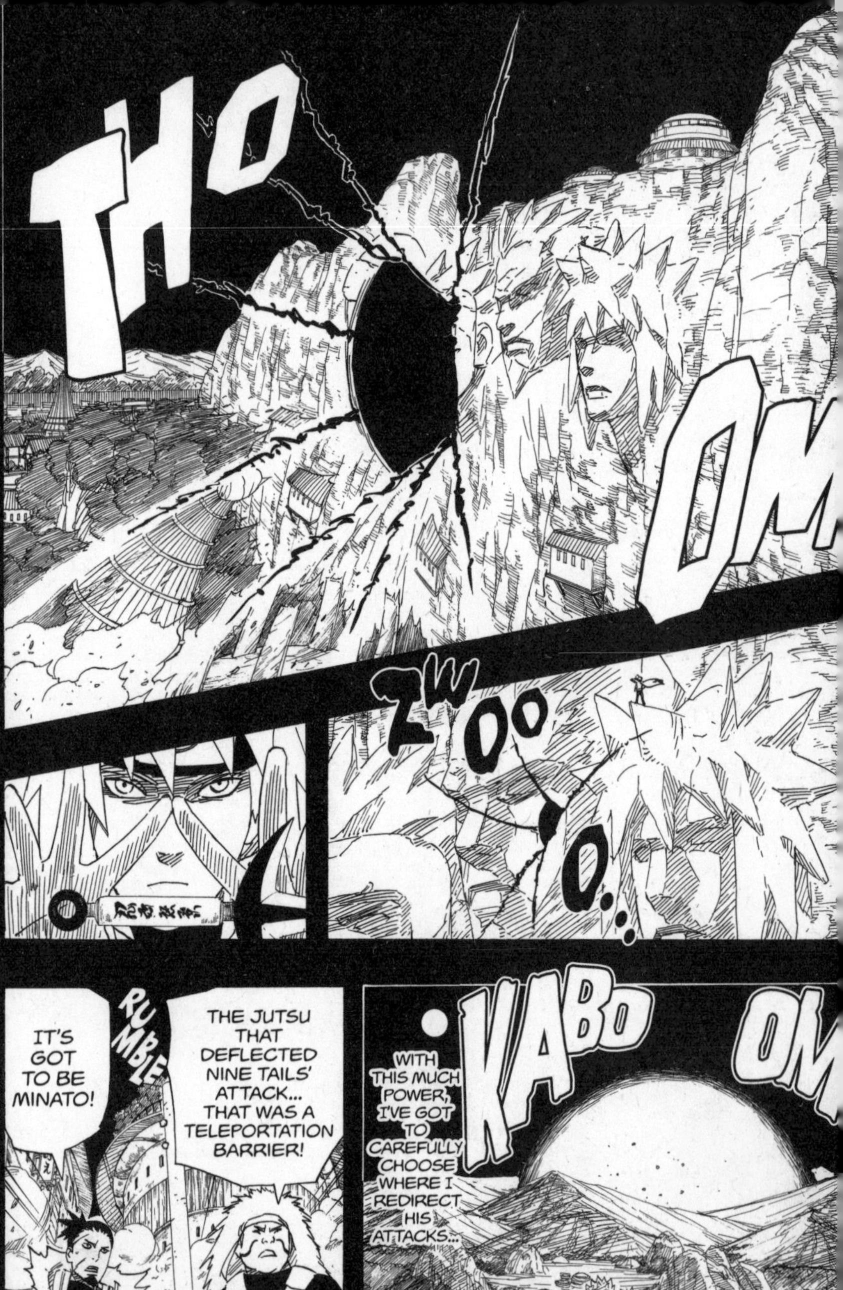
THO
OM
ZWOOO...
KABO
OM
WITH THIS MUCH POWER, I'VE GOT TO CAREFULLY CHOOSE WHERE I REDIRECT HIS ATTACKS...
THE JUTSU THAT DEFLECTED NINE TAILS' ATTACK... THAT WAS A TELEPORTATION BARRIER!
RUMBLE
IT'S GOT TO BE MINATO!

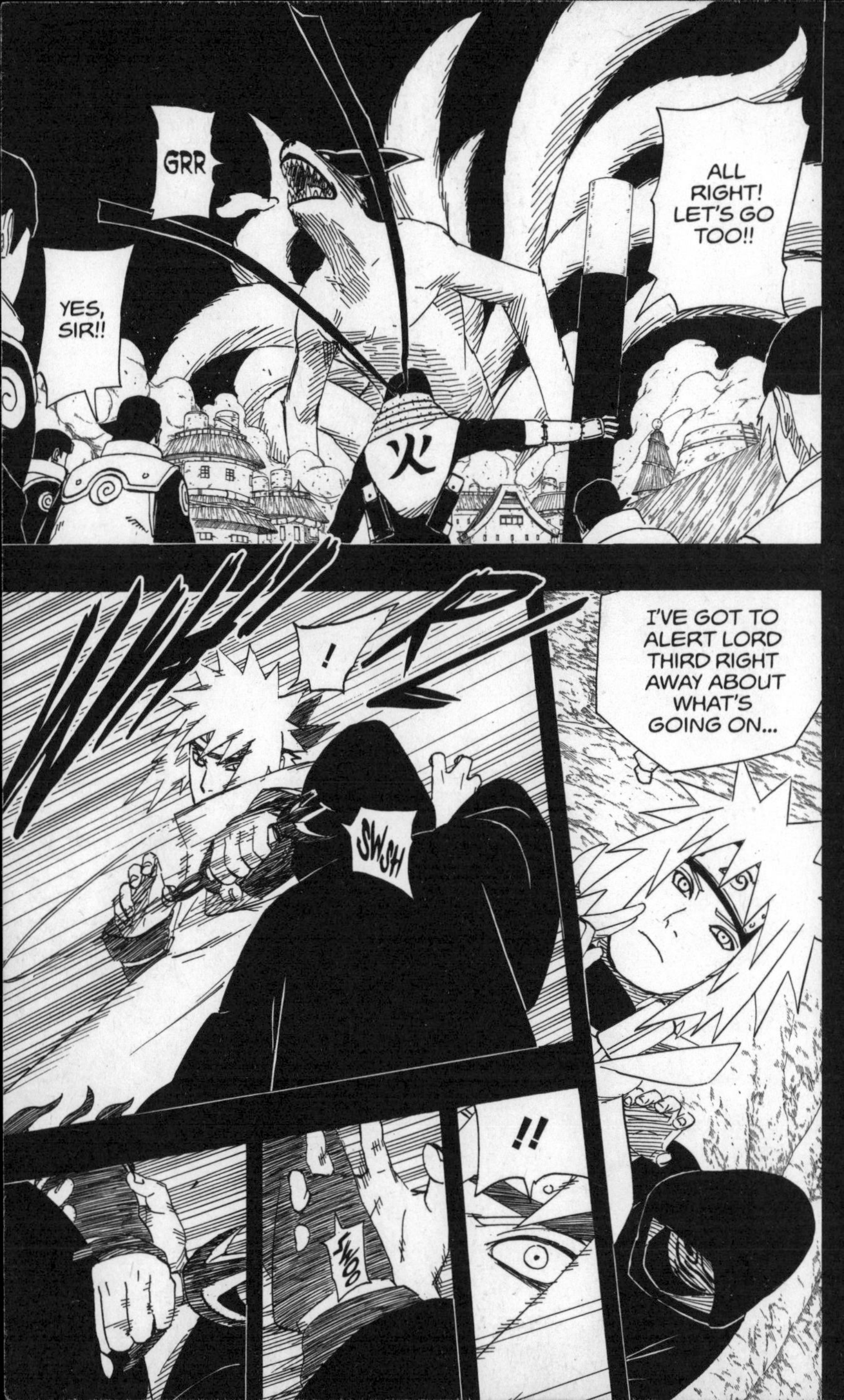
ALL RIGHT! LET'S GO TOO!!
GRR
YES, SIR!!
I'VE GOT TO ALERT LORD THIRD RIGHT AWAY ABOUT WHAT'S GOING ON...
!
SWSH
!!
SWOO

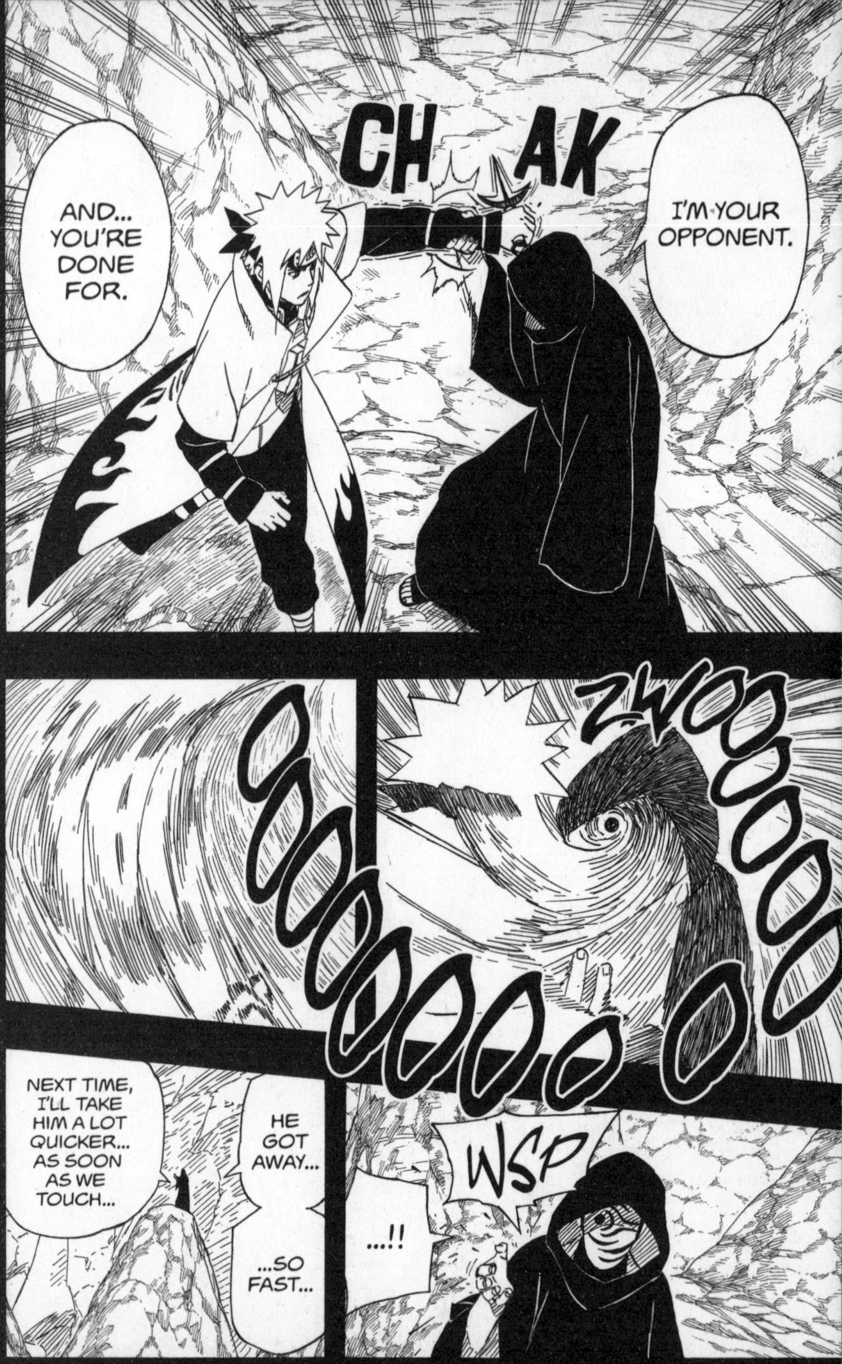
I'M YOUR OPPONENT.
CH AK
AND... YOU'RE DONE FOR.
ZWOOOOOOOOOOOOOOOO
WSP
...!!
HE GOT AWAY...
...SO FAST...
NEXT TIME, I'LL TAKE HIM A LOT QUICKER... AS SOON AS WE TOUCH...

READ THIS WAY

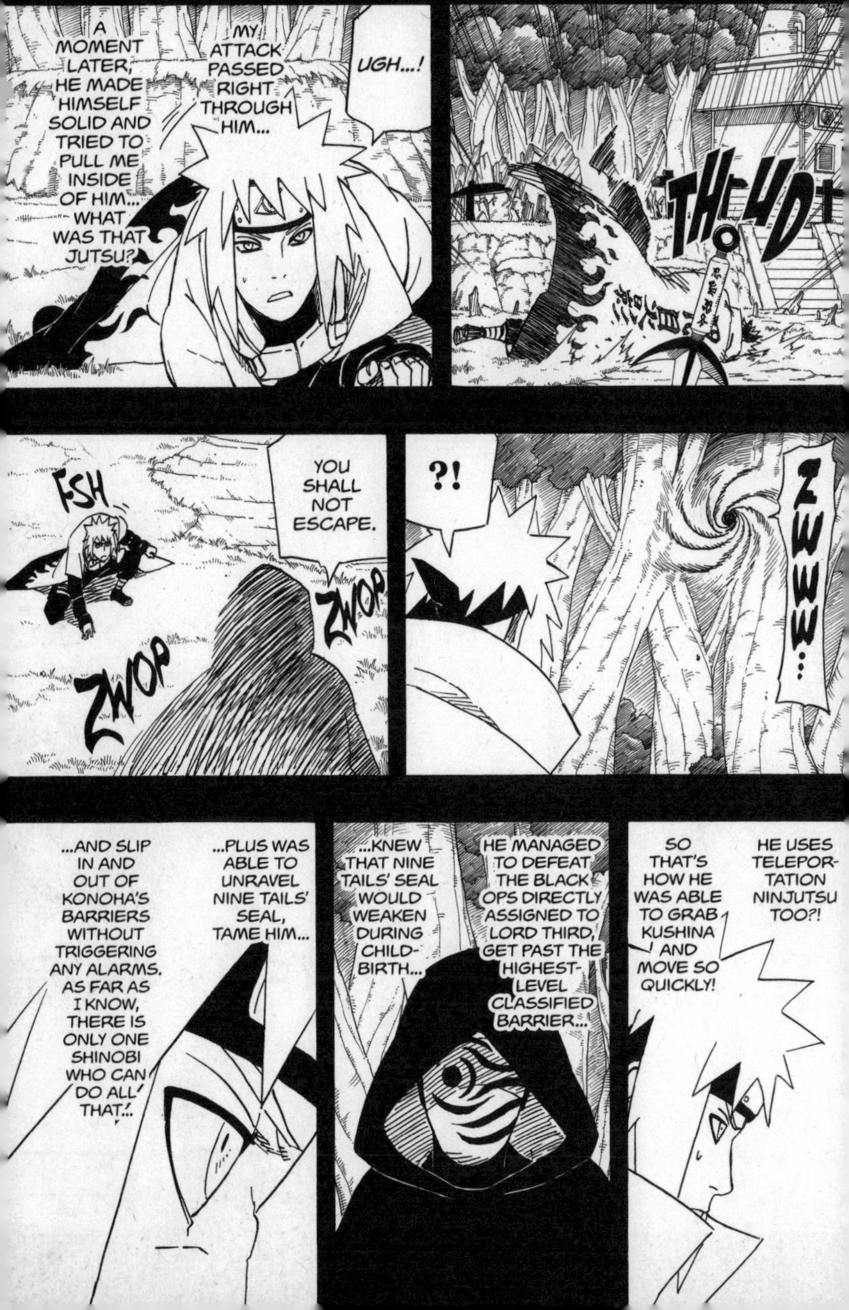
THUD
UGH...!
MY ATTACK PASSED RIGHT THROUGH HIM...
A MOMENT LATER, HE MADE HIMSELF SOLID AND TRIED TO PULL ME INSIDE OF HIM... WHAT WAS THAT JUTSU?
ZWWW...
?!
YOU SHALL NOT ESCAPE.
ZWOP
FSH
ZWOP
HE USES TELEPORTATION NINJUTSU TOO?!
SO THAT'S HOW HE WAS ABLE TO GRAB KUSHINA AND MOVE SO QUICKLY!
HE MANAGED TO DEFEAT THE BLACK OPS DIRECTLY ASSIGNED TO LORD THIRD, GET PAST THE HIGHEST-LEVEL CLASSIFIED BARRIER...
...KNEW THAT NINE TAILS' SEAL WOULD WEAKEN DURING CHILDBIRTH...
...PLUS WAS ABLE TO UNRAVEL NINE TAILS' SEAL, TAME HIM...
...AND SLIP IN AND OUT OF KONOHA'S BARRIERS WITHOUT TRIGGERING ANY ALARMS. AS FAR AS I KNOW, THERE IS ONLY ONE SHINOBI WHO CAN DO ALL THAT...

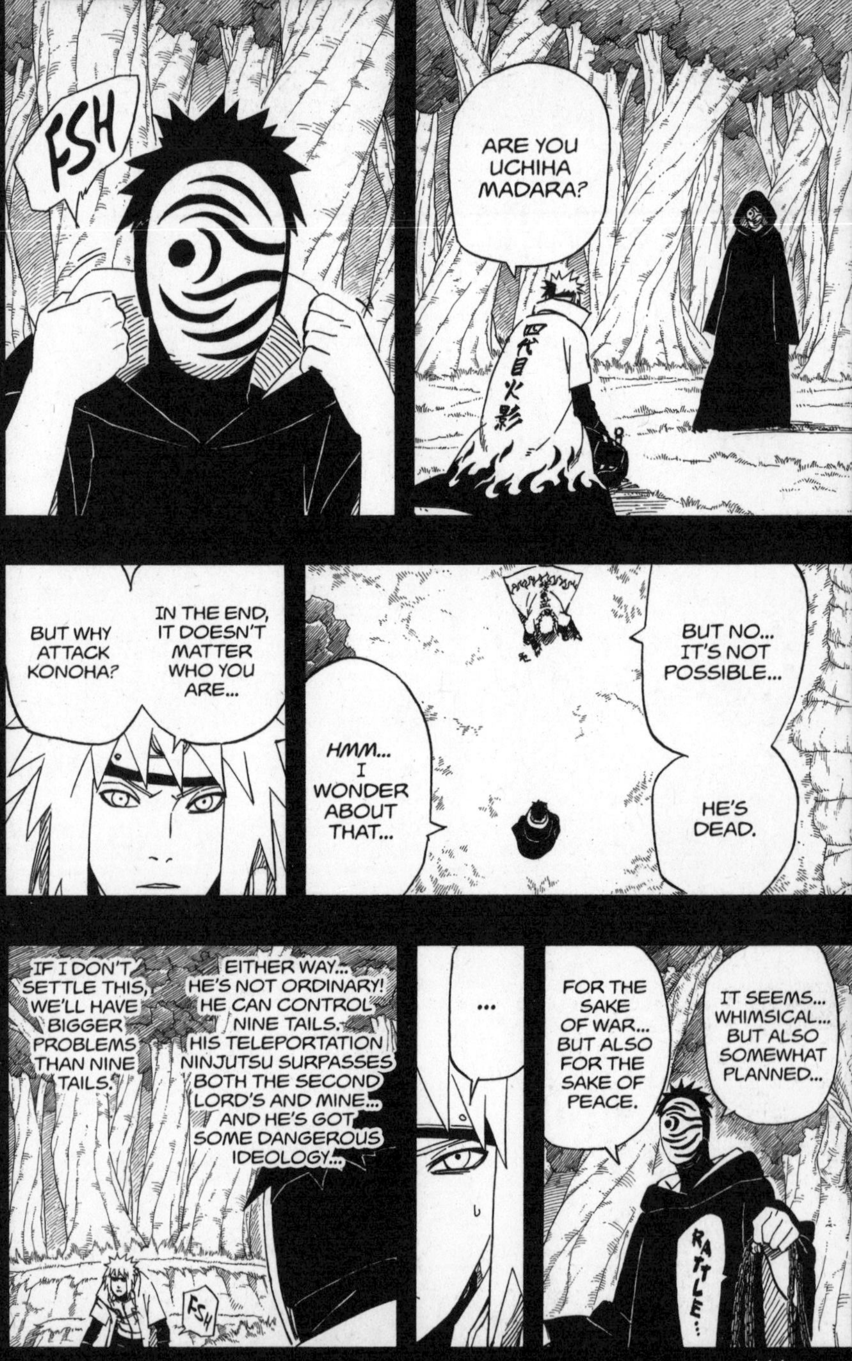
ARE YOU UCHIHA MADARA?
FSH
BUT NO... IT'S NOT POSSIBLE...
HE'S DEAD.
HMM... I WONDER ABOUT THAT...
IN THE END, IT DOESN'T MATTER WHO YOU ARE...
BUT WHY ATTACK KONOHA?
IT SEEMS... WHIMSICAL... BUT ALSO SOMEWHAT PLANNED...
FOR THE SAKE OF WAR... BUT ALSO FOR THE SAKE OF PEACE.
RATTLE...
...
EITHER WAY... HE'S NOT ORDINARY! HE CAN CONTROL NINE TAILS. HIS TELEPORTATION NINJUTSU SURPASSES BOTH THE SECOND LORD'S AND MINE... AND HE'S GOT SOME DANGEROUS IDEOLOGY...
IF I DON'T SETTLE THIS, WE'LL HAVE BIGGER PROBLEMS THAN NINE TAILS.
FSH

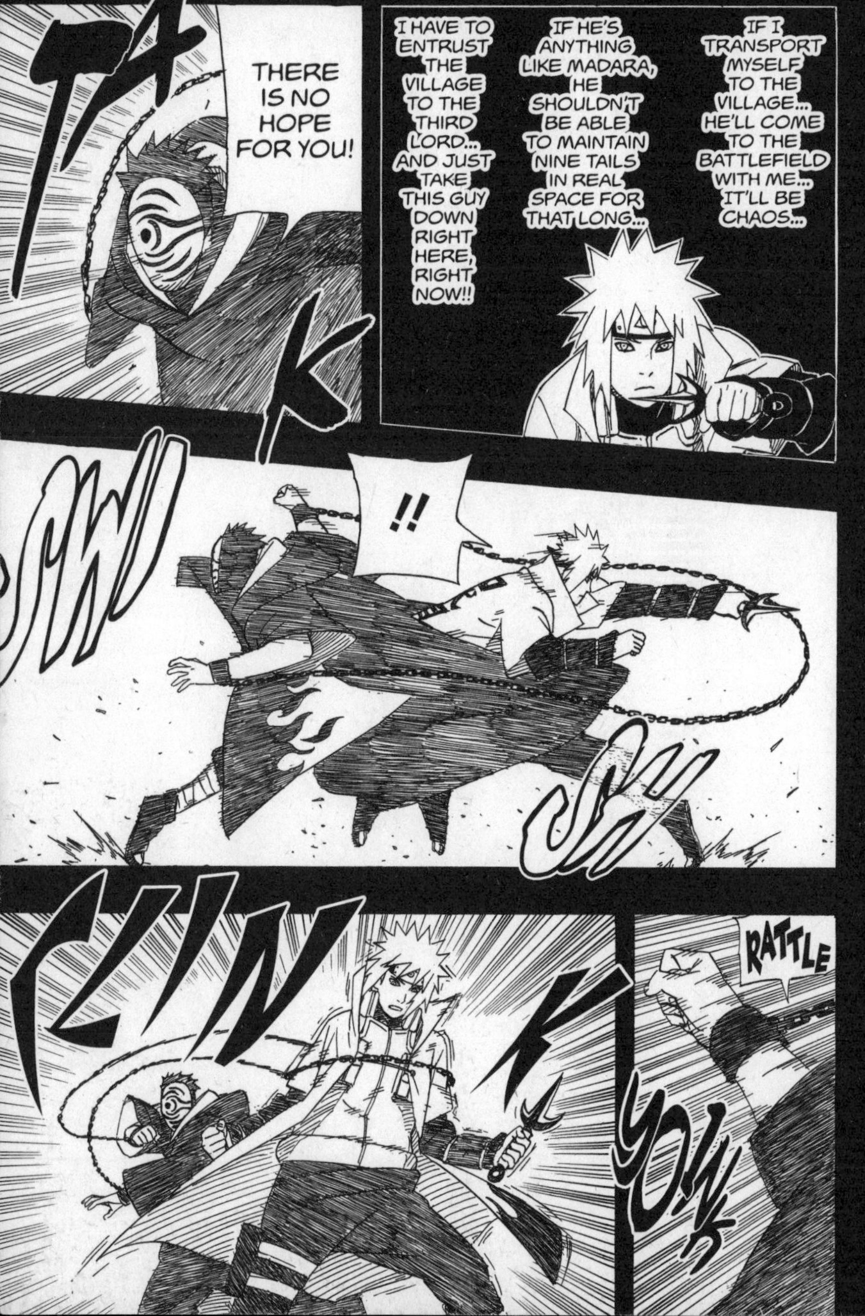
IF I TRANSPORT MYSELF TO THE VILLAGE... HE'LL COME TO THE BATTLEFIELD WITH ME... IT'LL BE CHAOS...
IF HE'S ANYTHING LIKE MADARA, HE SHOULDN'T BE ABLE TO MAINTAIN NINE TAILS IN REAL SPACE FOR THAT LONG...
I HAVE TO ENTRUST THE VILLAGE TO THE THIRD LORD... AND JUST TAKE THIS GUY DOWN RIGHT HERE, RIGHT NOW!!
THERE IS NO HOPE FOR YOU!
TAK
!!
SWSH
SWY
RATTLE
YOINK
CLINK

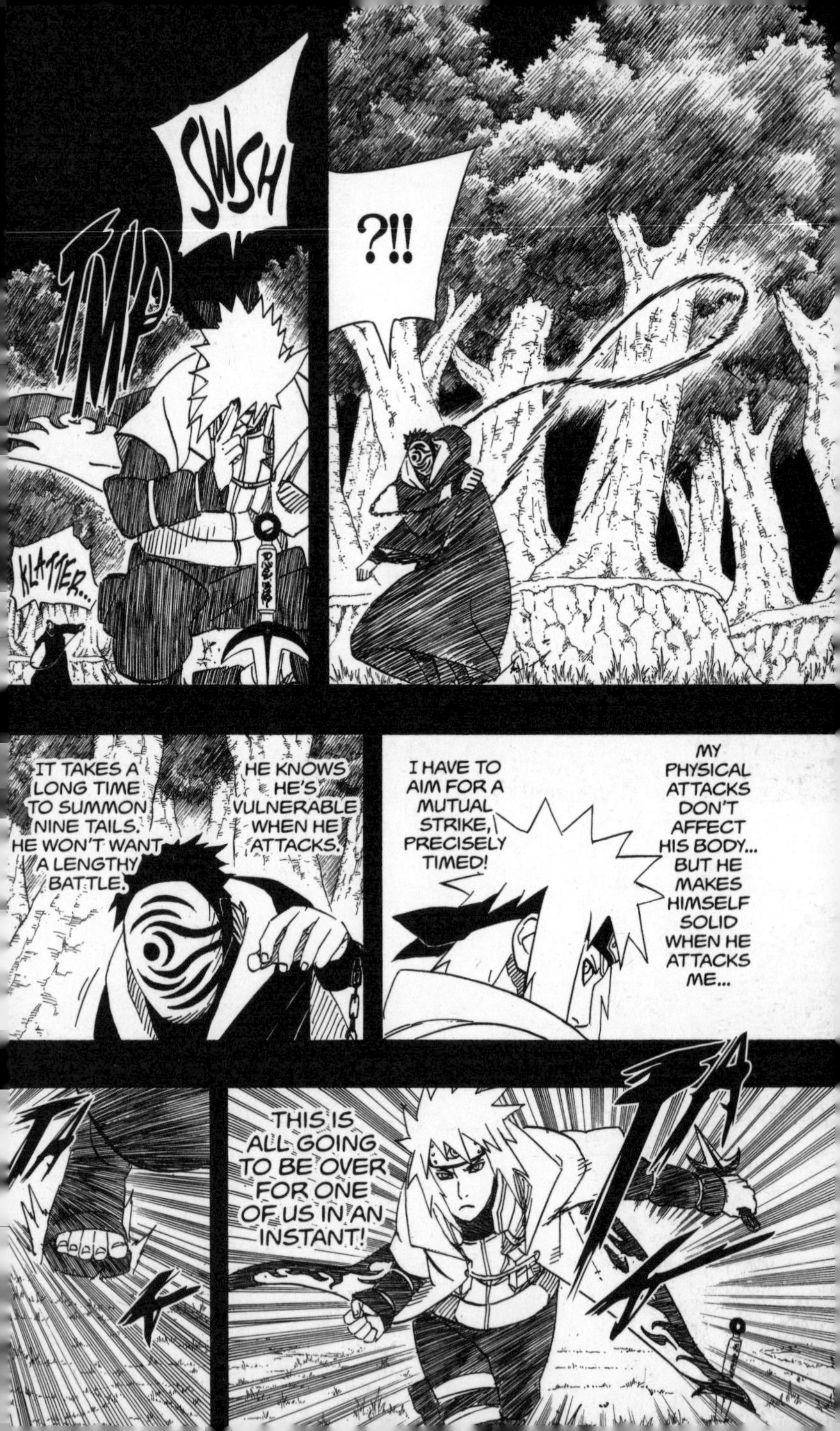
?!!
SWSH
TMP
KLATTER...
MY PHYSICAL ATTACKS DON'T AFFECT HIS BODY... BUT HE MAKES HIMSELF SOLID WHEN HE ATTACKS ME...
I HAVE TO AIM FOR A MUTUAL STRIKE, PRECISELY TIMED!
HE KNOWS HE'S VULNERABLE WHEN HE ATTACKS.
IT TAKES A LONG TIME TO SUMMON NINE TAILS. HE WON'T WANT A LENGTHY BATTLE.
TA
K
THIS IS ALL GOING TO BE OVER FOR ONE OF US IN AN INSTANT!
TA
K

READ THIS WAY

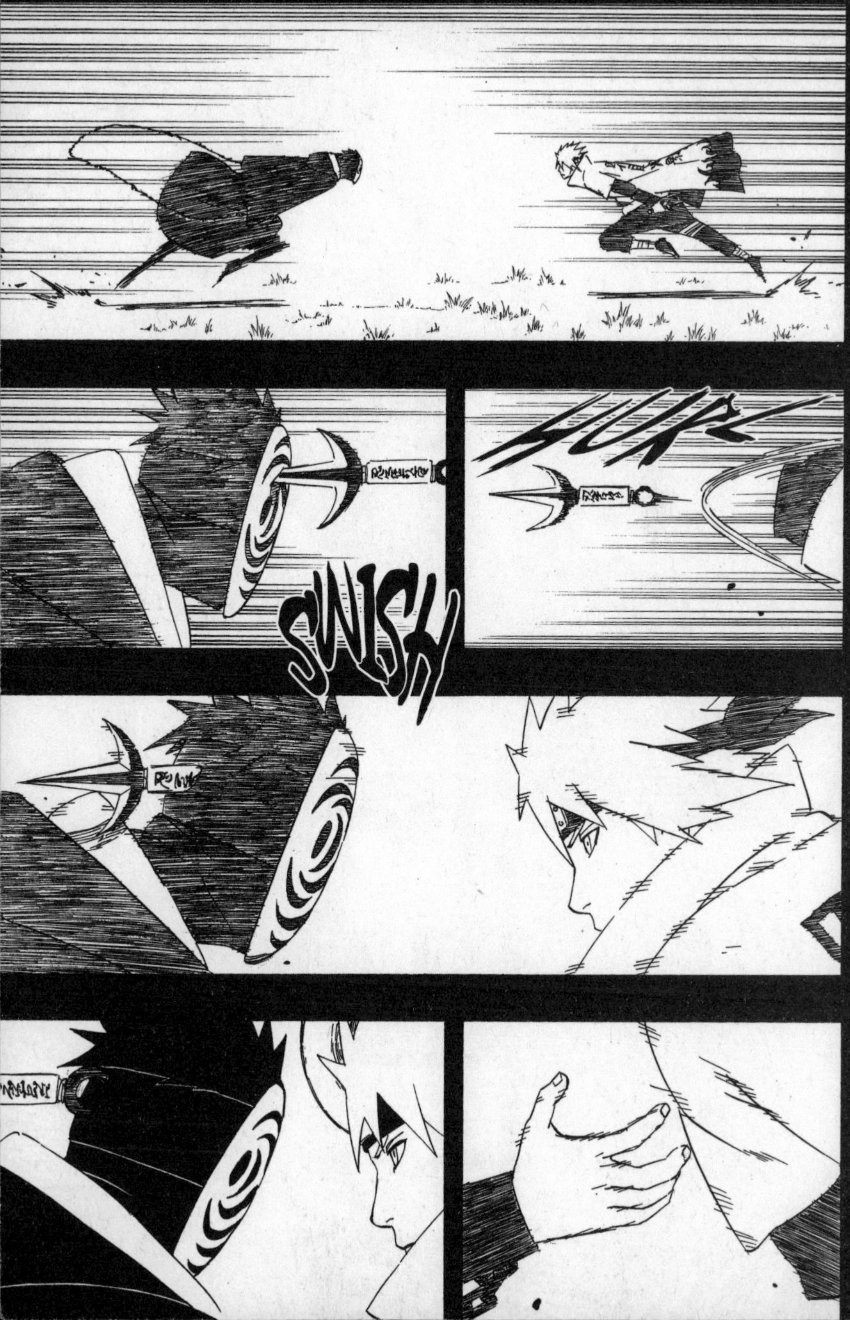
HURL
SWISH

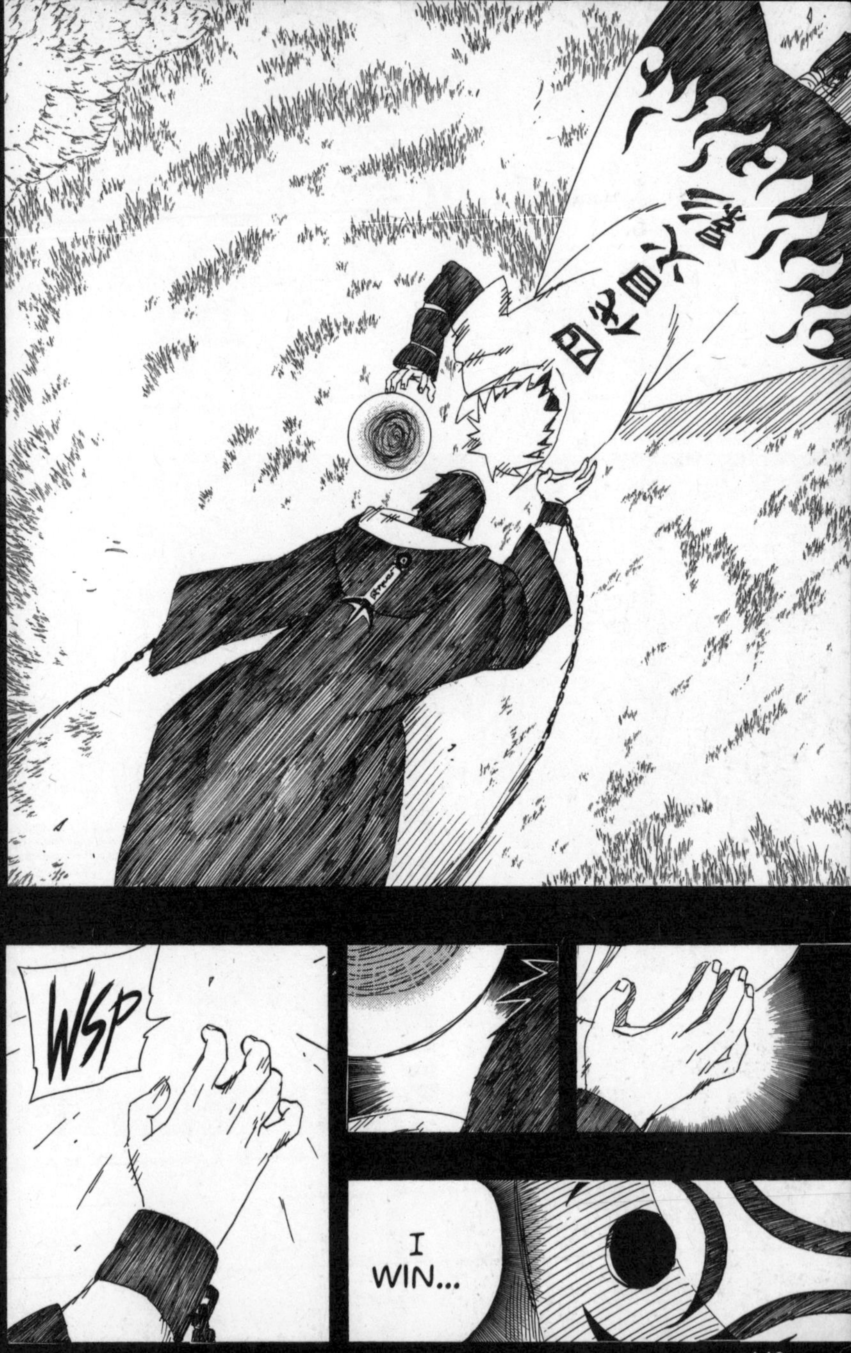
I WIN...
WSP

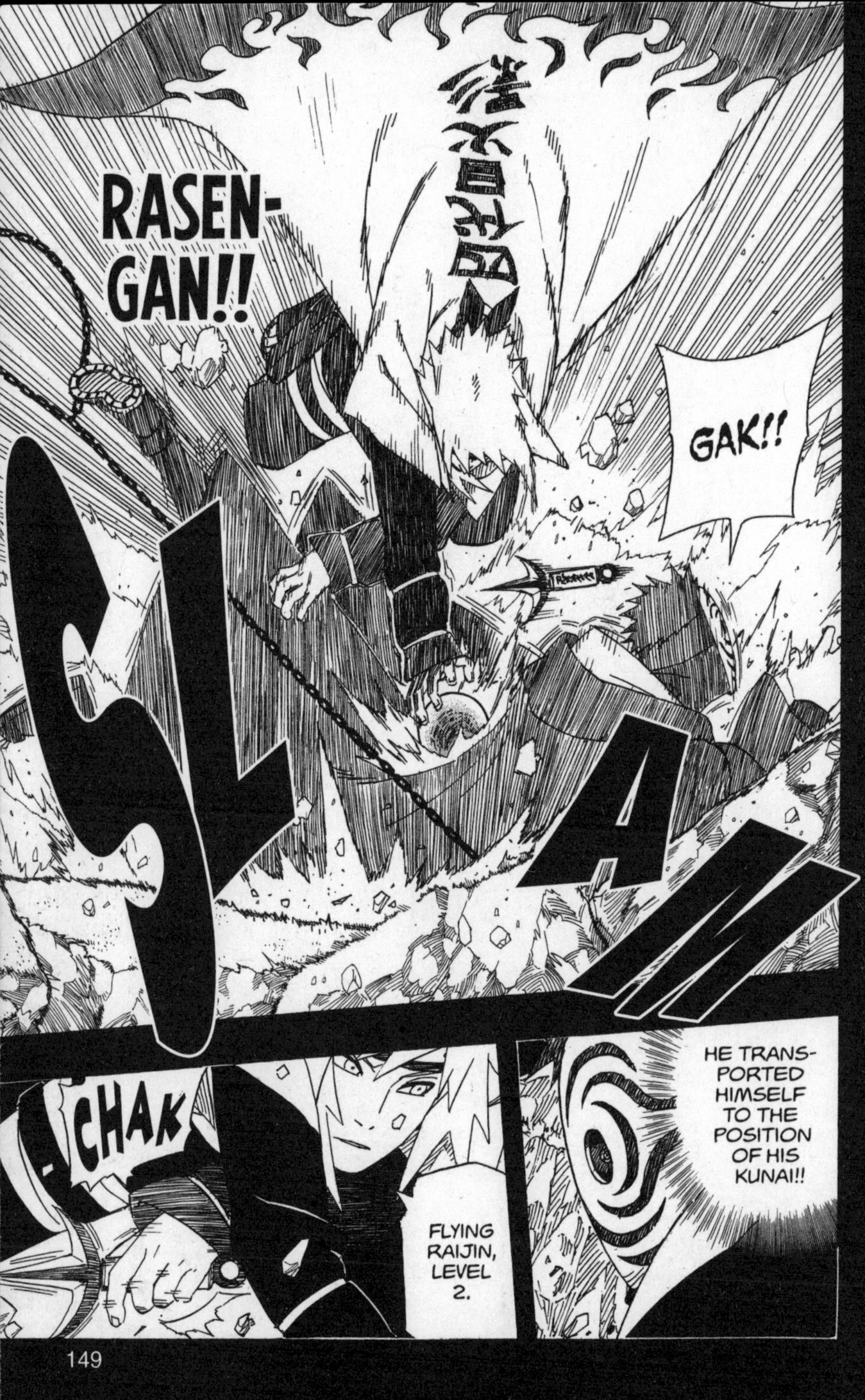
RASEN-GAN!!
GAK!!
SLAM
HE TRANS-PORTED HIMSELF TO THE POSITION OF HIS KUNAI!!
CHAK
FLYING RAIJIN, LEVEL 2.

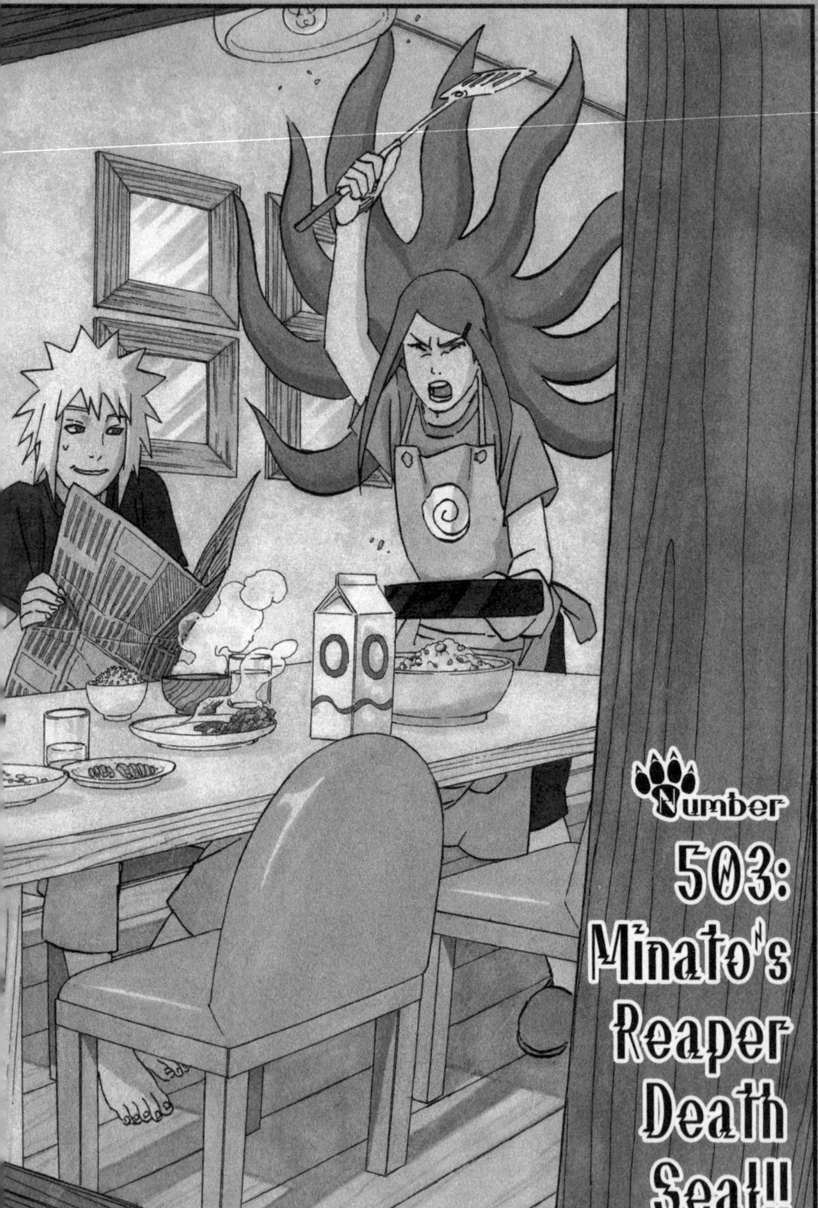
Number
503:
Minato's
Reaper
Death
Seal!!

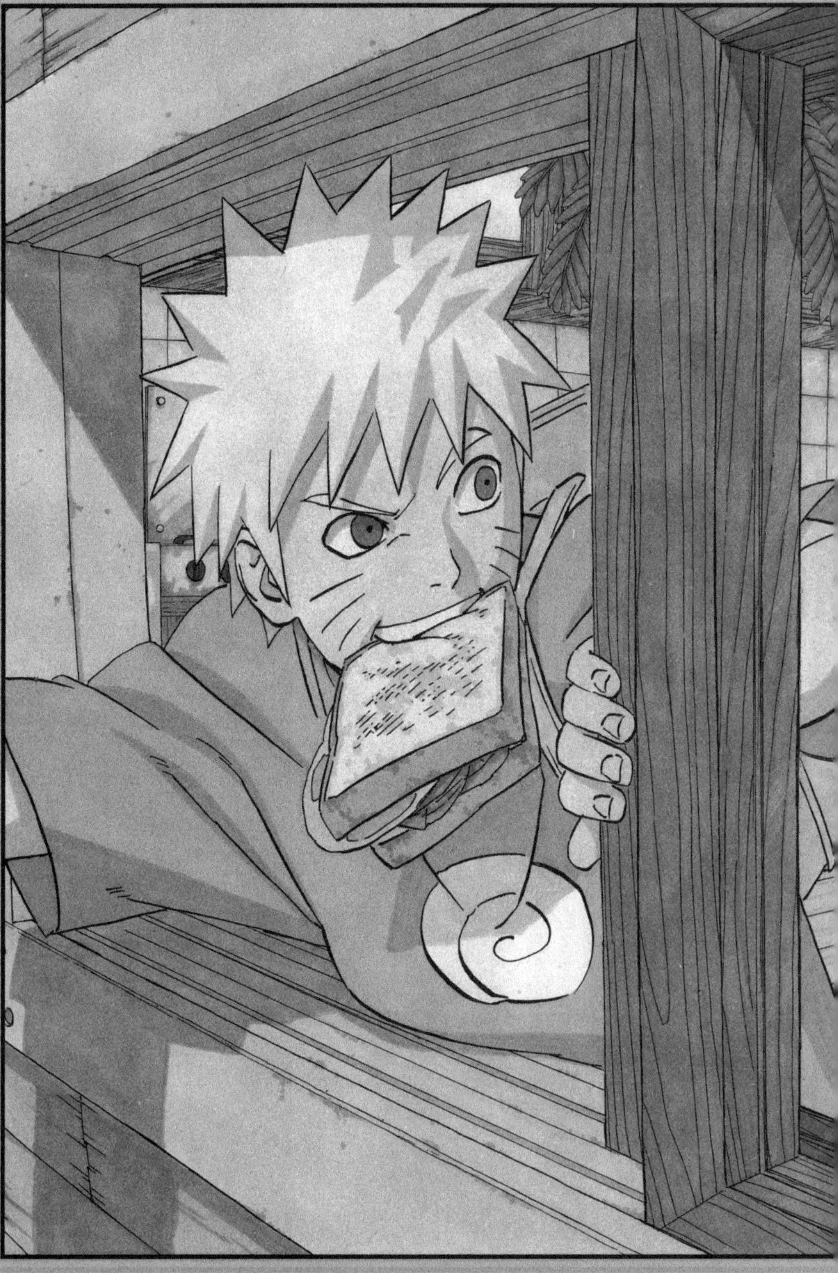

NARUTO

四代目火影

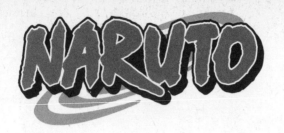

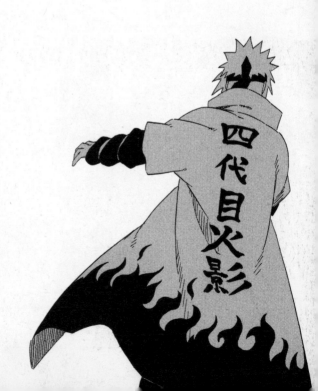

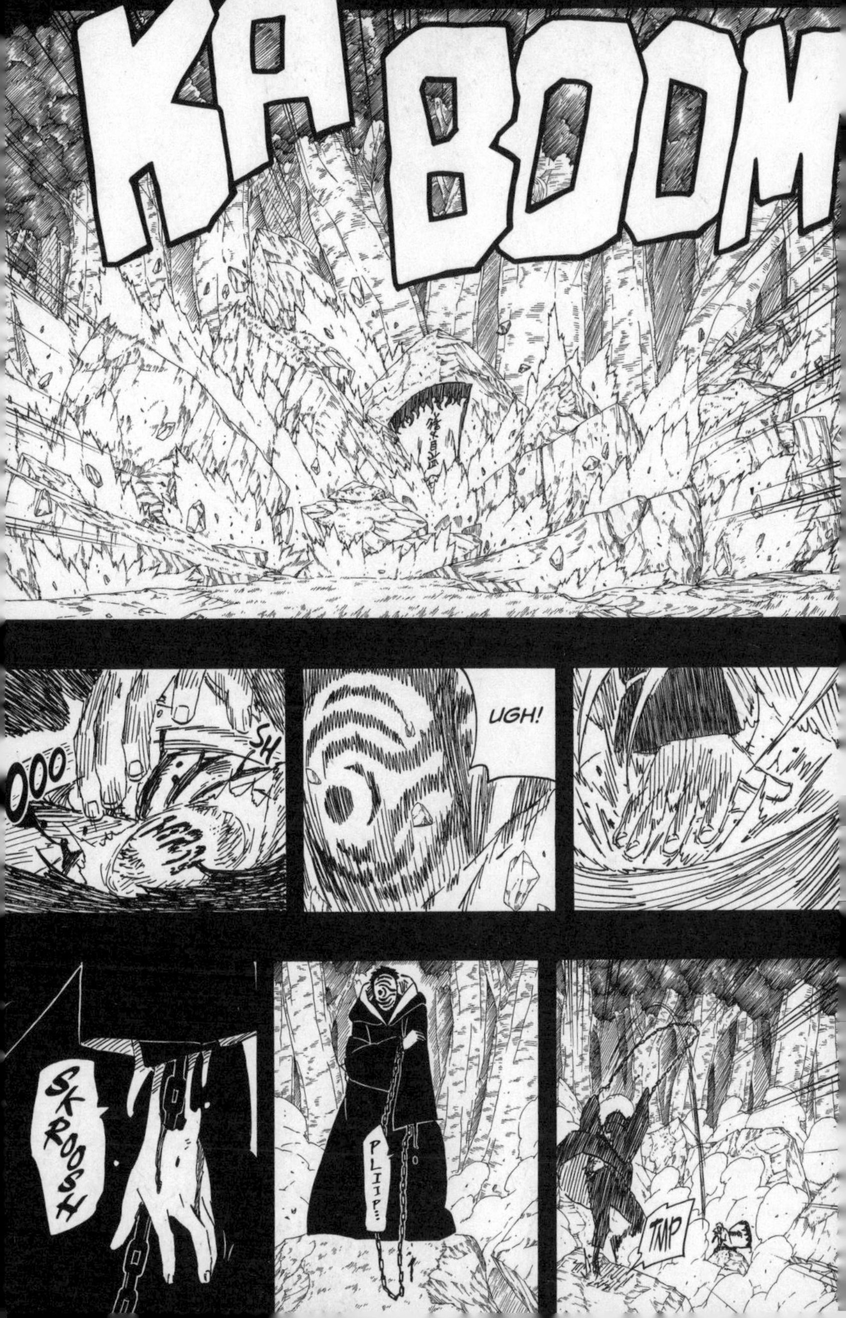
KA-BOOM
UGH!
SH
OOO
TMP
PLIIP...
SKROOSH

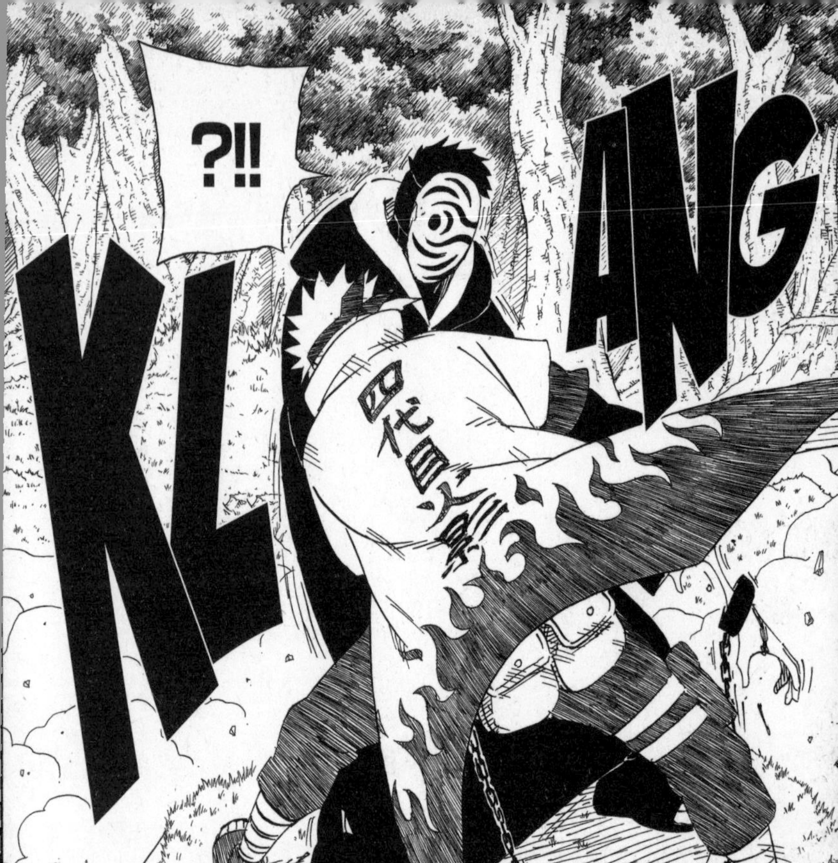
?!!
KLANG
四代目火影
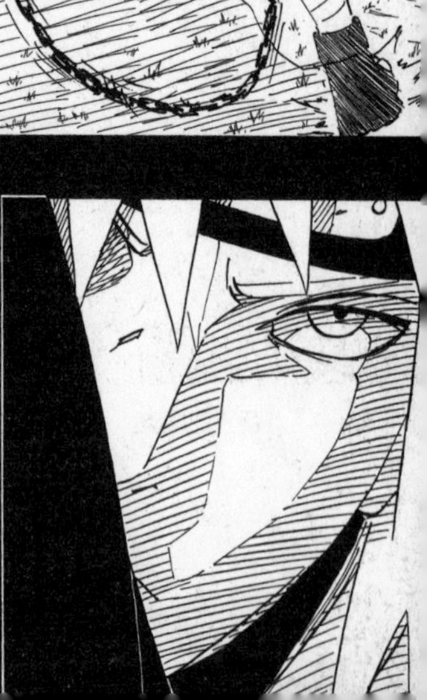
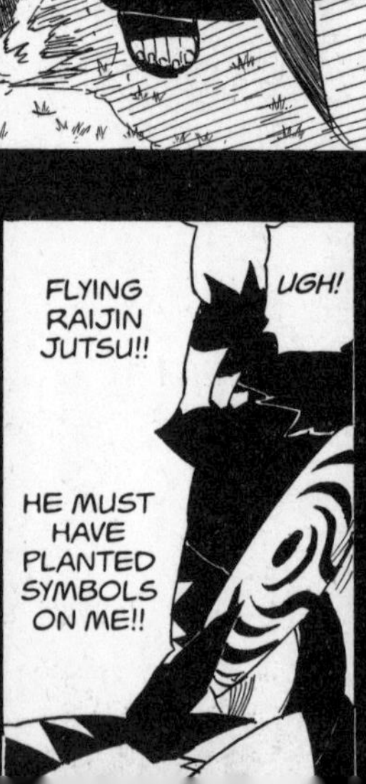
UGH!
FLYING RAIJIN JUTSU!!
HE MUST HAVE PLANTED SYMBOLS ON ME!!
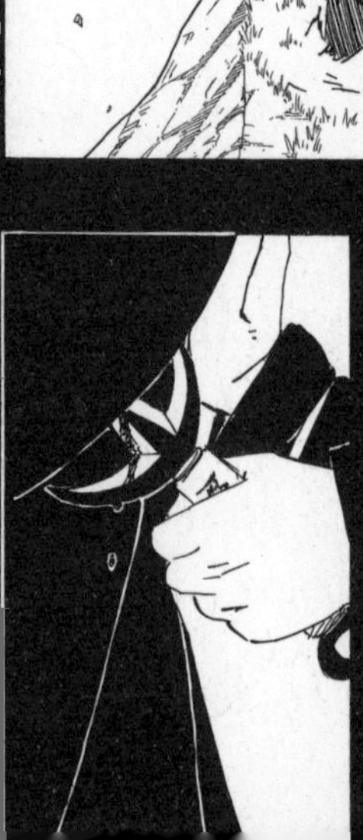

READ THIS WAY

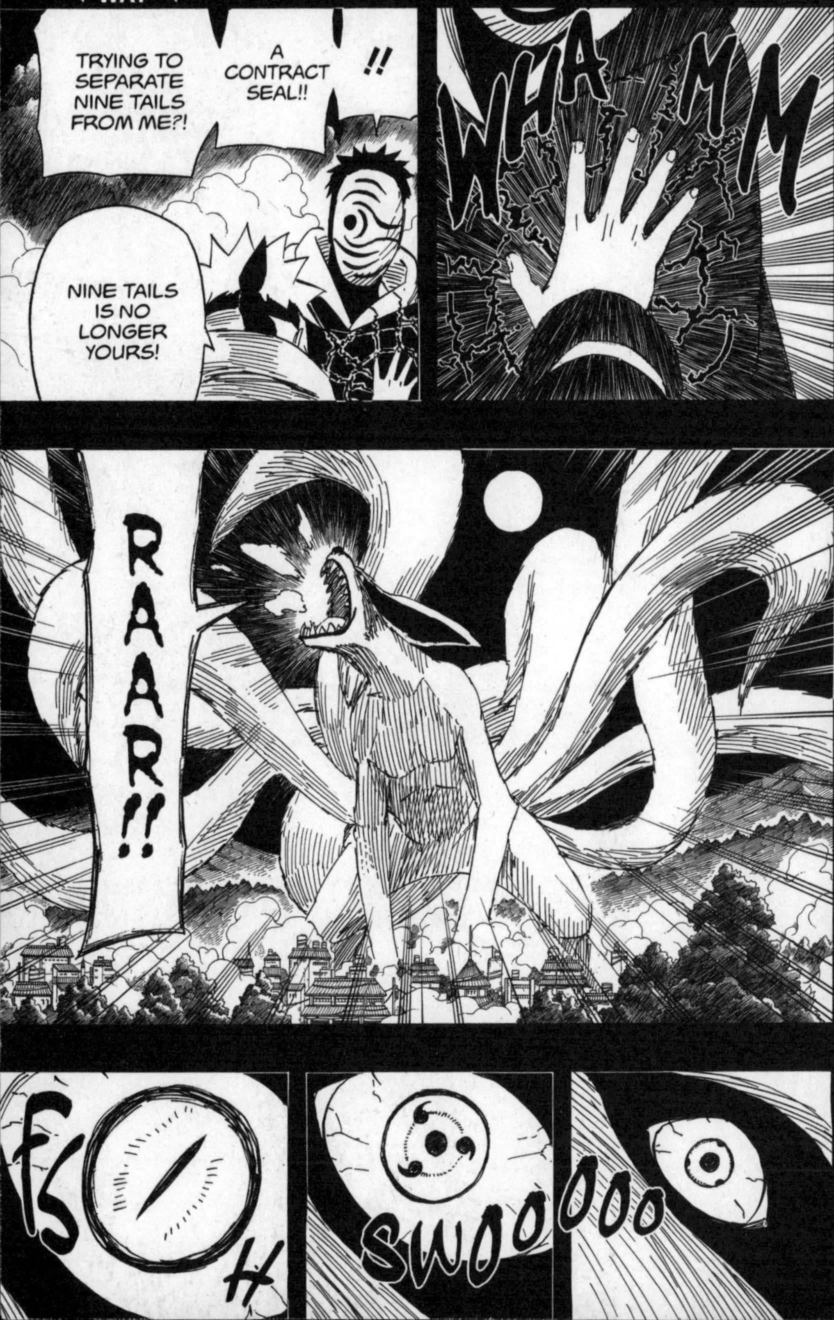

WHAMM
!!
A CONTRACT SEAL!!
TRYING TO SEPARATE NINE TAILS FROM ME?!
NINE TAILS IS NO LONGER YOURS!
RAAAR!!
SWOOOOOO
FSH

I **SHALL** RULE THIS WORLD...

THERE ARE PLENTY OF WAYS TO GO ABOUT IT.

YOU'RE WORTHY OF YOUR TITLE, FOURTH HOKAGE, INFLICTING INJURY UPON ME AND SEPARATING NINE TAILS FROM ME...

BUT HE **WILL** BE MINE FOR GOOD ONE DAY...

...HE'S NOT JOKING AROUND.

GIVEN HIS TONE...

SWOO...

PA AND MA ARE STILL FIGHTING!!

LET ME GO...!!

KEEP HIM OCCUPIED UNTIL LORD FOURTH GETS HERE!

LISTEN UP. YOU YOUNGER SHINOBI STAY AWAY FROM NINE TAILS...

THIS IS DOMESTIC TROUBLE, NOT A WAR AGAINST OTHER VILLAGES.

WHAT DO YOU MEAN?!

THERE IS NO NEED FOR YOU ALL TO RISK YOUR LIVES.

NO MORE PONTIFICATING!!

CALM... KURENAI!

RAAR!!

ZING

BEQUEATH THE WILL OF FIRE UPON MY FUTURE GRANDCHILDREN!

MAKE THAT YOUR OATH TO YOUR FATHER... FOR I DO BELIEVE IN YOU.

YOU'RE ALSO SHINOBI. YOU'RE NOT GOING TO LIVE FOREVER...

BUT, DAUGHTER... YOU'RE A WOMAN TOO.

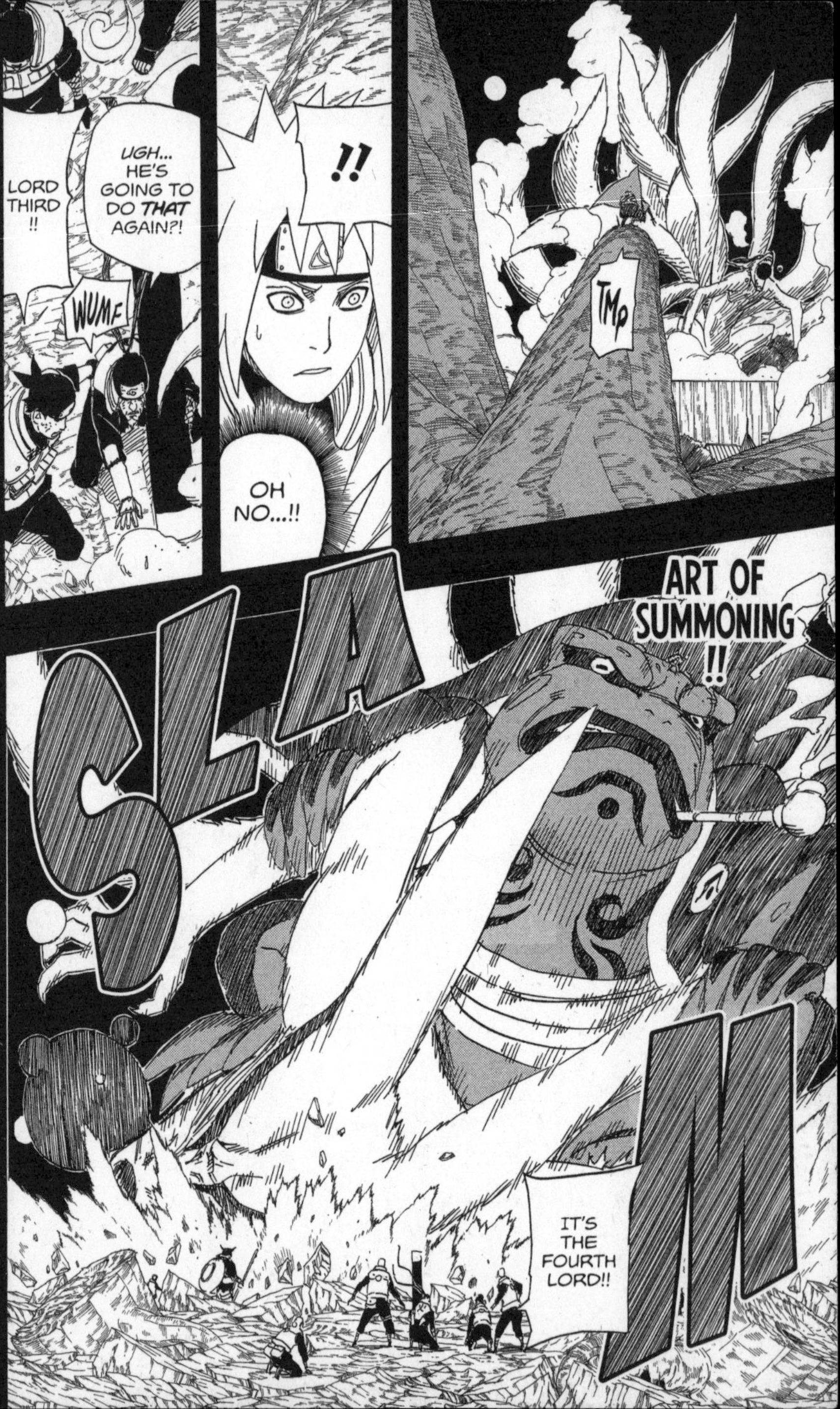
TMP
!!
OH NO...!!
UGH... HE'S GOING TO DO THAT AGAIN?!
LORD THIRD !!
WUMF
ART OF SUMMONING !!
SLAM
IT'S THE FOURTH LORD!!

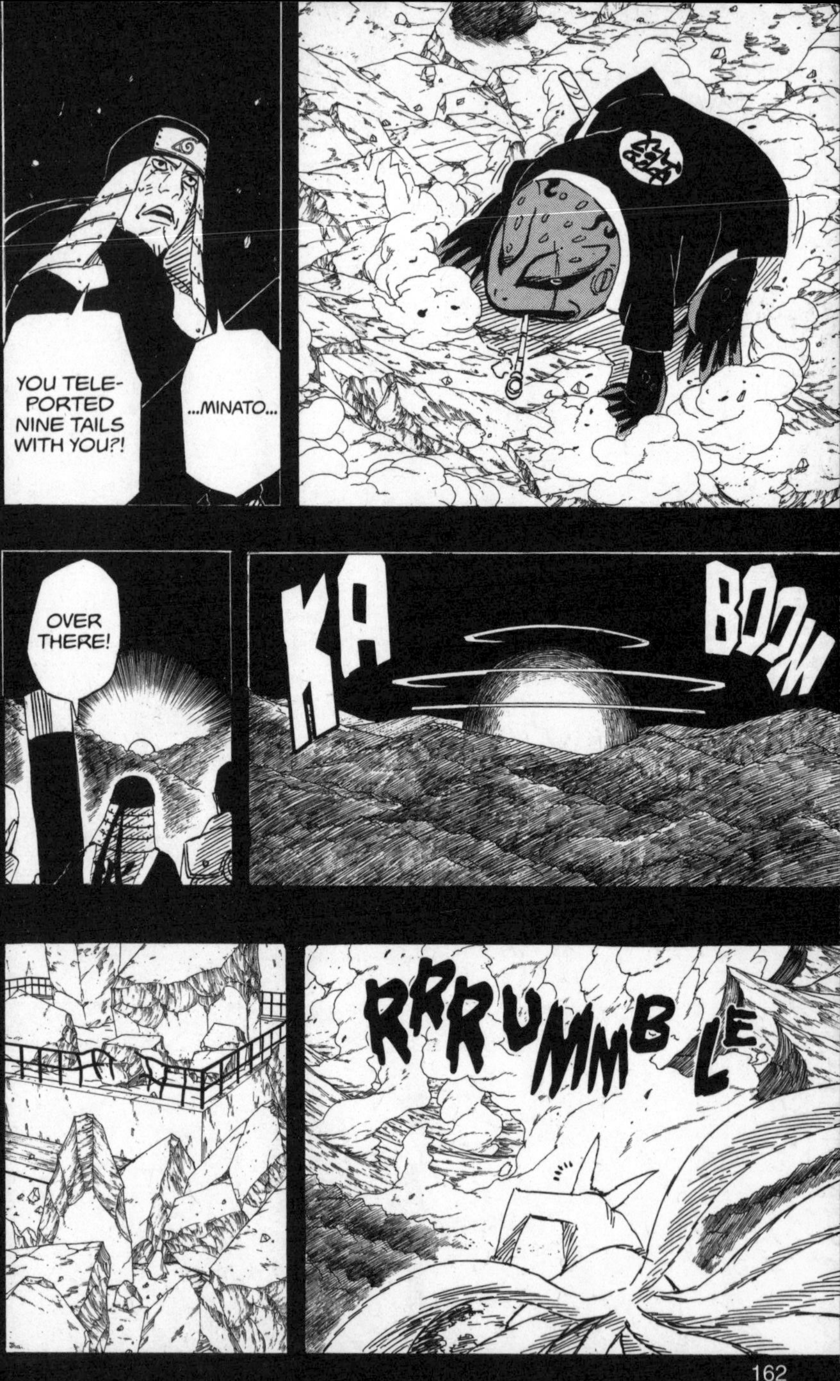
...MINATO...
YOU TELE-PORTED NINE TAILS WITH YOU?!
KA
BOOM
OVER THERE!
RRRUMMBLE

...I CAN'T SEE US... BEING ANYTHING BUT HAPPY...

MOST OF ALL... IF...I... WERE TO IMAGINE...

...ME ALIVE, AND OUR FUTURE... TOGETHER, AS A FAMILY OF THREE... THEN...

WAAH!

WAAAH!

WAAAH!

HUF

HUF

I WISH I COULD HAVE SEEN NARUTO... GROWN UP...

IF I WERE ALLOWED... JUST ONE... REGRET...

HUH...?

PRESERVE WHAT LITTLE OF YOUR CHAKRA REMAINS FOR YOUR REUNION WITH NARUTO...!

KUSHINA... THERE'S NO NEED FOR YOU TO DIE TO KILL NINE TAILS.

...

...WITH THE SEALING JUTSU THAT I CAN DO, NOT BEING A JINCHÛRIKI...

...THE SHIKIFÛJIN REAPER DEATH SEAL!

AND THEN *I'LL* TAKE NINE TAILS WITH ME...

IT'LL BE PART OF AN EIGHT-SIGNED SEAL.

I'M GOING TO SEAL THE REST OF YOUR CHAKRA INSIDE NARUTO.

BUT... THAT JUTSU RESULTS IN THE CASTER'S DEATH...

....!

WITH THE REAPER DEATH SEAL, WE CAN AT LEAST SEAL AWAY HALF OF NINE TAILS FOREVER.

AND THE OTHER HALF...

IF YOU TAKE NINE TAILS WITH YOU, THERE WILL BE NO JINCHÛRIKI UNTIL HE REEMERGES, AND THE BIJU BALANCE WILL BE UPSET, WHICH ISN'T GOOD.

PARTLY BECAUSE IT'S PHYSICALLY IMPOSSIBLE TO SEAL AWAY SUCH A LARGE VOLUME OF POWER...

...BUT ALSO BECAUSE IT'S NOT STRATEGICALLY WISE.

FURTHER-MORE... I'M ONLY GOING TO SEAL AWAY HALF OF NINE TAILS...

AND THE SAVIOR THAT SHALL EMERGE IS THIS CHILD OF PROPHECY...

IN THE FUTURE... TERRIBLE THINGS ARE LIKELY TO BEFALL THE SHINOBI WORLD.

HUH? THE WHAT?

PERHAPS... YOU'RE THE CHILD OF PROPHECY...

NARUTO

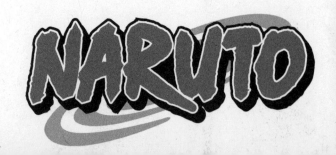

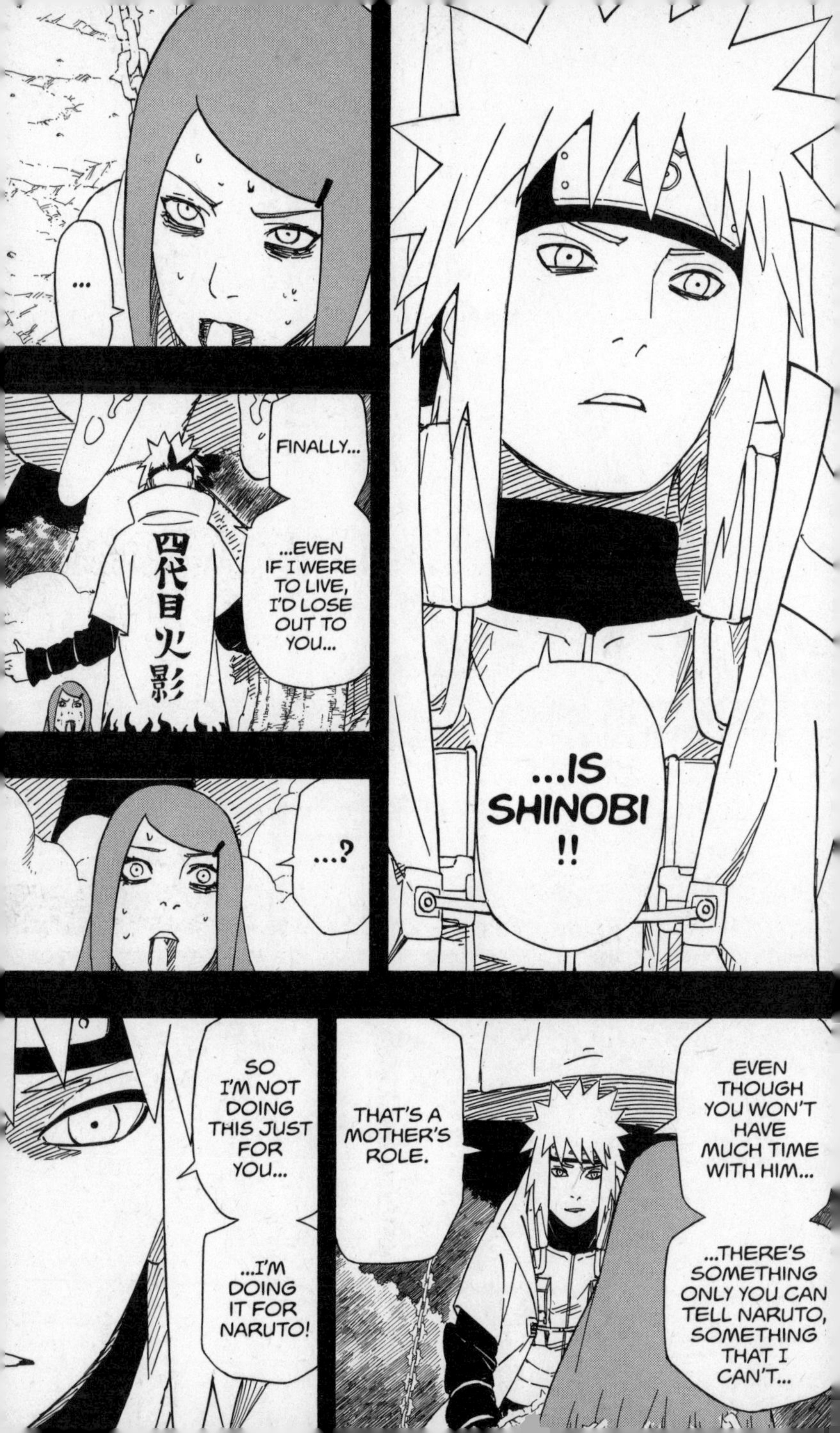
...IS SHINOBI !!
...
FINALLY...
...EVEN IF I WERE TO LIVE, I'D LOSE OUT TO YOU...
...?
EVEN THOUGH YOU WON'T HAVE MUCH TIME WITH HIM...
...THERE'S SOMETHING ONLY YOU CAN TELL NARUTO, SOMETHING THAT I CAN'T...
THAT'S A MOTHER'S ROLE.
SO I'M NOT DOING THIS JUST FOR YOU...
...I'M DOING IT FOR NARUTO!

SEAL!!

!

RAAAAR!!

SHUD DER

BUT NINE TAILS IS STILL ALIVE! HE COULDN'T SEAL ALL OF HIM AWAY?!

...ALTHOUGH HE DOES APPEAR SMALLER!

IT IS THE REAPER DEATH SEAL!

I DIDN'T THINK HE'D REALLY USE IT!

HUF

HUF

...I CAN'T BELIEVE HOW HEAVY HIS CHAKRA IS...

...MY BODY'S GOING NUMB...!

HUF

176

...TO SEAL THE REST OF NINE TAILS INSIDE NARUTO...!

ALL RIGHT... NOW FOR THE EIGHT-SIGNED SEAL...

BO

OF

GRRR

UNF...!

UGH...!

HUF

HUF

FSH

HUF

A RITUAL ALTAR! HE'S PLANNING TO SEAL ME UP AGAIN?! NOT INSIDE THAT BABY?!!

THERE YOU ARE!

?!

SHRRL...

TAK

SHRRL...

!

COUGH

HACK! HACK!

KUSHINA ?!

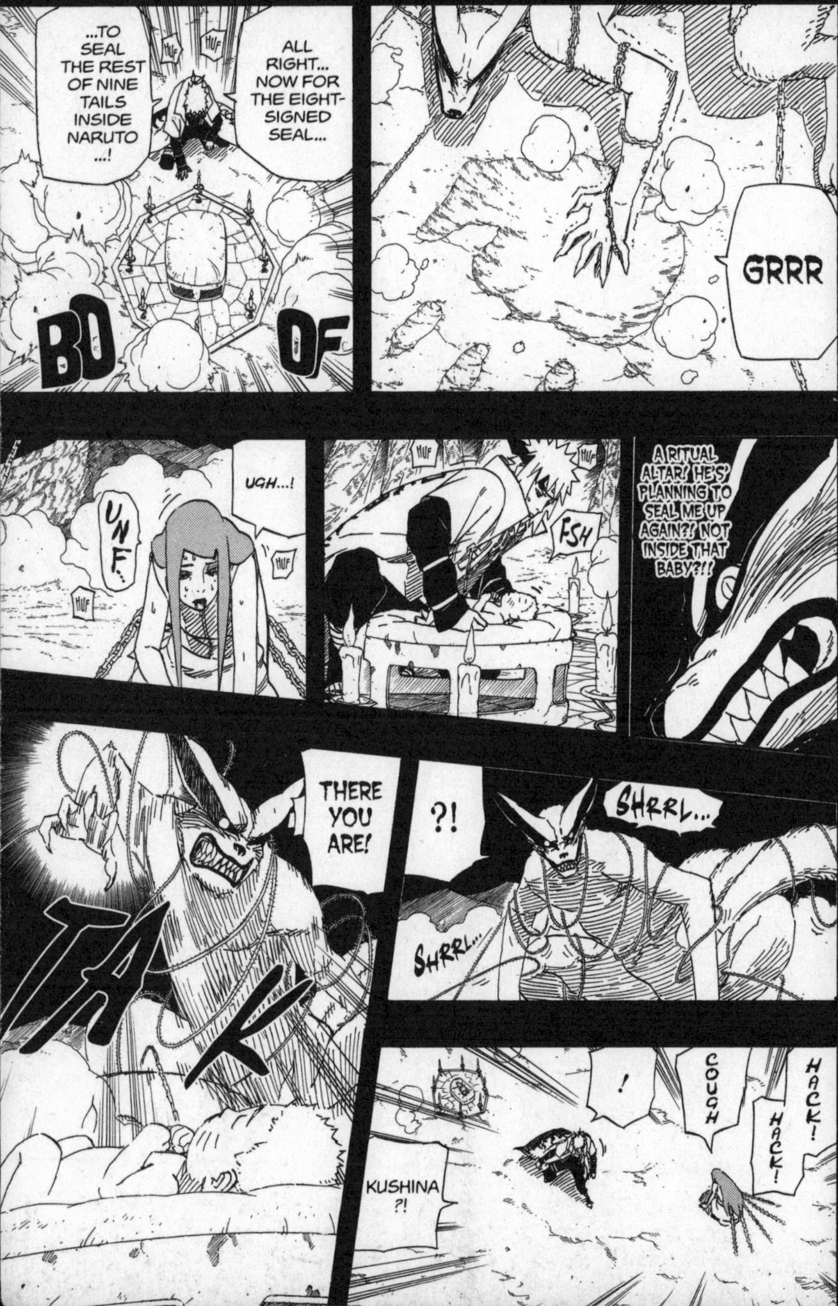

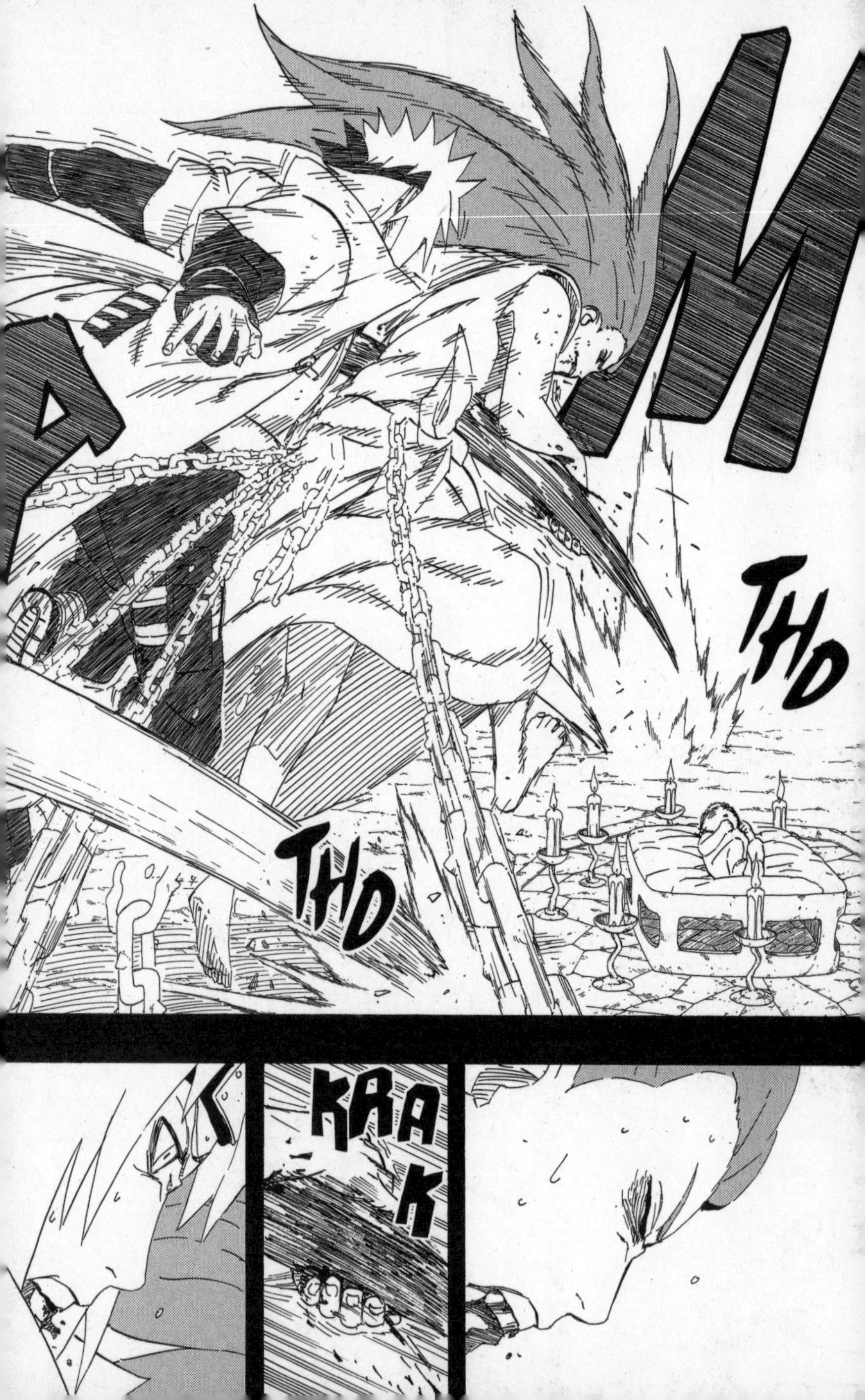
THD
THD
KRAK

HM?!

HOVER...

BOO**F**

ART OF SUMMONING!!

THANKS, KUSHINA...

DRIBBLE

SKOO SH

WHEN I'M DONE... GO STRAIGHT TO MASTER JIRAIYA... AND HAVE HIM TAKE YOU IN...

GAMATORA, I'M GOING TO GIVE YOU... THE SEAL SPELL KEY.

HEY, FOURTH! WHAT'S UP WITH YOU?!!

WHOA!! NINE TAILS!!

AND NOW... I'M OFF!

I AFFIRM THAT I'VE RECEIVED THE KEY!

MINATO PLANS TO SAVE THE VILLAGE BY MAKING HIS OWN SON THE JINCHÛRIKI!

THAT'S IT...!

FRRRR

RRR

182

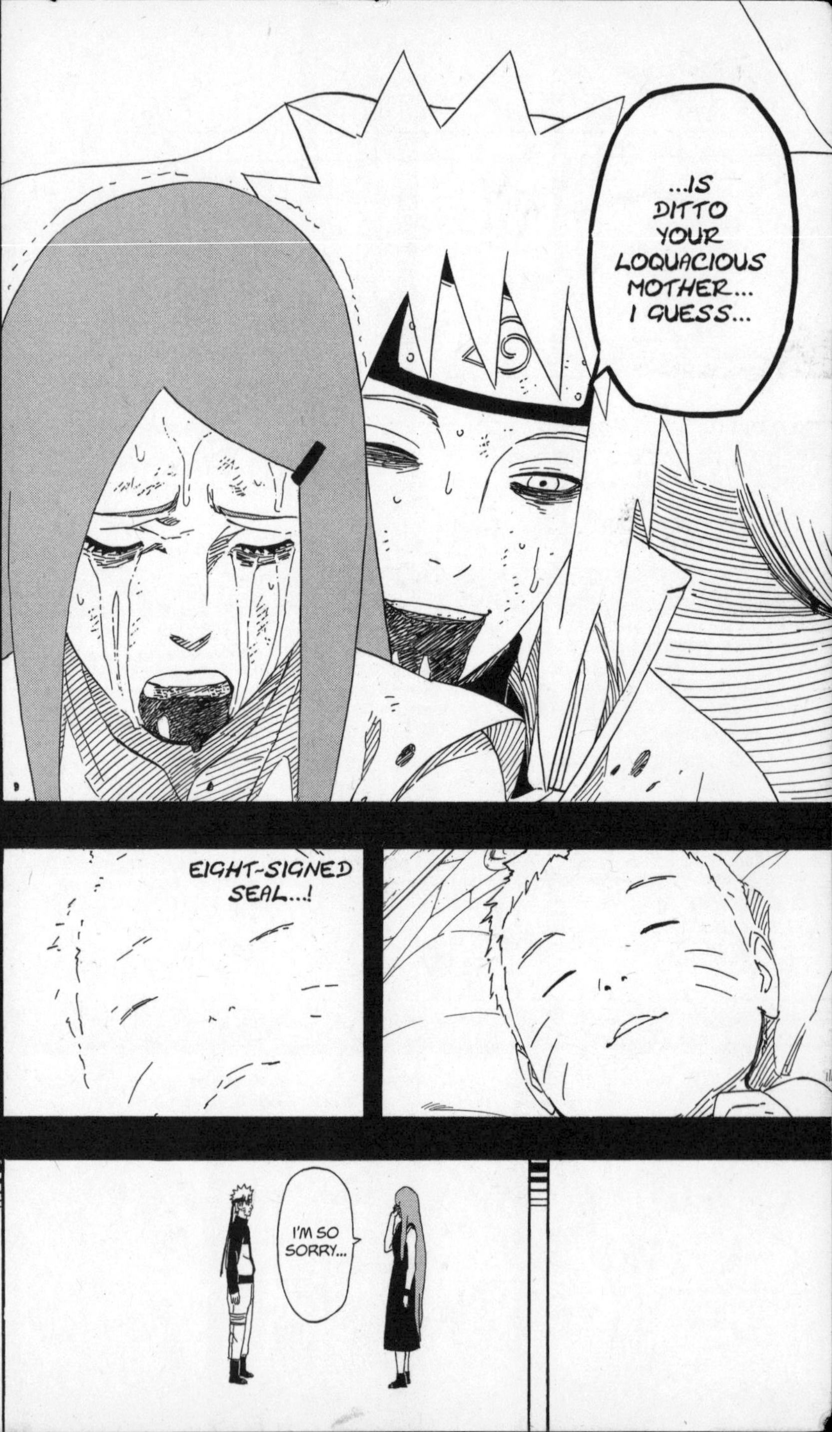
...IS DITTO YOUR LOQUACIOUS MOTHER... I GUESS...
EIGHT-SIGNED SEAL...!
I'M SO SORRY...

READ THIS WAY

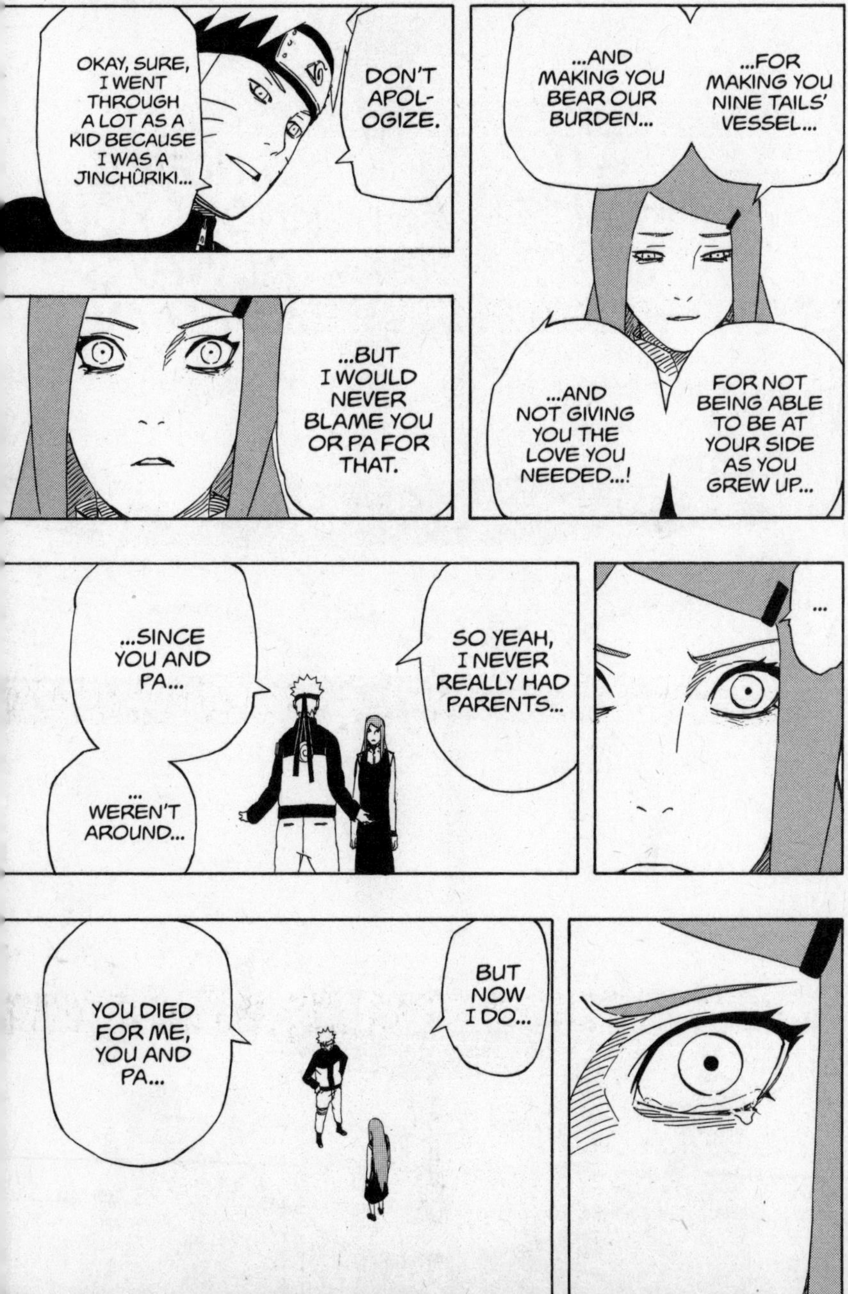

...FOR MAKING YOU NINE TAILS' VESSEL...
...AND MAKING YOU BEAR OUR BURDEN...
FOR NOT BEING ABLE TO BE AT YOUR SIDE AS YOU GREW UP...
...AND NOT GIVING YOU THE LOVE YOU NEEDED...!
DON'T APOLOGIZE.
OKAY, SURE, I WENT THROUGH A LOT AS A KID BECAUSE I WAS A JINCHÛRIKI...
...BUT I WOULD NEVER BLAME YOU OR PA FOR THAT.
...
SO YEAH, I NEVER REALLY HAD PARENTS...
...SINCE YOU AND PA...
... WEREN'T AROUND...
BUT NOW I DO...
YOU DIED FOR ME, YOU AND PA...

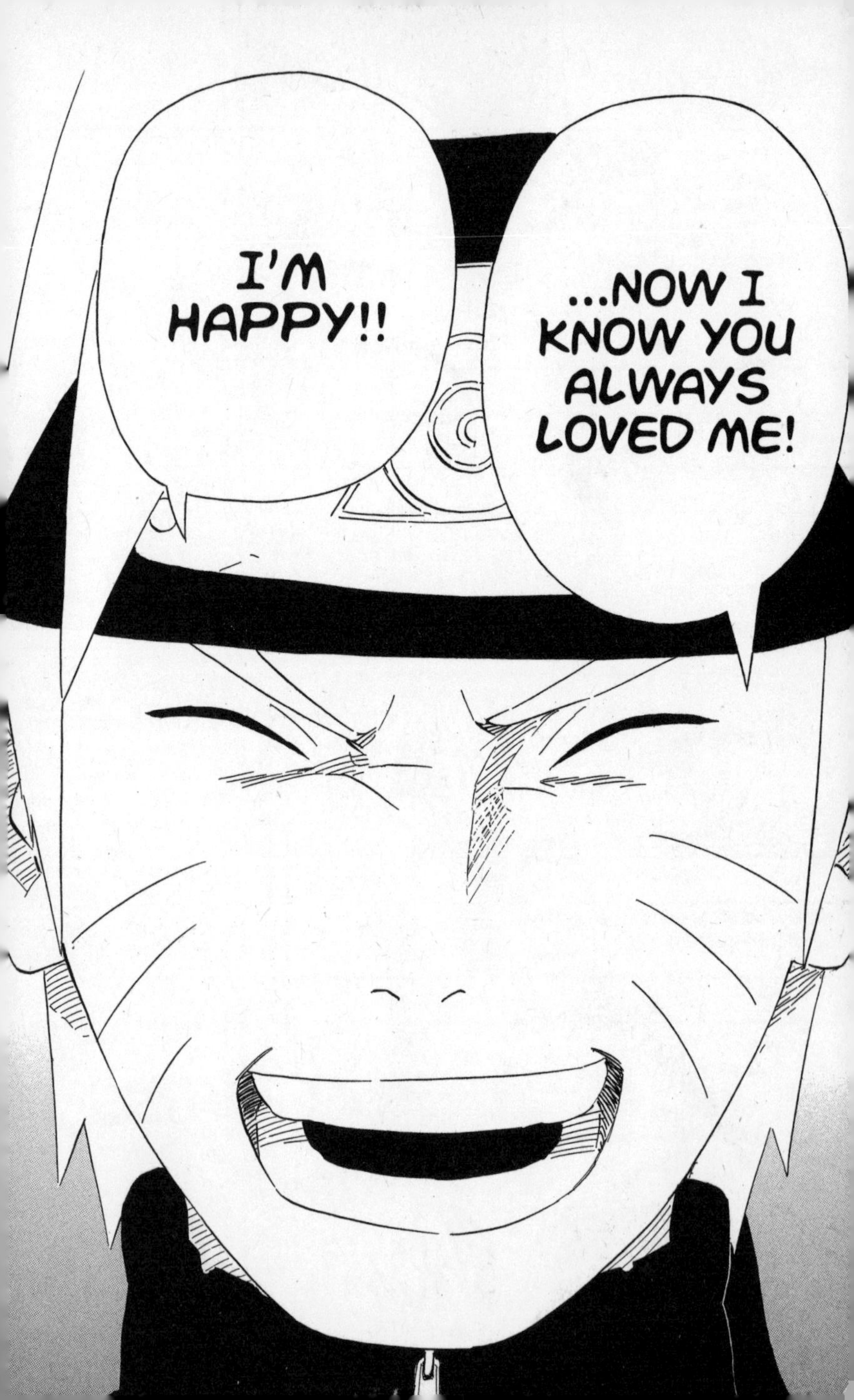
...NOW I KNOW YOU ALWAYS LOVED ME!
I'M HAPPY!!

I'M GLAD I'M YOUR KID!!

SSH...

FSSH

THANK YOU SO MUCH...

THANK YOU FOR LETTING ME BECOME A MOTHER... AND MINATO A FATHER...

SHOOO...

NARUTO...

OUR HOPES... DID REACH OUR BOY...!!

MINATO... ARE YOU LISTENING...?!

!

...FOR HAVING BEEN BORN TO US!!

SWOO...

TO BE CONTINUED IN *NARUTO* VOLUME 54!

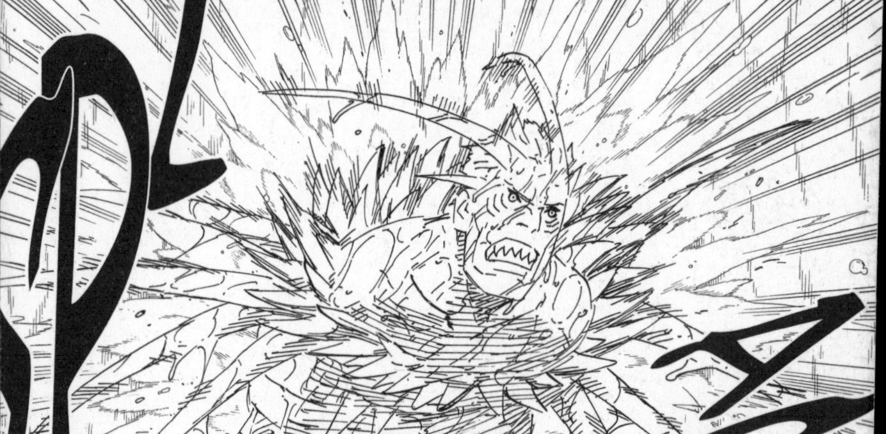
SPLASH

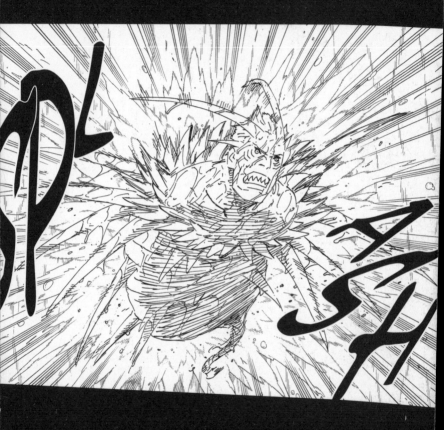

IN THE NEXT VOLUME...

PEACE VIADUCT

Naruto and his team engage in an intense battle with the Akatsuki organization as both sides seek the power to determine the future of their land. Internecine fighting weakens the Akatsuki, but will their power sideline Naruto?

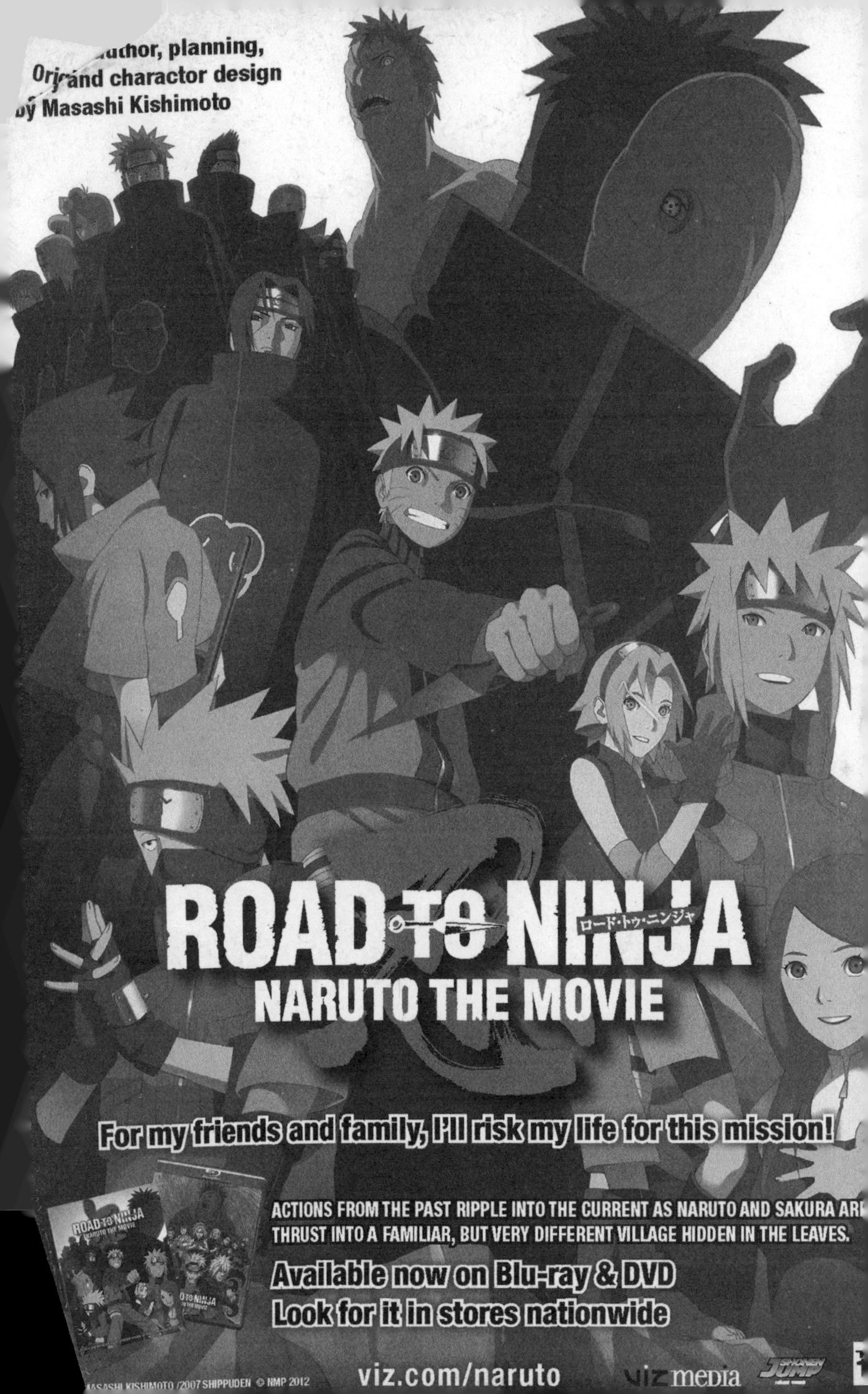
uthor, planning,
Ori and character design
by Masashi Kishimoto
ROAD TO NINJA
ロード・トゥ・ニンジャ
NARUTO THE MOVIE
For my friends and family, I'll risk my life for this mission!
ACTIONS FROM THE PAST RIPPLE INTO THE CURRENT AS NARUTO AND SAKURA AR
THRUST INTO A FAMILIAR, BUT VERY DIFFERENT VILLAGE HIDDEN IN THE LEAVES.
Available now on Blu-ray & DVD
Look for it in stores nationwide
viz.com/naruto
viz media
SHONEN JUMP
MASASHI KISHIMOTO /2007 SHIPPUDEN © NMP 2012

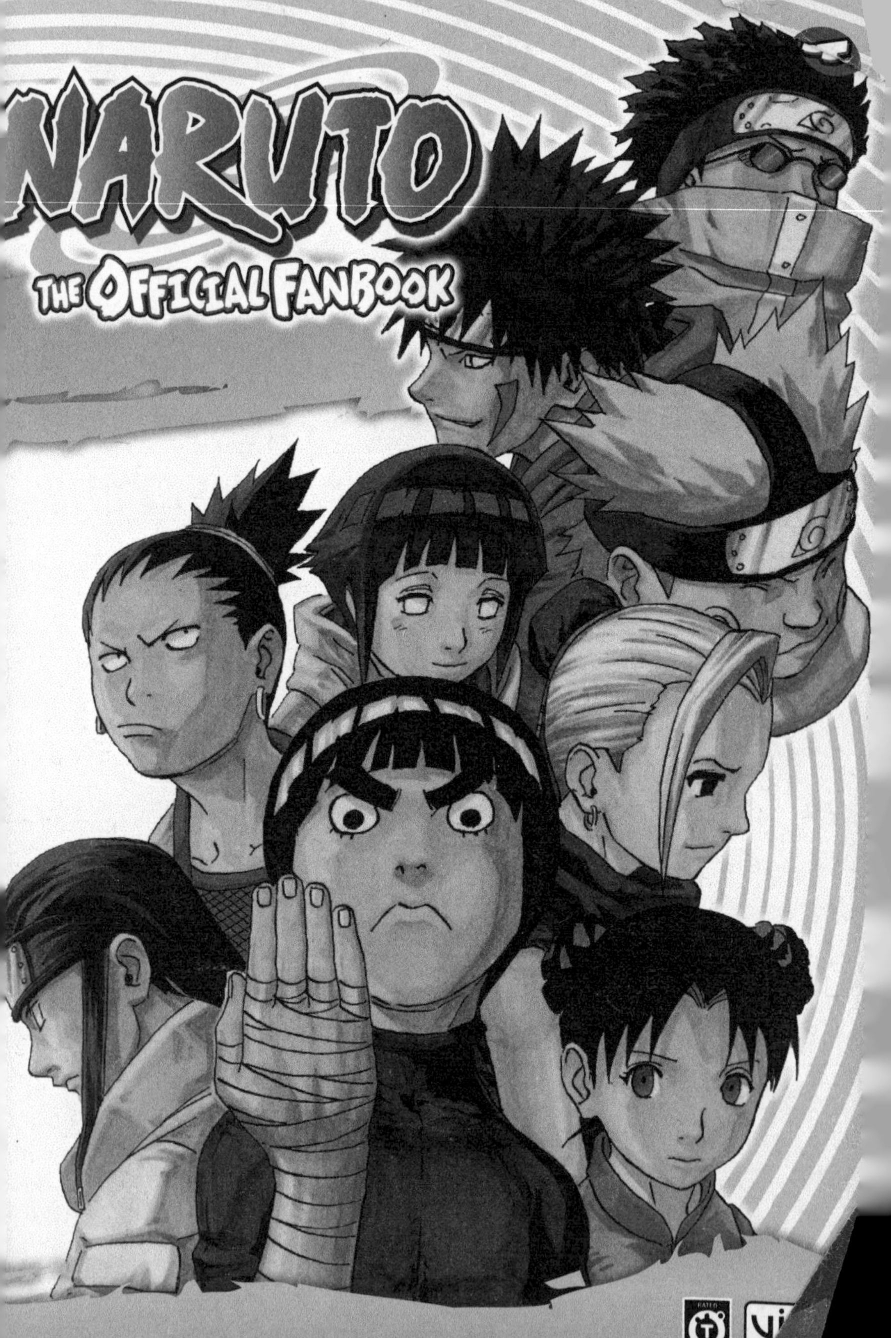
NARUTO
THE OFFICIAL FANBOOK